This book uncovers the rich, fascinating and complex world of Ottoman manufacturing and manufacturers in the age of the European industrial revolution. Using a wealth of sources from Ottoman, European and American archives, Donald Quataert explores the technological methods of producing cotton cloth, wool cloth, yarn and silk, how these changed throughout the nineteenth century, the organization of home and workshop production and trends in the domestic and international markets.

By focusing on textile manufacturing in homes and small workshops, the author reveals a dynamism that refutes traditional notions of a stagnating economy, which have been based on comparisons of Western and Middle Eastern factory production. Quataert demonstrates, to the contrary, that manufacturers adopted a variety of strategies to confront European competitors, protect their livelihoods and retain or regain both domestic and international customers. These strategies usually involved reducing production costs through a combination of cheap technological innovations and decreased wages, often involving women and children.

This book presents the first comprehensive study of Ottoman manufacturing from the beginning of the nineteenth century to the outbreak of the First World War. Fundamentally changing traditional thinking of late Ottoman manufacturing, it will be widely read by students and specialists of Middle Eastern studies and economic history.

Cambridge Middle East Library: 30

OTTOMAN MANUFACTURING
IN THE AGE OF THE
INDUSTRIAL REVOLUTION

OTTOMAN MANUFACTURING IN THE AGE OF THE INDUSTRIAL REVOLUTION

DONALD QUATAERT

Binghamton University

CAMBRIDGE
UNIVERSITY PRESS

PUBLISHED BY THE PRESS SYNDICATE OF THE UNIVERSITY OF CAMBRIDGE
The Pitt Building, Trumpington Street, Cambridge, United Kingdom

CAMBRIDGE UNIVERSITY PRESS
The Edinburgh Building, Cambridge CB2 2RU, UK
40 West 20th Street, New York NY 10011-4211, USA
477 Williamstown Road, Port Melbourne, VIC 3207, Australia
Ruiz de Alarcón 13, 28014 Madrid, Spain
Dock House, The Waterfront, Cape Town 8001, South Africa

http://www.cambridge.org

First published 1993
First paperback edition 2002

A catalogue record for this book is available from the British Library

ISBN 0 521 42017 2 hardback
ISBN 0 521 89301 1 paperback

To Jean Helen Quataert, with love and respect

Contents

Contents

Illustrations

Tables

Acknowledgements

This book has been in preparation since 1983 and I have many friends and colleagues to whom I am indebted for their numerous kindnesses and generosities.

The staffs of many archives and libraries made the work far more pleasant than it might have been. These include the Library of Congress and National Archives in Washington, D.C., and the Public Record Office in London, as well as at the Bibliothèque Nationale in Paris. At various times, the personnel at the libraries of the University of Houston, the University of Chicago, and of Binghamton University were very kind to me. I also am grateful for the efficient help given by the staff in the Zentrales Staatsarchiv in Potsdam of the former German Democratic Republic, who overlooked Cold War policies to render guidance. As always, my work at the Başbakanlık Arşivi, İstanbul, was indispensable to my research and I recall with pleasure the many friends I have made there.

Jim Jones gave me needed support and encouragement at a very early stage. Rifaat Abou El-Haj always has been a valued critic, from whom I continue to profit. At varying points in the research, the following have offered constructive advice: Çağlar Keyder, Şevket Pamuk, Faruk Tabak, as well as the participants in the Binghamton University 1990 conference on Ottoman Manufacturing, especially Jonathan Prude and Albert Feuerwerker. Both the Ottoman history reading group in the Fernand Braudel Center (and its director, Immanuel Wallerstein) and the History Department faculty at Binghamton have given me much valuable criticism. Among the latter, I single out Mel Dubofsky and the late Charles Freedeman. Mehmet Genç always has shared research findings and ideas. Andreas Tietze remains an inspiration.

For the carpet chapter, I owe particular thanks to Carol Bier, Victor Binns, the late Louise Davison, Brian Hufner and Annette Ittig. For the silk chapter, my special thanks to Beatrice Saint-Laurent.

The three anonymous readers at Cambridge University Press offered exceptionally careful and thoughtful comments. I count myself fortunate for the time they spent.

For various kinds of help in preparing the manuscript, my thanks to Bennie Ables, University of Houston, and to Lisa Fegley-Schmidt and Yavuz Karakışla,

Binghamton. Nergis Canefe Günlük helped prepare the maps. Faruk Tabak proof-read the final text and prepared the index.

Invaluable financial support was offered at the beginning by the University of Houston and by the Institute of Turkish Studies, then by the National Endowment for the Humanities – its Senior Fellowship was essential for the completion of this project. At the end, a Binghamton University Research Award gave me a needed semester away from teaching.

The arrival of my daughter Laurie's twins, as the manuscript neared completion, reminded me that life goes on, even after books are written. For the years with my son Eliot, who continuously gave me perspective on the importance of this scholarly undertaking, I owe very much.

Abbreviations

AA	Germany: Auswärtiges Amt
A&P	Great Britain: Parliamentary Papers, Accounts and Papers
AE	France: Archives du Ministère des affairs étrangères, Quai d'Orsay, Paris
AS	Great Britain: Annual Series
Aus	Austria
BBA	Turkey: Başbakanlık Arşivi, İstanbul
BCF	France: *Bulletin consulaire français. Recueil des rapports commerciaux adressés au Ministère des affaires étrangères par les agents diplomatiques et consulaires de France à l'étranger.*
BEO	Bab-ı Âli Evrak Odası
Bel	Belediye
BTTD	*Belgelerle Türk Tarih Dergisi*
Buhi	Germany: Deutsches Reich. *Handel und Industrie. Berichte über Handel und Industrie*
CC	Correspondance commerciale
Cev	Cevdet Tasnifi
CR	Consular Reports of the United States
Dah	Dahiliye
FO	Great Britain: Foreign Office
Fr	France
GB	Great Britain
Ger	Germany
HH	Hatt-ı Hümayûn
HHst A	Austria: Haus-Hof und Staatsarchiv, Vienna, Politisches Archiv (PA)
İ	İradeler
IJMES	*International Journal of Middle East Studies*
IJTS	*International Journal of Turkish Studies*
Kepeci	Kamil Kepeci Tasnifi
k und k	Austria: *Berichte der k. u. k. Österr.- Ung. Konsularämter über das Jahr*

Mal	Maliye
MM	Meclis-i Mahsûs
MV	Meclis-i Vâlâ
PA	see HHstA above
RCC	Rapports commerciaux des agents diplomatiques et consulaires de France
RCL	*La Revue commerciale du Levant, bulletin mensuel de la chambre de commerce française de Constantinople*, 1896–1912
ŞD	Şura-yı Devlet
UPA	University Publications of America
US	United States
VS	Vilayet Salnamesi
ZStA	Germany: formerly Democratic Republic, Zentrales Staatsarchiv, Potsdam, Auswärtiges Amt

Note on weights, measures and currencies

Weights

All weights are given in kg. or tons (1,000 kg). oke = 2.8 lb. = 1.28 kg.; 2.20 lb. = 1 kg.; cantar = c. 100 lb.; cotton bales: generally, 196 kg. or 5.09/ton.

Measures

Measures usually are in meters; arşın = ell = 28" = .68 cm.

Currencies

Currencies usually are in piasters, 100/Ottoman pound; 110/British pound sterling. Exchange rates, unless otherwise noted, are derived from Şevket Pamuk, "Money in the Ottoman Empire, 1326–1914," in Halil İnalcık and Donald Quataert, eds., *A social and economic history of the Ottoman Empire, 1300–1914* (Cambridge, forthcoming).

Introduction

Opening remarks

This book is about manufacturing and manufacturers in the Ottoman Middle Eastern world between *c.* 1800 and 1914. It is a study of events that happened, not about failures to industrialize according to a pattern prescribed from outside. Concerns of our own day frame this work, as Third World countries attempt, and too many fail, to improve their living standards through high technology industrial change. The locus of analysis is the Ottoman Empire, one of the original Third World countries, and its efforts to grapple with an expanding, highly efficient and competitive European industrial order. The geographic focus is on areas that remained within the Ottoman Empire until the twentieth century. Thus, the book includes manufacturing in Salonica, Macedonia and in the Anatolian, north Syrian and, to the extent possible, the Iraqi provinces. Since Damascus, south Syria and Palestine have a far richer literature, they were excluded except for comparative purposes.

Although there are fragmentary accounts of Ottoman manufacturing in various works, there has been no comprehensive examination of this fascinating and complex subject. In the following chapters are stories of manufacturing decline and failure, of adaptation, restructuring, growth and resistance. Four major regions of industrial activity bustled in the late nineteenth-century Ottoman world. Salonica and the Macedonian countryside formed the first of these, mainly concentrating on wool cloth and yarn production but increasing cotton cloth output towards the end of the period. Western Anatolia formed the second major manufacturing region and produced a wide variety of textiles, including raw and woven silk, carpets, and several different cotton cloths. The third and perhaps least important of the regions was clustered in a group of towns, some 100–200 kilometers south of the Black Sea coast between Samsun and Trabzon. Here, chiefly cotton cloth and some wool cloth production prevailed, with the addition of carpetmaking very late in the period. Likely the most important region centered in southeast Anatolia and northern Syria, where weavers focused on silk and silk-cottons, with a growing late-century emphasis on pure cotton cloth. Altogether, the tale of these four regions trace out once-unknown activities and demand a change in the way that we view the manufacturing sector of this last great independent Islamic state in the Age of Imperialism. Collectively, the details mass up to challenge and, I believe, refute the notion that Ottoman industry merely declined and/or stagnated in the era of European industrial hegemony.

The overall importance of manufacturing in the nineteenth-century Ottoman economy is not now and may never be susceptible to accurate aggregate measurement. It surely contributed far more than one-tenth of Ottoman GNP, as once was indicated in a pioneering compilation of Ottoman statistics.[1] Existing measurements of its overall significance are essentially worthless, in part, because the available Ottoman statistics generally are very poor and because manufacturing has not been a discrete object of study. But there are other, more substantive reasons. Most observers considered only two forms of industrial activities when they sought to measure or evaluate Ottoman manufacturing. To them, manufacturing was visible only when it was urban-based and either guild-organized or located in a factory setting. As seen below, this assumption is incorrect. Also, many Ottoman economic historians have been led astray by the agrarian nature of the Ottoman Empire. In the nineteenth century, more than 80 percent of Ottoman subjects lived in rural areas. The importance of manufacturing was grossly underrepresented because of a prevailing if unconsidered assumption that cultivators necessarily only cultivated. We now know from studies of the American, British, German, Chinese and other economies that manufacturing often is an integral, variously important, part of agrarian life.[2] Agrarian economies commonly were mixed and rural families engaged in both agriculture and manufacturing, both for subsistence and commercial purposes. Thus, the account of Ottoman manufacturing must tally rural industry as well as non-guild urban production; it must reckon the contributions of Ottoman households and workshops as well as those of factories and guild organizations.[3]

There are many important lacunae in the present study. The relationship between land tenure and manufacturing, for example, is discussed infrequently. Overall, most Ottoman cultivators were small landholders, a pattern that remained generally true over the period. We know very little, however, about patterns of landholding or agricultural exploitation at the micro-level. Therefore, we cannot properly link what we learn in this book about clusters of manufacturing to local agrarian structures. Readers, after seeing where industry was most successful and concentrated, hopefully will be prompted to explore the prevailing land tenure and cultivating patterns.[4] Many active manufacturing regions possessed poor soil and marginal agriculture but it seems that some held comparatively fertile soil and comparatively dense populations. Security of property generally did improve and near the end of the period there were nearly full property rights. The book frequently does speak about the relationship between changing outputs in agriculture and industry. It repeatedly shows that manufacturers, both for the local market and for Ottoman buyers outside their districts, expanded output when agrarian production in the market area increased and contracted in the presence of failed or poor crops.

There are gaps in the analysis regarding the mechanisms used to market Ottoman manufactured goods. Sometimes we do not know if the manufacturers were independent producers or participants in a putting-out network. There is distressingly little on the personal consequences of changes such as lost jobs in hand spinning or new jobs in cloth weaving, cloth printing or ready-made clothing assemblage. Presently there is no information, for example, that we can use to assess the impact of such changes on gender relations within the family. The issue of capital accumulation among peasant manufacturers is *terra incognita* on the Ottoman manufacturing history map. Therefore, our analysis does not discuss how their successes led either to land acquisition, further industrial activity, or higher levels of consumption. These and other deficiencies underscore the introductory nature of this book, a quality that I would like to stress at this point. While answering many questions, the book leaves others insufficiently explored.

The gap regarding state-owned and managed factories, however, is deliberate. These factories economically were not important. According to one enumeration, all Ottoman factories (both state and privately owned) employed perhaps 36,000 persons in 1913.[5] Moreover, the state-run factories were *sui generis* and their history is of very limited general applicability. They were founded to supply state needs and operated as protected, subsidized establishments with guaranteed markets. Any of them would make an interesting subject for a monograph, and there certainly is super-abundant documentation available. But the game does not seem worth the candle at this primitive stage in the development of Ottoman manufacturing literature. While many new and fascinating details surely would be learned from studying government factories, few new insights into the structure and nature of the manufacturing sector are likely to be gained.

State policy

To the extent possible, this book is not about Ottoman governmental policy towards manufacturing. State decision-making did exert influence upon the manufacturing sector and could be of critical importance to Ottoman manufacturers. Before the Tanzimat reforms, for example, sumptuary laws governed "the strange and fantastic costumes and headgear worn by the members of the Ottoman military and civil hierarchy ... "[6] and by others in the various occupations and religious communities. These regulations afforded Ottoman textile manufacturers a certain protection from foreign competitors and when Sultan Mahmud II abolished them in 1826, the consequences were devastating.

Ottoman clothmakers' market vanished literally overnight. They suddenly were compelled to compete with European manufacturers in supplying the new frock coats and uniforms worn by the Westernizing bureaucrats and soldiers.

Similarly, the state's need for revenues often meant oppressively heavy taxes on manufactures. In one instance *c.* 1850, some 16 of the 18 cloth-printing factories in the city of İzmir closed, allegedly because of excessive taxation which made it impossible to compete with foreign goods.[7]

Many Ottoman artisans and entrepreneurs fought prolonged battles to reduce or eliminate taxes and tariffs. Take, for example, the Aleppo merchants who fought for decades to obtain relief from state levies. A pair of petitions from Aleppo, in 1846, complained of excessive tariffs. The first complained about the 1839 Tanzimat decree that, for the first time, placed customs fees of 12 percent, on *kumaş* cloth of every kind.[8] As a result, they stated, merchants had stopped purchases, sales had evaporated and the industry had fallen to a weak and destitute state. The second petition, from the Greek Catholic patriarch and the merchants of Aleppo, bemoaned the collapse of the silk and silk-cotton cloth industry brought about by excessive customs charges. Foreign-made silk-cotton (*kutni*) textiles, they said, paid only 3 percent customs and an additional 2 percent at the point of sale, but locally made silk and cotton textiles paid heavier multiple taxes, including land customs on the silk and import duties on the foreign yarn and dyestuffs. Consequently, they said, people were buying the cheap imported goods. The petitioners requested removal of the customs duty as well as the new taxes on the dyehouse, the fulling house and the cloth-polishing house at Aleppo.[9] In 1862, a new treaty gave some relief and reduced export duties from 12 to 8 percent. But the 12 percent duty on shipments into the interior remained. And, since the new treaty raised the duty on British yarn and imported dyestuffs, it added to the final production costs of Aleppo textiles.[10]

In 1866, in two separate petitions, a group of Aleppo Muslim merchants (joined by one European) and the Muslim populace petitioned successfully against the new customs fees. They appealed to a previous regulation that had placed duties of 2 to 6 percent on Aleppo textiles, according to the amount of synthetic dyes used. The greater the proportion of synthetic dyes used, the lower the tariff. The government in this case agreed and ordered that Aleppo textiles made for domestic consumption would pay the lower sliding-scale rates and not the flat 8 percent duty.[11] A few years later, in 1874, the state abolished the 8 percent internal tariff since "many products of agriculture and native manufactures were suffering from that oppressive impost."[12] Aleppo merchants again petitioned in 1875 and won tariff reductions, from 6 to 4 percent, on textile exports via Alexandretta. The government noted that the petition had no legal grounds but approved it anyway in order to help trade, maintain the Aleppo looms and increase production.[13] In later years, the abolition of tariffs on domestic seaborne trade was said to be playing a major role in the booming prosperity of this city's textile exports.[14]

Thus, as this extended example from Aleppo shows, tariffs and taxes could play an important role in the health of the textile industry. Such accounts must be treated cautiously since they may reflect other agendas. In the İzmir example, the author of the account likely was an Ottoman partisan of higher duties. The stress on tariff policies, in my view, is another way of giving primacy to the actions of the state in shaping economic development. Insistence on tariffs as the culprit distracts attention from the larger complex of international political and economic relationships that prevailed between Europe and the Middle East during this period.

It also is true that the state retained some importance in the manufacturing sector although its control slipped quite considerably over the nineteenth century. During the first half of the century, it enlisted tribes in western Anatolia to supply wool for a cloth factory that it was seeking to build. At this time, the networks of centuries past that had provided sail cloth to the navy still partially functioned, for example on the Gallipoli peninsula and in northern Anatolia. Quite a high proportion of all the mechanized factories built before *c.* 1900 were at the state's behest, both at İstanbul and everywhere else in the empire.

To determine just how important the state was remains quite another matter. Debates on the centrality of the state's role in economic development are familiar enough and rage in areas of historical inquiry far more developed than Ottoman history. For example, many have contrasted Japan's extraordinary leap to the status of a mature industrial power with that of continuing underdevelopment of India. To understand the differences between the performances of the Indian and Japanese economies, some scholars have focused on state policies as the crucial, determining variable. They have contrasted Meiji subsidies and support for industrialization with Indian *laissez-faire* policies. But others argue against such an effort and deny that state policies are crucial. They instead insist on explanations that stress the changes that percolated up from below rather than those that seeped down from above.[15]

The Ottoman state is important but does not need to be brought back in because, to misuse Theda Skocpol's oft-quoted remark, it never had left. The state always has been at the very center of Ottoman historiography and of Ottoman historians' consciousness. Ottoman scholars in fact have overly focused on the state and its concerns and the story of manufacturing has been no exception. Recounting state policy too often is merely recording what the state intended or wished reality to be, a vision very far removed from the actuality of the industrial sector itself. While such plans and programs have significance and interest, they are not our focus.

The following is a brief sketch, a guide to Ottoman state policy towards manufacturing; it is not, however, an exhaustive account.[16] In the era before the nineteenth century, according to one formulation, Ottoman economic policy generally aimed to provide a cheap, good and abundant supply of goods to the state and its urban populations, particularly those in İstanbul.[17] Complex control mechanisms embraced every part of the empire, seeking to direct the flow of raw and finished materials, ranging from wheat to shoe leather to wool cloth and most commodities in between. The state contracted with a host of different groups in Ottoman society, including nomads who provided wool and yarn and merchants who supervised putting-out networks. To facilitate control, the state characteristically worked with guilds not only in the big cities of İstanbul, Aleppo, Bursa and Salonica but also in small towns such as Merzifon in the Black Sea region. Guilds provided goods and services. They also cooperated in assessing and collecting government taxes on the manufacturing sector. For example, at Merzifon in the 1840s, guilds made certain that their textiles either paid a stamp tax for local sale or customs duties if sent outside the home district.[18] In exchange, they received production-distribution privileges and monopolies and government assistance in their maintenance.

The reforming statesmen of the nineteenth century, or at least some of them, sought to abandon this policy in favor of free trade. The official turning point, however, was neither the 1838 Anglo-Turkish Convention nor the Tanzimat decree of 1839, usually cited as such in the literature. These were only some more nails in the coffin of the prevailing "provisionist" policy. Rather, the decisive turning point in policy already had taken place. It occurred in 1826, when the government attacked and destroyed the Janissaries, whom the state and its chroniclers considered thugs, a vulgar and violent rabble. Indeed, the state had cause for concern since Janissary violence guarded the interests of urban guilds against encroachments by the state and the elites. The destruction of the Janissaries in 1826 was no mere removal of reactionary opponents to military and political modernization, as it generally has been considered. This state action had profound economic consequences, for it destroyed the armed protectors of guild privilege and thus facilitated implementation of now-favored *laissez-faire* policies. With the disappearance of these Janissary defenders of popular sovereignty, the state could promote free trade, hence the 1838 treaty and the 1839 decree.

State policy in the nineteenth century thus turned in 1826. But a fundamental inconsistency towards promotion of a free market economy characterized most of the remainder of the period. This inconsistency derived from a split within the Ottoman elite, between the free traders and the protectionists, who perhaps simply were later-day provisionists. The battle in part was fought on the field of tariffs, with the protectionists seeking to re-erect customs barriers demolished in 1838 and 1839. They won some successes with increased tariffs in 1861–62, when the state also employed other means to stimulate manufacturing, and again in 1907 and 1914. The inconsistency also shows up in government responses to urban guild artisans' appeals for assistance. On some occasions, officials responded by pointing to the Tanzimat decrees, reiterating that guild privilege officially was dead and open competition now prevailed. But, in many other instances, the state maintained the monopolies and privileges of the petitioning guilds. Similarly, the state continued to require possession of a certificate (*gedik*) in order to operate a shop, although this system clearly was incompatible with a free market economy. It repeatedly re-affirmed the legitimacy of these certificates into the 1860s, for the revenues they generated and sometimes from considerations of equity.[19] The extent to which the certificates actually hindered guilds and urban manufacturing, however, is not clear since the government repeatedly allowed their number to increase and permitted shops to open without them.[20] The certificates nonetheless did conflict with free market principles being promoted by the state. Another example of government inconsistency comes from a monopolistic method used to regulate and tax urban textile production, that persisted into the final quarter of the nineteenth century. Since 1805, cloth finishing in a city legally had been performed only at a single centralized location. There, the state recorded, taxed and stamped the cloth being polished, a procedure that also helped the guilds to restrict competition. Driven by fiscal considerations, the system had continued deep into the free trade era in a number of cities, including Diyarbakır, Erzurum and Harput. It was abandoned only in 1878, many decades after free market principles officially had been adopted.[21]

The historiography of Ottoman manufacturing

Our understanding of the Middle Eastern economy and its manufacturing sector has been influenced profoundly by now-discredited stereotypes concerning the inferiority of Islam as a religious system and the general stagnation and backwardness of the region. In this false vision, just as Islamic civilization underwent permanent decline after the 1,001 Arabian Nights, so did its economy, seen as equally incapable of dynamism and change. If the door of independent thinking (*ijtihad*) in religion had been closed, so too was the possibility of economic evolution. The economic institutions of the Islamic classical age, like the political ones, were assumed to have continued nearly unchanged into later centuries. Any shifts were seen as corrupted deviations from Golden Age norms. These stereotyped notions of Middle Eastern political and cultural life now largely have been abandoned in favor of more accurate depictions of internal evolution and change. But, in the realm of economic history and particularly manufacturing, these static conceptions have left a powerful and largely intact legacy.

This inheritance of older Orientalist prejudices concerning backwardness and

7

modernization has shaped our understanding of nineteenth-century Ottoman manufacturing particularly in regards to guilds and their importance. There has been too much implicit insistence on the history of guilds as representative of Ottoman manufacturing in general. Still worse is the tendency to regard nineteenth-century Ottoman guilds as unevolved versions of their sixteenth-century predecessors, virtually identical in structure and function everywhere in the empire (except in Egypt). This stress on guilds also derives from an acceptance of the Ottoman state's vision of industrial reality, a perspective fraught with significant consequences for our understanding of manufacturing. The dominance of this official vision no doubt is due partially to the incredible abundance of the source materials in the Ottoman archives, which, more generally, capture state perspectives, policies and activities. Indeed, the ability of the İstanbul government to largely dominate the political and cultural life of the empire for most of its existence probably reinforces widespread scholarly acceptance of the government view. Ultimately, however, state reports and documents tell us only about activities that the regime thought were important and/or were able to record. In the case of manufacturing, state concerns focused on urban areas and particularly on the guilds that played various administrative, supply and/or tax-collecting roles. Hence, the government recorded their activities. But, too often, the documentation grossly misrepresents the guilds' actual economic importance.

There are other grave dangers in relying on guilds as the sole barometer of manufacturing. Most of the extant literature relating to them suffers from a serious fault. It insists that since guilds declined in the nineteenth century, so did manufacturing overall; and, it ignores non-guild forms of industrial activity. Their restrictive qualities in fact made guilds comparatively inflexible and particularly unable to meet mounting Western competition. As the economy worsened during the late eighteenth century, the guilds began losing out but used the Janissary Corps to mobilize in self-defense.[22] Many Ottoman guilds, their rigidity making them exquisitely vulnerable, subsequently vanished or declined in the face of European competition. Contemporary and modern-day observers too often falsely equated the fate of the guilds – the most fragile components of the industrial sector – with manufacturing in general. They concluded that because many guilds had collapsed, so had Ottoman industry.[23] And, it is not even true that all the guilds collapsed; many continued throughout the nineteenth and some into the twentieth century. What they had become, however, is not at all clear; these late survivals probably were perpetuated thanks to their social functions, not to their economic logic.[24]

There were a great variety and number of manufacturing activities that fell outside the purview of guilds, both in urban areas and the countryside. Surely these must be considered in any study of manufacturing. The task is difficult if not impossible, however, if we rely solely on government records, or, to put it more accurately, on those currently available. Manufacturing activities carried on outside guilds were not particularly well-controlled, that is, counted by the state. These forms of production thus are nearly invisible in the government documents typically examined, sources that have remained at the heart of much of the literature on manufacturing.[25] For at least part of the nineteenth century, the state quite imperfectly taxed non-guild urban artisans. Also, it does not appear to have taxed commercial household industry in the countryside, at least in some of the locations where we know it was present. For example, if male members of the family performed military services, their household's commercial manufacturing output was exempted from taxation. And, because they were tax exempt, this production for the marketplace went unrecorded. Thus, such manufacturing activities have been neglected in virtually all the historical accounts.[26] In order to compensate for the silent official sources, this study examined a wide body of alternative materials that indeed do speak of Ottoman manufacturing.

The historiographies of Ottoman economic decline and de-industrialization have deep indigenous roots. Ottomans' beliefs in their own economic decline are nearly as old as the Ottoman Empire itself. These conceptions are embedded in the accounts of the empire's political and military woes, reported by the official and unofficial court historians of the Sultans. During the later sixteenth century, these chroniclers already were detailing a long list of factors – corruption, the reward of incompetents, rule by women – that, they said, were destroying the empire from within. These accounts powerfully affected views of the Ottoman economy since readers assumed, not illogically, that economic decay accompanied this reported political decline. Barkan's famous 1975 article on the Ottoman price revolution, for example, seems to imply that the late sixteenth-century crisis described therein initiated a centuries-long and permanent economic decline. The crisis is not discussed as a short-term, if severe, dislocation that may have passed. Thanks to recent scholarship, we now know that the court historians were not objective observers of Ottoman decline but rather partisans who represented events to serve their own causes.[27] Often the losers in elite political struggles, these authors wrote biased and dark tales of political decay to win their way back into power or, at least, to carp at the winners. That is, their stories of decline are tracts serving personal political agendas and are not reliable indicators of political or economic conditions.

In the nineteenth century, Ottoman political weakness in the international arena had become real and Ottoman histories of that decrepitude no longer simply were projections of personal political failure onto a larger stage. But the use of nineteenth-century court chroniclers' accounts remains risky for economic historians. Sometimes, in common with their predecessors, this is because they were participants in the struggles they recorded. Take, for example, Mehmed Esad's account of the Janissaries' demise in 1826. Less than one year before the slaughter of the Janissaries, this reporter was promoted to the post of official chronicler (*vakanüvis*) precisely because he was opposed to that group. He personally took part in their destruction in 1826 and was enriched and honored for it. His description of Janissary economic activity, to put it mildly, is highly biased.[28] So too are the accounts of industrialization and manufacturing by the chroniclers Lütfi and Cevdet, as well as by the great recorder of İstanbul events, Osman Nuri, who provides perhaps the most detailed account.[29]

The distortions in their accounts, at least in part, come from a different source: the ongoing adoption of modernization models by Ottoman elite circles during the nineteenth century. As is known, modernization, i.e., westernization, in the political realm meant a large and effective military, the centralization, increase and extension of state power into every area of life, and the rationalization and specialization of function of the bureaucracy. In the industrial sector, modernization meant manufacturing according to European methods and even with Western mentalities! Take, for example, this 1852 Ottoman inspector's report on industrial conditions in western Anatolia.

I travelled around studying industry and, in most of the areas where I observed, the majority of artisans were restricted in the kinds and types of manufactures. They have not reached the stage of development to invent other things, as is the case in Europe, where there is an era of renewal and the capabilities and mental dispositions of the people are suited to invention. For this reason, some ancient industries are abandoned and neglected and are profitless.[30]

Whatever their stance on specific issues, Ottoman modernizers shared a definition of manufacturing as properly understood. It ought to be machine-based and factory-located.[31] If not, it had little legitimacy and hence visibility in the eyes of nineteenth-century Ottoman recorders of Ottoman industry.

There are exceptions. For example, the author Salaheddin Bey does enumerate the many Ottoman handicrafts exhibited at the 1867 Paris exposition. But his willingness to discuss non-machine manufacturing derives not from his sensitivity to such activities but rather from his determination to record the Ottoman contribution to this international meeting.[32] There is the Ottoman industrial survey, taken in 1913 (and again in 1915), that enumerates either those factories with inanimate power sources and ten workers or those with animate power and twenty workers. In this latter case, therefore, centralized production on some scale was a key variable and not simply the machinery.[33]

Generally, however, officially inspired accounts of nineteenth-century Ottoman manufacturing discuss only mechanized factories. Most historians note the establishment of state-run factories early in the century and then jump to the private factory foundings after *c.* 1880, with attention to the burst of activity in the early twentieth century. They hardly ever discuss home or workshop manufacturing, in common with the state documents and perspective on which they are based.

Until *c.* 1970, there were few scholars in modern Turkey interested in nineteenth-century Ottoman economic history. Most of those who studied the nineteenth century preferred political events, specifically, the modernization of the Ottoman state. Hence, when discussing economic affairs, they, in common with most nineteenth-century Ottoman authors, discussed only (1) the role of the modernizing state in the economy and (2) efforts to form a factory-based industrial order.[34] An influential article by Sarç appeared in 1940, as part of a volume honoring the 100th anniversary of the official 1839 beginning of Ottoman westernization. This account reflects both the nineteenth-century Ottoman modernizers' bias in favor of big factories and its twentieth-century Kemalist republican variant. Written in the late 1930s, the article reflected recent efforts by the Turkish administrative elite to industrialize from above. Sarç's view is that of the modernizing Turkish state and transmitted to another generation the standard account of failed factories and economically inept Ottomans. This Tanzimat-republican Turkish tradition is alive and well in the present-day. Önsoy's 1988 book on Ottoman industry and the politics of industrialization is a latter-day version of Sarç, Osman Nuri and the nineteenth-century court historians, a study of mechanized factory industrialization from above.[35]

Heavy emphasis on mechanized, factory-based manufacturing, of course, is hardly unique to Ottoman and republican Turkish writers. Rather, it is part of an intellectual tradition that, until recently, held sway in Western scholarship on manufacturing. Indeed, as is well-known and readily acknowledged, the interpretations of Middle Eastern scholars have been shaped profoundly by European economic historians, a part of the westernization process itself. Moreover, European and American literature concerning other regions of the globe has provided the intellectual inspiration for scholarship produced within the territories of the former Ottoman Empire.[36]

Thus, in addition to their indigenous origins, the historiographies of Ottoman decline and de-industrialization also are heavily indebted to Western historiographical traditions concerning modernization and the Industrial Revolution. For the mainstream of Western writings on manufacturing, the Industrial Revolution was machine-driven production and an easily demarcated event that overwhelmed, outmoded and replaced (or soon would replace) existing, more primitive methods of manufacturing. Highly efficient, large-scale, capital-intensive factories *were* the Industrial Revolution that, in a triumphant march to a better world, outcompeted, out-produced and under-sold the artisans of the globe.

The high-tide of confidence in this future occurred in the 1960s, as victorious big-factory industrial capital was seen to be sweeping all before it. At this time, influential, benchmark studies appeared in both European and Middle Eastern economic history, works that scholars in both areas have profited from and struggled against ever since. In 1965, David Landes eloquently and compellingly summarized the progressive, technological vision in his study of British and European industrialization.[37] The Landes research exercised an exceptional influence because of its own merits and because it fit so well into a vision of the future shared by most intellectuals and policy planners in both the West and the rest. In Middle East economic history, Landes' 1965 study was sandwiched between Hershlag's 1964 survey account and Issawi's 1966 book of readings.[38] The three formed a chorus emphasizing machine-based, factory-located production as the sole, only truly valid, category of analysis in the industrial sector. Issawi's work became the better known of the two Middle East texts. In his book of readings, Issawi excerpted selections from a group of European and Ottoman writers who had remarkably similar visions of nineteenth-century Ottoman manufacturing history. His choices powerfully influenced a whole generation of young scholars (including this author) and roughed out a framework of analysis for Ottoman economic history and manufacturing history. By translating and reprinting these earlier accounts of hapless Ottoman industrialization, Issawi gave new life and broader currency to longstanding accounts – some of them more than a century old. In using Sarç's account of the failed industrialization drives of the Ottoman state, partially derived from Osman Nuri's account, he re-cycled the Tanzimat reformers' definition of manufacturing and vision of what they had been seeking to achieve in the industrial sector. Here, ironically, Ottoman and republican Turkish borrowers of Western economic models helped, in translation, to perpetuate those models among a Western audience. By quoting Ubicini, whose early nineteenth-century analysis is allowed to stand for the entire late Ottoman era, Issawi depicted the collapse of Ottoman industry from the perspective of an advocate of British economic liberalism. From the Marxist strain of liberalism, Issawi chose Smilianskaya's account that seems so similar to Ubicini's vision of hopeless industrial retrogression and decline. And yet, in the midst of these woeful and distressful accounts of Ottoman manufacturers and their inevitable failure, Issawi makes a number of his own comments about the resilience of Ottoman industries in Syria.[39] He thus reveals himself to be sensitive to the possibilities of alternatives to decline and collapse. But this fails to dilute the message delivered by his selections. The final impression that he leaves with us is very clear. A true son of Adam Smith, he presents a world in which economies that are not based on mechanized factories are less advanced, further down the evolutionary scale and less worthy of study than economies that are. It is, moreover, largely an urban industrial world, of inadequate factories and decaying guilds. In the best of all possible worlds, factories remain superior forms of organization, the emblems of progress.

The studies of Landes and Issawi obtained canonical status but, within a decade, a changing world order began to bring forward alternative views. The oil crisis of the 1970s, the Iranian revolution and the reemergence of allegedly dead, so-called traditional values all mocked the self-confidence of the industrial powers. In Middle Eastern studies, Owen's long-awaited economic history text (1981) gave a new stress to the resilience of local manufacturers, Manchester notwithstanding, and to the continued significance of small-scale, hand manufacturing.[40] Owen's industrial world was quite different from that of his predecessors in Ottoman Middle Eastern economic history. His was not a universe of sparsely scattered factories being ineptly managed by incompetent bureaucrats. Rather, his manufacturing pages, that are too few for such a lengthy survey, also are populated by artisans, active in town and country, vigorously participating in the economic life of their times. Owen also speaks of volitional factors, of human actions, not just impersonal market forces. For example, he noted how Syrian weavers were able to *expand* output during the world depression of the 1870s. He also discusses the eagerness of regional entrepreneurs to recapture or hold markets, their creation of styles and fashions not duplicable on a mass scale. Some of these factors are mentioned in Issawi's 1966 readings, but Owen gives them far greater weight and places them nearer to the center of his story. For Owen, human agency becomes part of the tale of Middle East manufacturing, one that includes decline and failure but also dynamism, adaptation and success. Despite the thin coverage, his depiction of manufacturing reveals a sector that survived and changed during the age of European industrial hegemony.

In 1982, Issawi published his own analysis of nineteenth- and twentieth-century Middle East economic history, not a book of readings. This more recent work reflects some shift in his views on manufacturing and leaves the door slightly open to perspectives different from those in his 1966 reader. Thus, while the de-industrialization of the Ottoman Empire remains a critical event, he now offers greater emphasis on the gradual and slow nature of the process. A great deal of industry remained in the region, he concludes, and "neither the speed nor the extent of the devastation should be exaggerated."[41]

The 1987 book by Pamuk is exceptionally useful in delineating nineteenth-century trade patterns. Its single chapter on manufacturing shows, if often from great macroeconomic heights, the continuing evolution of Ottoman economic history towards a greater appreciation of hand manufacturing and its vitality in the age of European expansion.[42] He speaks of "mechanisms of adaptation and resistance employed by the indigenous forms of production."[43] And, building on Owen, he estimates that the volume of hand-woven cotton cloth doubled between 1880 and 1914. Despite these accomplishments, his treatment of manufacturing is unsatisfactory. Pamuk offers elaborately derived tables of imported and locally made cotton yarn and cloth. These calculations, he asserts, demonstrate an overall nineteenth-century deindustrialization of the Ottoman economy, the essential disappearance of Ottoman handspinning. The methodology employed to produce the statistics that justify his assertions is very sophisticated.[44] But, to this reader, the calculations and the consequent analysis regarding manufacturing remain unconvincing. This is not mere academic squabbling. Pamuk has massively under-represented levels of hand-spun yarn production (see chapter 1, table 1.1.). Since his handspinning figures are incorrect, so are his calculated levels of handwoven cloth production and aggregate Ottoman cloth consumption. These estimates are far too low and must be discarded. This leads to the second and equally important point – Pamuk assumes that imports of yarn and cloth represent jobs that were lost to the Ottoman economy. He does not allow for the possibility that yarn and cloth imports created jobs, a theme explored below (in chapters 1–4 and also 6). Ultimately, in common with Issawi and the Ottoman chroniclers before him, Pamuk remains convinced that Ottoman textile manufacturing surely *must* have declined in the nineteenth century.

This brief survey of the historiography of Ottoman manufacturing suggests that although assaults on the fortress of mechanized, urban, high technology, factory thinking have been launched, the walls remain unbreached. Historians of Europe (and of the United States), however, have made far more effective encroachments on the factory orthodoxy of manufacturing history.[45] A turning point, perhaps, was the 1981 publication of Pollard's *Peaceful Conquest*, a textbook on the complex process of European industrialization. On the one hand, in common with and building on the earlier work of Landes, Pollard remains deeply committed to the centrality of technological change for successful manufacturing. On the other, he utilizes the 1970s studies by Mendels, Medick and others and devotes considerable space to rural manufacturing and to its low-technology, labor-intensive forms of production.[46] A few years after the appearance of the Pollard survey, Berg published her important 1985 book (that critiqued Mendels for his teleological approach). In common with Mendels, although in a different way, Berg (and Greenberg) downplayed the importance of high technology and emphasized the gradual nature of technological change. These new interpretations challenged views that had insisted on the abrupt character of the Industrial Revolution and its overnight replacement of hand manufacturing with "large scale, capital-intensive factories and mechanization."[47] The new scholarship demonstrated that the shift was very prolonged. It also showed that many output increases once attributed to mechanization in fact derived from "a whole series of industries whose technologies were based on traditional handicrafts or new skills – leathermaking, shoemaking, glove- and hatmaking ... "[48] A speed-up of manual work processes rather than mechanization and technological efficiency often had accounted for rising manufacturing production.[49] During the eighteenth century, British industries grew as much in the old framework of home and artisanal manufacturing as within the more noticeable new factories.[50] Similarly, many industrial sectors in Britain between 1760 and 1830 substantially increased output *not* via mechanization but through improved hand tools and more systematic exploitation of labor.[51] In the British heartland of the new industrial order, factory and domestic forms of industrial organization continued to coexist, often within the same industry.[52] Tens of thousands of cotton hand-loom weavers in Britain still worked at home, as late as the 1850s.[53]

As will be clear, the above findings powerfully influenced the questions that I formulated regarding nineteenth-century Ottoman manufacturing history. Widespread rural industry and hand production in town and country had been an integral part of European manufacturing during the nineteenth century. Surely that could be the case in the Ottoman Empire as well. The question remained, how and where to find the evidence? Thus, these recent works by European economic historians both prompted and legitimized the present study of home, workshop and factory manufacturing in the Ottoman world.

Ottoman manufacturing in comparative perspective

Sharing the common fate of nations in the nineteenth century, Ottoman manufacturers competed under conditions that increasingly were framed by the international economy. As elsewhere, the specific circumstances and patterns of the Ottoman experience prompted interactions with global forces that created patterns of economic change unique to the area. That is, to use a writing metaphor, the international economy provided the general outline of the plot but the region furnished the details of the script. Thus, the Ottoman proximity to Europe rendered it especially sensitive to the effects of the Continental Blockade and to the end of the Napoleonic Wars. Later in the century, along with producers in India, East Asia and Latin America, Ottoman manufacturers confronted an opportunity of sorts with the price depression of 1873–96. As agricultural prices fell and local peasants reduced their purchases of imported goods, domestic manufacturers found new internal markets for their goods, if they were able sufficiently to reduce costs. Producers on several continents similarly found new market niches as the maturing industrial economies of Europe, after the mid century, turned away from textiles to capital equipment production. Thus, many countries – including India, Italy and the Ottoman Empire – significantly increased their mechanized production of cotton yarn, an arena in which competition with the British once had seemed unimaginable. At the end of the century, to give a final example, Ottoman and other manufacturers watched their domestic markets expand in the general price inflation of the post-1896 era.

Facing the extraordinary competition of British and, later on, other west European producers, Ottoman manufacturers and those in every region of the globe struggled to cope, adopting an equally extraordinarily varied set of responses and adaptations. On one end of the spectrum is Japan, with its massive, technologically sophisticated factory networks, that has out-industrialized the West. On the other, we might place those economies that entirely de-industrialized and switched over to the agricultural or emerging service sectors of the new, Third, world.

In the nineteenth-century Middle East manufacturing world that capitalism made, the Ottoman experiences fall somewhere in between. The Ottoman industrial sector did not mechanize on any significant scale; nor did it disappear. As this book will make abundantly clear, nineteenth-century Ottoman manufacturing scarcely was moribund. Indeed, aggregate production levels were greater in 1914 than in 1800. On the one hand, the international export market truly had disappeared for the wool, cotton and linen cloth makers. At the end of the period, these produced hardly anything for the west and central European buyers who once had been important consumers of their goods. At least partially offsetting these losses, however, were impressive exports of rugs, lace, embroideries and raw silk – late nineteenth-century entries into the international market. There is a distinct possibility that the absolute value of exported Ottoman manufactures was *greater* at the end of the period than its beginning.[54] The internal market, however, is the key to understanding the history of the manufacturing sector during the nineteenth century. Most Ottoman textile workers wove, printed and dyed for the domestic consumers who, despite the huge territorial losses endured by the empire during the nineteenth century, still numbered an impressive 26 millions in c. 1914.

These clearly are important, indeed crucial, issues in considering the fate of Ottoman manufacturing. Thus, the remainder of the book is divided into two sections, separately treating, as much as possible, production for domestic and foreign consumers. Part I deals with yarn and cloth production, almost exclusively for the domestic Ottoman market. Part II treats the silk and carpet industries, that (except for silk cloth) served to meet the needs of foreign consumers.

While the histories of often-rising production for the domestic market and of the sharp increases in certain textile exports form the story told in the pages of this study, they do not suggest that Ottoman industry had experienced an "industrial revolution" or maintained its relative global position. Rather, it is quite clear that Ottoman manufacturing was less important internationally in 1914 than it had been previously, c. 1800. The Ottoman industrial economy expanded in size but steadily shrank in global importance during the post-1750 period. The Ottoman Empire accounted for a share of world trade that already was minuscule in 1830, 3 percent; by 1910, this share had dropped to under 1 percent.[55] In examining Ottoman manufacturing, we are treating an industrial sector that played a marginal and diminishing role in the international economy of the nineteenth century.

This should hardly surprise us. Here, recall the many studies that arose in response to Franklin Mendels' seminal work, seeking to confirm but ultimately refuting his proto-industrialization thesis. Often these researches demonstrated that vibrant manufacturing activities led nowhere and did not provide the basis for mechanized, factory-based industrial production.[56]

There were other non-West European states that enjoyed more visible successes. India, for example, entered into the fiercely competitive world of cotton textile exports and increased the value of such shipments by more than seven-fold between 1860 and 1900, becoming an important if secondary supplier on the international market. By comparison, Ottoman cloth production at this time perhaps doubled, output that remained focused completely on the domestic market.

Japan, of course, became the first non-Western country to emerge as a major industrial economy and important textile producer. Between the 1870s and World War I, the clothing and textile share of all Japanese exports rose from 4 to 34 percent. Japanese exports of silk cloth rose spectacularly after the 1880s, some twenty times in just two decades. And, they sold the cloth in the very backyard of their European competitors. The output of Ottoman silk cloth production did rise in the nineteenth century (contrary to all previous accounts of this industry), but it was only for domestic buyers.[57] The Ottoman raw silk industry registered impressive achievements in the export sector during the nineteenth century. But the Japanese (and Chinese) first surpassed and then dwarfed this output; by 1913, these East Asian sources were producing at least eight times as much as their Middle Eastern counterparts.

Unlike in India and Japan, the textile industries of the Ottoman Empire (except raw silk and rugs) and Spain relied on the domestic market. In both the Ottoman and Spanish cases, substantial markets vanished because of imperial failures; the Spanish lost most of the overseas empire in America while the territorial extent of the Ottoman realms shrank by more than one-half during the nineteenth century. Just as the loss of its Balkan possessions dealt a shattering blow to the Ottoman economy, the Spanish defeat in Cuba negated the last-ditch effort to save the final remaining long-distance market, on which manufacturers had come to depend to maintain their growth rates. During the nineteenth century, British competition prevented both textile industries from making up for imperial losses with new international markets.[58] But in the Ottoman case, as we shall see, export producers moved into non-competing sectors (rugs, silk, lace). Such similarities aside, the structures of (at least) the cotton textile industry in the two states were quite different. The Ottomans' remained overwhelmingly based on handicraft production scattered about in a number of locations. The Spanish industry, by contrast, centered on one area – Catalonia in the northeast – and featured big, mechanized factory production.

How can we use the experiences of these other textile industries for understanding the Ottoman record of competition with British hegemony during the nineteenth century? The answer is not clear and, frankly, there does not seem to be a great deal of room for optimism. The problem rests in the sharp disagreements that prevail among development economists and economic historians over what happened and why – e.g., the character and causes of Japanese industrialization and/or Indian underdevelopment. According to some Japanese specialists, as seen, the answer to industrialization there is not to be found in government policies. Instead, the key to the phenomenal growth of the Japanese textile industry is said to rest in the fact that Japanese handicraft producers were focused on supplying the internal market. Therefore, in this argument, mechanized mill owners could focus on the export market. But others disagree, pointing to the Chinese example, where handicraft production for the internal market was considered not as a stimulus but rather as a brake on the domestic textile industry! Still others argue for rates of capital accumulation that were very high indeed, because of the particular evolution of certain groups in rural Japan. This emphasis points to the extent of the structural transformations that created and distributed the surplus. The debate over Japanese industrial evolution has raged, apparently to the point of despair.[59] In one argument, the example of Japan is said to hold no useful lessons for those present-day states seeking industrial development.[60] A similar stalemate has emerged in Indian studies. Whether Indian manufacturers' achievements occurred because or in spite of British rule is debated among specialists who are unable to come to closure on the issue.[61] Put less positively, the argument centers on the role of the British imperial system in the Indian inability to achieve the status of a mature industrial economy in the twentieth century.

Among some who study the evolution of Japan and India, it seems that a certain consensus has evolved, independently in the two cases. It is now posited that specialists have not explained the success of Japan or the failure of India, only described it. In the Japan example, they have read back from successful industrialization in order to demonstrate how all the major events in Japanese history have assisted in achieving the happy result. In the India case study, similarly, some have proven the inevitability of the flow of industrial history.

Several issues in the India debate seem particularly relevant here. The first begins with the now-familiar assertion that the evolution of manufacturing in a given country should not be seen as a series of steps down a unilinear path. Rather, the evolution consists of a series of "ceaseless improvisation," a series of decisions made by actors in the particular region. This perspective assumes the continuing occurrence of conscious choices. It focuses attention on actions in the periphery rather than in the industrialized core countries.[62] A second aspect of the India debate should be particularly sobering for Middle East specialists – that revolving around the term "deindustrialization" to describe the changes in manufacturing in the subcontinent between 1850 and 1947. Some India scholars suggest that the term be abandoned altogether because its meaning is not clear.

They argue that there are too many holes in the data to support the level of generalization that use of the term implies. Time series of absolute values and volumes of output are required; similarly unknown are sectoral output shares, as well as, i.e., sectoral and total employment.[63] Thus, some India scholars are uncertain about the path taken by manufacturing. This hesitation exists despite a truly vast, impressive and sophisticated body of literature, at least compared to that in Middle Eastern and Ottoman studies. Surely the continued unsureness of these specialists about Indian manufacturing should be a caution for proponents of Ottoman "deindustrialization."

PART I Manufacturing for the domestic market

General introduction

Cloth production

Ottoman textile manufacturing retained a strong vitality during the nineteenth century despite falling prices, changing technologies and fashions, and severe foreign competition. The remarkable decline in yarn and cloth prices in Europe, at first in Britain, derived from a number of factors. These included the introduction of the machine-spun yarns and synthetic and artificial dyestuffs (chapter 1) and, later, machine-made cloth as well (chapters 2 and 3). In addition, the fall in prices owed much to the vast expansion in the supply of very cheap raw materials from the United States to Britain.[1] In the Ottoman world, these distant innovations prompted shifts from one textile to another, usually cotton at the expense of other materials. Thus, cotton largely replaced silk and mohair as the fabric of choice for the Ottoman upper classes. Among workers and peasants, the use of home-spun cotton yarn declined as did that of wool cloth, animal skins, and mohair cloth. The adoption of Western fashions in clothing accompanied and stimulated these shifts from one to another textile. And so, Ottoman imports of cotton yarn and cloth grew enormously over the century, to levels that are very impressive on an absolute scale. Over the nineteenth century, imports of cotton yarn increased between 25 and 50 times, depending on whether a base year during or after the Napoleonic Wars is adopted (chapter 1). Cotton cloth imports have been estimated at 4,100 tons a year during the 1840s; by 1909, they had risen over tenfold, to more than 49,000 tons.[2] Early in the century, Britain drove its Indian competitors from Ottoman marketplaces, where they had sold for centuries.[3] Thereafter, British producers always dominated the overall textile import market. But, i.e., the Swiss, Germans, French and Austrians offered greater and lesser competition over the century in certain cloths and segments of the market; these states, as well as India and Italy, competed to fill Ottoman cotton yarn needs.[4]

Ottoman manufacturers survived because the story of Ottoman yarn and cloth is more complicated than the preceding, familiar, account suggests. Cotton yarn imports did soar but homespinning remained important and, at the end of the period, still provided a full one-quarter of all Ottoman cotton yarn needs (chapter 1). The rise of cotton cloth to the first rank did occur but some other textiles hung on. The use of mohair cloth seems to have vanished almost entirely but that of linen did not and in fact rose over time. Similarly, use of silk and silk-cotton cloth persisted for much of the century and then significantly increased, on a per capita basis, towards its end. Wool cloth, for its part, retained considerable popularity, as demonstrated by the continuing vitality among Balkan weavers of the stuffs. Also, the wearing of "traditional" clothing – here only meaning non-Western styles – by both men and women, of all communities, remained very common. This is true despite ongoing westernization and our assumption that it meant disappearance of existing modes of behavior (and dress). Western-styles at first found favor among the urban-based elites and only gradually, in a process continuing until the present, spread into provincial towns and the rural countryside. European manufacturers in fact recognized and responded to the continuing appeal of local fashion, devoting quite considerable energies to learning and copying local patterns. Much of the imported cloth was not at all of the modern and Western design, but rather were European imitations of Middle Eastern patterns and styles. Ottoman styles also continued because some wore them as a form of protest, seeing the economic danger to Ottoman manufacturers posed by Western-style clothing.[5]

Ottoman textile manufacturers employed several survival strategies. A major theme of their story is the relentless drive to reduce prices. Hence, they employed rural and household labor and also more intensely exploited workshop labor. Producers frequently purchased machine-made yarn (at first European and later Ottoman and Indian as well) to obtain the price, quality and regularity advantages that such yarns offered. At the same time, for various textiles that required a particular texture or other characteristics, producers continued to use homespun. Many manufacturers used varying mixes of machine and hand-spun yarn for the warp or the weft, in order to produce desired qualities in a particular fabric. Also, they employed huge quantities of factory-made dyes and, over the century, became increasingly sophisticated in their handling of these new and inexpensive dyestuffs. Especially during the later part of the period, they readily used these to dye on the spot rather than import colored yarn. And, in a few locations, local manufacturers began producing their own synthetic and artificial dyestuffs. Through these mechanisms, they not only dropped prices but also obtained the precise colors demanded by their consumers. Many Ottoman weavers focused on making the non-Western clothing still beloved by so many of their customers. Here, the producers both encouraged the maintenance of unique local fashions and created new ones as well. It turns out that some patterns were hardly traditional, in the sense of longstanding, at all. Ottoman merchants had invented them, trying to keep their European competitors off-balance by rapidly changing fashions and creating patterns difficult to replicate in a factory.[6] It was not only that producers found refuge in weaving and dyeing particular cloths in the small quantities that were not worthy of European manufacturers or that they underbid them for the bottom of the market.[7] This often did occur. Many Ottoman producers survived because of the tiny niche in the market they filled; this especially was true of wool cloths and those made of silk and silk-cotton. Some wove the coarsest textiles at extremely low prices, an effort that is a critical part of the story of Ottoman cloth production. But these alone are not adequate explanations. Ottoman manufacturers sometimes outcompeted the Europeans for products sold in quantities that were extremely large indeed, winning because they better understood their customers' wants. Also, the Ottoman product often was slightly more expensive and won favor because of durability and/or style.

1 Raw cotton, dyestuffs and yarn production

Raw cotton

For centuries, Ottoman cotton yarn and cloth producers had benefitted from abundant supplies of the raw materials, both raw cotton and dyestuffs. Important centers of cotton cultivation historically had included southern Arabia, the Mesopotamian steppe, north Palestine, north Syria and the Adana region, the Aegean littoral, as well as the Thessalian plain and the Zekhua and Serez regions of Macedonia. From the time of the Crusades, many of these areas had supplied both regional and European textile makers. Levantine cotton seeds were transplanted in the soils of colonial Virginia, Delaware and Louisiana and helped give rise to these global centers of cotton production. But still, cotton production in the Levant during the late eighteenth century exceeded, by a factor of nearly thirty, that in the American colonies. Ottoman raw cotton exports then were considerable and there were plentiful supplies of raw cotton remaining for local manufacturers. At the beginning of the nineteenth century, the city of Salonica exported 22,500 bales of raw cotton while supplying another 15,000 bales to local manufacturers. During the 1830s, the Adana region produced c. 1,900 bales of raw cotton for domestic hand spinners.[1] Somewhat later, in the 1850s, Asia Minor altogether produced c. 50,000 bales of cotton, and about one-quarter of it was spun locally. By contrast, the Palestine port of Jaffa then exported only c. 500 bales. Macedonia, for its part, produced 9,700 bales, half of it for export; Thessaly, on the other hand, consumed virtually all of the 3,500 bales of cotton grown locally. In 1879, Anatolia exported some 85 percent of its production, then estimated at 27,000 bales.[2] In the early 1890s, aggregate Ottoman cotton production totalled 60,000 bales but, by 1904, the provinces of Adana, Syria and West Anatolia alone yielded some 80,000 bales. Stimulated by booming international textile production that caused severe raw material shortages, raw cotton output increased sharply in some regions during the early twentieth century.[3] Between 1906 and 1914, for example, production on the Adana plain rose 250 percent, from 50,000 to 250,000 bales, and had risen four-fold since the late 1880s. But at İzmir, by contrast, production held stable after 1888 and, in 1914, totalled c. 29,000 bales. In the Syrian regions, cotton cultivation was neglected

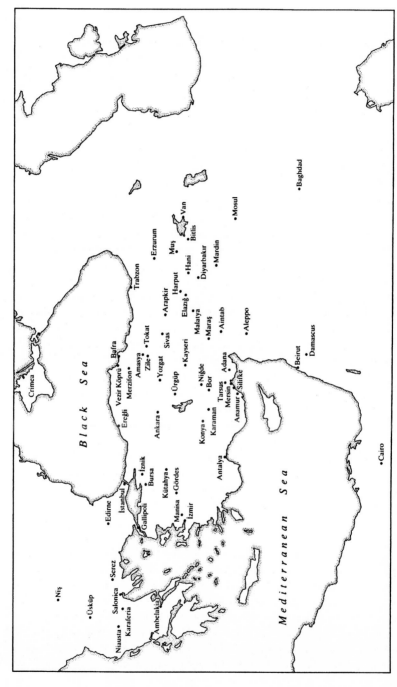

Map 1. Cotton and wool yarnmaking in the nineteenth century.

in the nineteenth century: in 1913, output at Aleppo was only *c.* 10,000 bales while that of Palestine was about one-half that level.[4] Egyptian raw cotton output, on the other hand, completely overshadowed that of the Ottoman lands during the nineteenth century. Raw cotton exports there averaged over 100,000 bales during the 1850s and, with violent fluctuations in between, reached a phenomenal 1.7 million bales on the eve of World War I.[5]

Dyestuffs

Textile producers historically also had access to richly abundant supplies of most of the dyestuffs they required. The most important of these was madder root, the source of the famed "Turkey-red" color so valued by European and Ottoman consumers. The madder dyestuff itself came from many regions, such as the mountains south of Konya that shipped to İzmir, to Europe through the Taurus mountains and met the needs of local dyers as well. Aleppo in the earlier nineteenth century received large quantities of madder root from Ereğli, two days the other side of the Taurus range. The region around Gördes in western Anatolia, *c.* 1800–40, supplied the İzmir dyeworks and foreign markets with some 8,000 bales of the root, ideally 3–6 years old when extracted.[6] Other notable dyestuffs of the late eighteenth century included yellow berries. England once had relied on the European provinces of the Ottoman Empire for this material but switched over to fustic wood from the Caribbean. The Kayseri region, however, continued to supply important quantities of the berries for local yarn and cloth producers and for export to Holland and the Germanies.

The development of artificial and synthetic dyes during the 1850s and 1860s, first in England and then Germany, had enormous consequences for Ottoman textile producers. The first breakthrough had been in the 1820s and, by the 1850s, it had become possible to produce alizarin, possessing some 36 times the color strength of madder, in the laboratory. Factory production of this widely used and highly prized color soon followed. It was molecularly identical to the natural substance and had the advantage of being obtainable in unlimited quantities from the factory. Other new colors thereafter steadily emerged out of European laboratories. In addition, there were the new coal-tar, aniline, dyes. These came into existence in the 1850s and were photo-sensitive substitutes for, but not the chemical equivalents of, natural dyestuffs. The anilines, if used properly, were color-fast and very cheap artificial coloring materials. Synthetic dyes cost somewhat more. Use of the new dyes was not without problems (see chapters 2–3 and 5). Illiterate peasants could not read the directions; and mordants were left out, sometimes deliberately to save money. Merchants did not always provide proper instruction in use of the anilines or synthetics, resulting in poor color fastness and other problems. But there were many advantages. Synthetic dyes freed Middle East textile producers from the often-laborious task of gathering and preparing natural dyestuffs, or paying others for the work, and it liberated them from the vagaries of nature. The new dyes enabled them to color their yarns and cloths with very inexpensive materials that, compared to the natural substances, were simple to apply. Since, by the third quarter of the century, Ottoman consumers largely had switched over to imported yarn, these new dyes had a particular importance. Ottoman textile producers using imported yarn benefitted from European technology that provided a steadily cheaper basic material that was superior in strength and regularity to home-spun yarn. By importing undyed yarn and using these easily handled dyes, they could cut costs since imported undyed yarn cost from one-fifth to one-third less than dyed yarn of the same size. Part of the savings could be retained by dyeing the yarn locally with the new materials. Use of the aniline dyestuffs avoided the duty on red yarn, that was higher than duties on the imported undyed yarn and dyestuffs together. Textile makers now could bypass professional dyehouses, at some risk to quality and fastness, but with considerable savings. Locally dyeing the yarn transferred the labor input from Europe to the Middle East, where it was cheaper, hence commercial textile producers could enhance their marketplace position. The product was acknowledged as imperfect but served the lower end of the market.[7]

The impact on natural dyestuff production and usage was impressive although the evidence is mainly indirect. Madder, yellow berries and other dyestuffs disappeared from the world market as well as many regional ones. Madder production in Asia Minor had totalled as much as 80,000 bales in the early 1860s. For decades, the export of madder root annually had averaged *c.* 10,000 bales, worth *c.* 12.0 million piasters. But by the mid-1880s, shipments to foreign markets had fallen to *c.* 0.4 million piasters/year. İzmir had exported 5,000 tons of madder roots in 1830 and 7,000 tons in 1856, when it was the second most important export. Between 1905 and 1911, by contrast, madder root exports averaged only 94 tons.[8] Indigo imports from India suffered first from aniline competition in some areas and later when the synthetic equivalent was formulated.[9] Saffron, once a favored and extensively cultivated dyestuff, was grown only as a spice by World War I. Yellow berry production also suffered. The competition of aniline colors lowered the price of yellow berries some 90 percent in just a few years. At the end of the century, cultivators hardly bothered to harvest the berries and began cutting down the bushes in some regions.[10] The hilltops of the Ankara districts once were covered with yellow berry shrubs but reportedly became barren as demand faded. In the later nineteenth century, European travellers were to report that yellow berries grew wild on the hilltops of the Kayseri region, affording a source of income with scarcely any labor. This, however, had not always been the case. Before the development of synthetic dyes and the collapse in the price of natural dyestuffs, great plantations of yellow berries had been cultivated carefully and were well-cared for since this notably enhanced output.[11]

Regional use of imported dyed yarn varied considerably, depending on the manufacturing speciality of the area (see chapters 2–3). Several important textile production centers continued to dye locally, while some others imported their colored yarn needs. In Mardin district (*sancak*) during the early twentieth century, for example, local dyers annually colored 94 percent of the yarn imported while at Maraş, some 43 percent of all yarn imported already was dyed, of the better qualities.[12] At Trabzon, *c.* 1900, producers dyed substantial quantities of cotton yarn with cochineal, indigo, campeche and alizarin. But for better quality and specialized goods and for colors the local dyers could not provide, they imported colored yarns.[13] The important textile center of Tokat, at the end of the century, imported only red yarns from Switzerland and Germany. Otherwise, local dyers colored the imported plain yarn, imparting a fastness considered more durable than the European.[14]

Until late in the nineteenth century, residents of the land behind İzmir still used "a large quantity of vegetable dyes."[15] Imports of colored yarn into the port city were reduced when factories for yarn dyeing opened in the early twentieth century, one each for dyeing cotton yarn and wool carpet yarn.[16] One of the factories employed some 25–50 workers and produced in all colors; by 1912, it had "shut out [imported] colored yarns to a large extent."[17]

At several locations including Diyarbakır, dyeing with natural indigo, that had to be imported, remained significant. At Aleppo, the indigo dyers, who worked with Manchester yarn, were singled out for their prosperity at the end of the nineteenth century.[18] By then, there were only indigo dyers in the city, working in about 100 shops. With the development of synthetic indigo just a few years later, the blue dyers in Aleppo continued to thrive, using the new discovery as well as the natural indigo.[19]

Some textile producers alternatively abandoned and then resumed local dyeing in their efforts to find the most marketable combination of product and price. In the 1880s, for example, Aleppo producers started buying large quantities of aniline and alizarin dyes to undercut their Aintab competitors by dyeing locally. But, after losing customers, they resumed colored yarn imports within two decades. By contrast, the Aintab producers imported a recently developed and cheap synthetic dye for its lower-end textiles, while importing dyed yarns for their higher qualities (see chapters 2–3 for details).[20]

Handspinning

Introduction

Ottoman cotton yarn producers labored in a context of (nearly) steadily falling yarn prices. Whatever their identity – Ottoman, British, Italian or Indian – suppliers of yarn to the Ottoman market continuously were challenged by competitors who offered approximately comparable goods at a lower price. During the late eighteenth and early nineteenth centuries, Indian and Ottoman yarn lost out to British goods. Thereafter, for most of the century, England nearly totally dominated the import of unbleached yarns while, for a time, Belgium supplied most of the balance. In the 1870s, unbleached English yarns formed 90 percent of all yarns imported into İzmir. England then also provided all the red-dyed thread imported to that city. Subsequently, Britain lost its virtual monopoly in red-dyed yarns as Germany, Switzerland and Austria-Hungary emerged as important suppliers. Elberfeld in Germany became particularly important.[21] In unbleached yarns, Britain encountered stiff competition near the end of the century, when Italy suffered from overproduction of yarn and sought new markets in the Middle East. Thanks to lower labor and transport costs, the Italians drove Belgium totally out of Anatolia, winning real successes in the coarser numbers of unbleached yarn, selling them for 5–10 percent less.[22] At Bursa, Italian mills won the lion's share of the market in low price, coarse yarns, sharing sales with producers from Salonica and Germany. Italian thread also sold well at Edirne, but at Harput it captured only 10 percent of the total market in the first years of the new century.[23] Despite these advances, Britain remained the primary supplier of imported yarns and, in 1901, the Ottomans were Britain's third most important customer in both yarn and in piece goods. The United Kingdom then supplied over half the total yarn imports, sending over 8 million kg. of thread while Italy provided some 5 millions.[24]

At the turn of the century, *c.* 1902, resurgent Indian spinners entered the Ottoman market, undersold the British and struggled with the Italians. Totally unknown before 1900, Indian yarn quickly occupied an important place in the Ottoman market, supplying some one million kg. of yarn by 1904.[25] Its price advantage was fractional, not even 2 percent less than British yarn of the same number. But, thanks to this differential and dumping, Indian yarns quickly dominated the İzmir market in the lower numbers, while England continued to prevail in the finer grades. Bombay spinners, selling at a loss, began making inroads into the Iraqi markets *c.* 1908; by then, Aleppo weavers already had shifted away from the Manchester yarns to inferior but cheaper Indian grey twists and Italian mercerized yarn. As World War I approached, India accounted for as much as one-fifth of all Ottoman yarn imports.[26]

Toward the end of the century, a number of mechanized Ottoman spinning mills emerged. Utilizing technology more readily available than in the past, and employing very cheap female and child labor, these factories captured about one-quarter of the total Ottoman market (see below). By the period's end, Ottoman suppliers of machine-made cotton yarn were competing, often successfully, with British, Belgian, Italian and Indian producers. Amidst the price-cutting wars of the machine producers of yarn, hand spinning both by wheel and by hand persisted remarkably in many districts.

Ottoman handspinning before Manchester

In the waning decades of the eighteenth century, Ottoman cotton-yarn makers dominated the domestic marketplace; Indian yarns were ranked second while European, mainly Dutch, suppliers ranked a poor third.[27] Local weavers generally obtained their yarn supplies from this combination of Ottoman, Indian and Dutch yarn producers, although there were many regional variations. The silk weavers of İstanbul, for example, used Indian, as well as Dutch and local, cotton yarn. They bought the yarns from Muslim and non-Muslim Ottoman merchants who imported all numbers of Indian yarn, separated those that were too fine for local use and forwarded them to Europe. Many customers, such as these weavers, turned to cheap, good quality English yarn that, as early as the 1790s, had become one of the largest Ottoman imports.[28] The Syrian textile industry, for its part, placed considerable reliance on the Indian yarns, more so than in most other parts of the empire.

At the turn of the eighteenth-nineteenth centuries, Ottoman spinners produced important quantities of cotton yarn in very many areas, for personal use and for sale to domestic and foreign buyers and to the state. In addition to the towns of northern Anatolia, these included the central districts (*sancak*s) of Hamit, Bozok, Kayseri, Yozgat and Niğde. In the European provinces, the Gallipoli peninsula at the Dardanelles, the Ambelakia region, and the area of Salonica particularly were active,[29] while, in the Syrian provinces, Aleppo excelled.[30]

The yarn was produced through a variety of organizational forms that differed in the many cities, towns and villages of its origin. Free labor spun the yarn in thousands of village homes, often for family use or casual sale in nearby markets. But merchants also organized substantial putting-out systems, involving large numbers of village and town spinners. The Kayseri merchants operated a very widespread network, buying cotton from Adana (some 70 percent of its total output) and distributing it to spinners throughout central and northern Anatolia. In some cities, guild labor may have provided the yarn although this seems unlikely since non-guild female labor accounts for most of the hand-spun yarn used by commercial and subsistence weavers alike. Labor of various kinds made yarn in government workshops. In the Eyüp quarter of İstanbul, for example, about 60 non-Muslims spun in a state-run factory, rewarded by exemption from the poll tax (*cizye*) (and perhaps cash payments as well).[31]

To overcome the chronic problem of finding sufficient numbers of workers in an economy characterized by its scarcity of labor, the Ottoman state resorted to a number of other mechanisms. State factories (*rіştehane-i amire*) regularly employed several hundreds of orphaned children to spin yarn for the Ottoman fleet. The children were "suitably paid" and worked in the factories for short, specified periods of time, on a rotational basis. Initially, Armenian Orthodox children from around Erzurum, Van and Sivas were employed but when their numbers proved inadequate, some 100 Greek and 100 Catholic orphans were summoned from the Ankara-Ürgüp-Niğde regions of central Anatolia. In the 1850s, this yarn factory used persons convicted of misdemeanor offenses, who worked off their sentences and then were released. Other spinners worked under government orders, e.g. those on the Gallipoli peninsula who received piece work wages to supply yarn to the tentmakers' guild in İstanbul.[32]

At the end of the eighteenth century, Ottoman yarn producers not only prevailed in the internal market, but also shipped substantial quantities of yarn abroad. Exports of cotton thread totalled some 2.5 million kg., mainly from the regions around Serez, Salonica and Thessaly. North Anatolian yarn spinners exported massive quantities to the Crimea while İzmir, for its part, exported one million kg. of yarn, in approximately equal shares of red and white, to Marseilles alone. Towards the end of the Napoleonic Wars, the İzmir hinterland was exporting some 250,000 kg. of hand-spun yarn. Arriving at the port in hairsacks of *c.* 67 kg., each sack contained 4–5 different numbers of yarn. The yarn arrived in the grey state and was dyed red in the city, for export to Russia. Formerly, great quantities of the "Turkey red" yarn had flowed to France and the German lands, but ceased in the face of protectionist measures that were enacted in those areas.[33]

Ottoman yarn exports had rested on well-guarded techniques of red yarn dyeing, secrets so valuable that English manufacturers allegedly had offered five thousand pounds sterling for the formula. The secret technique involved boiling the cotton in olive oil and then in a mild alkali, before immersing it in the madder dye.[34] The so-called "Edirne red" had predominated but gave way in the late eighteenth century to the products of İzmir, "some towns in the interior of Asia Minor" and, most of all perhaps, to Ambelakia. The brilliant yarn-manufacturing center at Ambelakia, to the south of Salonica, provided perhaps one-quarter of late-eighteenth-century Ottoman yarn exports. Thanks to booming European demand for its famed red yarn, the population of the town had trebled between 1783 and 1798.

Every arm, even those of the children, is employed in the [twenty-four] factories; whilst the men dye the cotton, women prepare and spin it.[35]

They exported the yarn to Vienna, Leipzig, Bayreuth and other cities in south Germany and had offices in Salonica, İzmir and İstanbul.[36]

But the European industrial vibrancy that boosted the Ambelakia and Anatolian yarn industries also caused their destruction, and that of Ottoman spinning in general. As early as 1765, the French government obtained and publicized the secret red formula.[37] Thus, means were found

within a short time, in our French manufactories, to give spun cotton a red colour full as beautiful and as durable as that which is given to it in Turkey.[38]

Beginning in *c.* 1790, English machine-made yarn started substantially to underprice the Ottoman and Indian products, thanks to steam-power and increasingly exploitative labor employment practices. The price of English yarn fell by two-thirds between 1792 and 1812 and its production increased at least 250 percent.

Ottoman yarn exports abroad ceased forever by the mid-nineteenth century. As a result, production centers that had focused on the foreign trade, notably Ambelakia, were abandoned by the organizing merchants and fell into near ruin. The spinning families emigrated in large numbers to expanding industrial centers, such as Serez.[39]

The Ottoman import of machine-made yarns from abroad increased by leaps and bounds. By 1810, the annual volume of yarn imports equalled some 250 tons.[40] During the next decade, these annually averaged 450 tons and then shifted, nearly incredibly, to some 2,650 tons in the 1840s. Thus, in a mere three decades, according to one calculation, Ottoman use of foreign yarns had risen ten-fold.[41] Important changes continued until *c.* 1870, when nineteenth-century Ottoman yarn production probably reached its nadir. During the great mid-Victorian boom years of the 1840s–70s, yarn imports reportedly tripled again, to an annual average of 7,750 tons and then rose to 12,550 in the final years before World War I.[42]

The growth of European yarn production caused huge dislocations in Ottoman yarn spinning and, more generally, the Ottoman textile sector. Inflationary spirals driven by Western demand forced up the cost of raw materials, increases that European makers could better absorb since their labor input costs were dropping. These raw material price increases badly hurt many Ottoman guilds. For the products they provided, the guild received fees that were fixed and could be adjusted only with official consent, a procedure that, if prolonged, could be damaging in times of rising raw material prices. Because of increased raw cotton prices, in one period of less than three years during the mid-1840s, the government granted a full 33 percent increase in the price that it paid for thread used in tents.[43] During the 1830s, the price of copper, starch and indigo that the Muslim dyers guild (*İslam boyacı esnafı*) of İstanbul used to color tenting cloth rose exceptionally. After absorbing these rising prices for seven years, they obtained a 25 percent fee increase from the state. Within a year, the guild won another increase, of 20 percent, only to return again, four years later, to petition for yet another raise. This time, they received increases of *c.* 17 and 40 percent for dyeing several different kinds of cloth. Invariably, there was some time delay between the increase in raw material prices and state approval of the fee hikes, during which the workers had to absorb the rising costs.[44] In the early 1840s, the European market had become so attractive that some imported logwood dyestuffs virtually were unobtainable within the Ottoman economy and various guilds scrambled to control the limited supplies of other dyestuffs available.[45] The diminished supplies of dyestuffs in turn adversely affected the producers of mordants to make fast the colors. For example, some 400 households processed alum at a centralized workshop in the Kütahya district, receiving piece wages according to the quantity of each grade produced. They also received military service and tax exemptions, until these were eliminated in the legislation of 1845–46. Alum production, however, stagnated because of the lack of demand and workers' wages remained unchanged between the 1830s and 1860s.[46]

The critical shortage of dyeing materials prompted a series of private and government efforts to expand existing supplies. In 1845, several Ottoman Jews obtained tax privileges to grow and process indigo in western Anatolia (İznik).[47] At the same time, the government launched a major search to locate, identify and exploit mineral sources of dyestuffs. Samples were taken at locations in northwest Anatolia and the Üsküp and Niş regions of the European provinces that could provide green, yellow, white and red dyes, and plans were formulated to hire local workers for wages.[48] A decade later, the state initiated plans to import indigo from Egypt for cultivation in the Baghdad region, with the intent of replacing existing Indian supplies.[49]

Ottoman handspinning in the era of European industrial hegemony

The combination of competition from foreign yarn producers whose prices steadily fell and the rising cost and scarcity of raw materials was devastating. During the first decades of the nineteenth century, profits in Ottoman yarn making plummeted by as much as one-half.[50] Ottoman handspinning was abandoned, rapidly and permanently, in some areas. At places such as Ambelakia, the Ottoman export trade in yarn evaporated immediately and the decaying town became a symbol for the decline of Ottoman industry in general. Northern Anatolia, at the end of the eighteenth century, began losing its yarn markets in the Crimea to English producers. Indian and Dutch yarns similarly disappeared very quickly from Ottoman markets.

But the replacement of British for Ottoman yarn was not a uniform process; rather it occurred with considerable variations in timing and extent. More surprisingly, perhaps, the manual spinning of Ottoman yarn persisted at levels, often extremely difficult to assess and measure, that were significant nonetheless. Geography played some role but was a far less important factor than has been assumed. The presence of putting-out networks as well as poverty played greater roles in delaying acceptance of the foreign yarn. The merchants of İzmir, for example, still were exporting some 14.9 million piasters of cotton yarn to England and Trieste in 1843, suggesting the enduring vitality of that particular network.[51] Rural households, generally, were slower to accept the imports than town or city textile manufacturers. The availability of alternative manufacturing and/or agricultural opportunities certainly promoted the shift from locally to foreign-made yarn. Similarly important were economic cycles affecting agricultural and manufactured goods.

In some areas, the process of adopting British yarn was completed or well-advanced by the mid-1830s, for example, at the textile-producing centers of Tokat and Yozgat as well as Arapkir, where yarn imports gave birth to a new weaving industry (see chapter 3).[52] Residents of the Bursa region were among the first to switch, nearly totally, to British yarn.[53] Here, as in many regions, customers

appreciate its advantages, and the waste of time spared in spinning cotton of native growth, for making stout articles of common wear ...[54]

But there were other, more specific reasons for the early changeover, explanations linked to the booming foreign demand for raw silk. Bursa cotton spinners, caught in a cycle of declining profits, had a ready alternative in the world of silk spinning, one long familiar to area residents. At this critical transition time, moreover, silk spinning was not the ill-paying activity that characterizes it generally, but a lucrative occupation, one offering high wages to attract badly-needed workers (see chapter 4).

The manufacturing empire of the Kayseri merchants fought a bitter but losing rearguard action against European yarn imports. In the mid-1830s, they still were shipping Adana cotton to north Anatolian towns, such as Vezir Köprü, where large quantities of yarn were made. Some of the yarn was used locally and the balance sent to nearby Merzifon and Bafra. Amasya weavers at this time used local yarns exclusively, to make coarse dyed and printed cottons. Similarly, workers at Zile received large quantities of Adana cotton from the merchants at Kayseri, spinning it and then weaving coarse calicoes for export to the Crimea. A half decade later, the Amasya industry annually still used 100,000 kg. of Adana cotton to spin yarn for tent canvas and sails and for coarse calico.[55] In the mid-1840s, Kayseri merchants continued to buy a substantial amount, some 3,000 bales, of Adana cotton for distribution to hand spinners. But by the middle of the next decade, the marketing networks of the city and its importance as a center for organizing manufacturing had withered away.[56] Similarly, the famed Diyarbakır cloth industry, oriented to production for sale, had switched over to British yarn by the mid-1830s.[57]

The use of Ottoman homespun elsewhere, however, continued. In some areas, its use persisted for a few decades more than in locales where British yarn immediately had been adopted. In yet other regions, hand spinning was present until the end of the Ottoman Empire. At Malatya, in the mid-1830s, homespun provided enough yarn to supply some 800 looms commercially weaving cloth.[58] Domestic spinners in the Diyarbakır area continued to work at home for decades after, as the following demonstrates.

All the Koordish women during the winter employ themselves in spinning the native twist of which the above cloth [*bez*] is made. The poverty of the mass of the country people is however so great that they can rarely afford to buy the cotton of which the twist is made, so that numbers of women endeavour to find employment in gathering and picking cotton, for the sake of a small portion which is given to them. Thus a woman being possessed of, for instance, six pounds of cotton, turns it into twist as soon as she can, and brings it into town, where she exchanges it for nine pounds of raw cotton; this she converts again into twist, and exchanges again, in the same proportion, against raw cotton; until by these means she becomes possessed of a certain quantity of twist, which the husband converts into cloth, using for his family what is necessary, and selling the rest.[59]

Northeast of Diyarbakır, at Hani, some 300 Muslim and 150 Armenian families in 1839 spun cotton yarn imported from Harput and Erzurum and then wove it into cloth for sale in nearby villages as well as in Diyarbakır and Muş.[60] In the region of Bitlis at this time, Persian cotton (from Shirvan, Harzan and Khvoy), was spun in very large quantities, enough to make several hundred thousand pieces of heavy calicoes. At Bor, southwest of Niğde and just across the Taurus Mountains from the Çukurova plain that produced the cotton, spinners were using Adana cotton into the mid-1840s.[61] At this time, north Syrian spinners used local cotton to produce yarn of ordinary quality to make coarse clothes, underwear, shirts, mattress coverings, and stockings. Weavers there, however, also employed British yarn for the better kinds of goods and Aleppo annually was importing *c.* 230,000 kg. of British yarn, Nr. 10–30 and 40–60.[62]

Much of the surviving spinning industry rested in the hands of rural women, who spun for their own needs and sold the surplus, for example, women of the Aleppo area. Many used only their own homespun to weave cloth. The practice described in detail for the area around Niğde during the later nineteenth century probably prevailed in most Ottoman regions. In the district of Niğde, most homes held both a spinning wheel (*çıkrık*) and a loom. "Young girls, each of them planning on motherhood," bought cotton, spun it on the wheel and wove cloth on the loom, either for their trousseaus, for members of the family or for sale. But, as the use of the factory yarn, so-called water yarn, increased, the spinning wheels gradually disappeared.[63] Around Kayseri, although the region is not mentioned as a major source of yarn, cotton (and wool) spinning remained an everyday part of women's skills until World War I.[64]

Although many wove for family use, commercial weavers also used hand-spun yarn, in combination with factory yarns, to produce cloths of a certain desired strength, fineness and price. Women spinning at home in Sivas province during the early 1890s used "the modest kind of spinning wheels," and annually utilized 10,000 bales of cotton from the provinces of Adana and Harput to produce yarn for a coarse cloth used in men's trousers.[65] A steady decline in the price of imported yarn was continuing to erode demand for raw cotton from Harput at the turn of the century. By 1907, one account suggests, local yarn only occasionally was being used for the warp while Adana factory yarn more usually was employed.[66] At Aleppo, cotton spinners numbered 6,000 persons in the late 1850s, employed in 400 shops. In the first decade of the twentieth century, weavers in the city still used regionally spun yarn for warp thread in many of the coarser textiles. Women working at home for "supplemental" income provided the yarn, earning 0.4–0.8 piasters a day. Annual yarn output totalled an estimated 100,000 kg.[67] Bitlis spinners annually produced 650,000 lb. of cotton yarn for local weaving during the 1860s. In the 1870s, Erzurum weavers regularly used a mix of local and English yarns to produce the lower-grade towels.[68]

Yarn spinning in the districts surrounding Diyarbakır, as seen, retained great vitality among the Kurdish tribal population who depended on the income it produced. In the early twentieth century, the district (*sancak*) of Diyarbakır still produced over 16,000 *top* of red yarn, shipping two-thirds of it to Ottoman customers. Spinners in Mardin district (*sancak*), in the mid-1880s, made *c.* 7,700 kg. of red yarn and 10,000 kg. of white yarn, using three-quarters of each type locally and sending the balance to other Ottoman buyers.[69] Two decades later, in *c.* 1907, Mardin district yarn output had more than doubled and spinners provided local weavers with more than twice as much yarn, an estimated 45,000 kg. Local weavers used the hand-spun for the warp in the coarse natural colored textiles and in the striped *alaca* cloths as well.[70]

At Harput, impressive quantities of locally spun yarn were used *c.* 1905, often in combination with the machine-made. Employing cotton gins that replaced the old hand gins in the late nineteenth century, villagers then hand-carded the cotton and spun it on small wheels for use on home looms. These spinners utilized over 700,000 kg. of local raw cotton. Unlike weavers in Sivas province and at Aleppo who used hand-spun for the warp, Harput weavers employed it for the weft (and for candle wicks).[71] During the mid-1890s, hand spinners in villages around Mosul annually produced *c.* 665,000 kg. of yarn for sale to weavers in the town. Women "and men" even in the villages spun the yarn "when they are not employed in other profitable occupations."[72]

At Maraş, home-spun prevailed until the 1850s, when Manchester yarn, found to be cheaper and better, reportedly "almost entirely" superseded the local product. But, *c.* 1906, local hand spinners still were producing some 46,000 kg. for sale to local weavers.[73]

Spinning yarn does not constitute a profession properly speaking; it is done in all the poor homes – that is, among nearly all families – the occupation of women who are at the spinning wheel during their spare time moments ...[74]

For the work, they daily earned *c.* 0.50 piasters; the most active might gain up to 0.75 piasters, about the same as the women who spun for the Aleppo industry. The yarn was very coarse and irregular, suitable for weaving but not sewing and sold for 10 percent less than approximately equivalent size factory thread from Adana.[75]

Table 1.1. *Handspun cotton yarn production (available data), c. 1900*

place	date	original qty.	in tons
Diyarbakır district (*sancak*)	1900	16,000 *top* (red yarn)	?
Sivas province	1890s	10,000 bales	2,000
Aleppo city	1900	100,000 kg.	100
Mardin district	1907	45,000 kg.	45
Harput district	1900	700,000 kg.	700
Maraş district	1900	46,000 kg.	46
İzmir region	1901	4,000 bales	800
Mosul area	1896	50,000 *batman*	666
		TOTAL (IN TONS)	4,357

Sources: see references in text. Pamuk (1987), p. 115, calculates annual average Ottoman cotton yarn imports at *c.* 11,000 tons in 1894–96. He mistakenly calculates Ottoman handspun yarn production at only 1,500 tons.

The picture of Ottoman handspinning thus is quite different from that suggested by the standard accounts of deindustrialization. The handmaking of cotton yarn hardly had disappeared. Rather, it remained an important source for Ottoman textile producers and accounted for a considerable proportion of all cotton yarn being used in the empire, at least 25 percent in *c.* 1900 (see table 1.1). At this time, the known quantity of handspun cotton yarn production exceeded 4,000 tons. The actual total surely is much higher since the statistics presented are hardly a systematic compilation but those randomly encountered in the sources.

Ottoman spinning mills

Introduction

Hand spinning survived in part because some of its makers could not afford to purchase yarn at any price, as in the example of the Kurdish female spinners around Diyarbakır in the 1850s. Also, many families did not give monetary value to the time spent spinning, counting as net savings the sums not spent to purchase yarn. But, as seen, much of the spinning activity that did survive was aimed at the marketplace, for sale to regional and distant consumers. The spinners continued working because their yarn undersold the European product. It was not yarn of comparable quality, but yarn of the coarsest kind, that nonetheless had a wide variety of uses. Since the price of imported yarn and textile goods fell steadily over the century, so too did the prices of hand-spun yarn and the wages received by the surviving spinners. In the final quarter of the century, Ottoman hand spinners encountered new competitors, while continuing their battle with Manchester and the other foreign producers.

Mechanized Ottoman yarn factories emerged, carving out a market by undercutting the European products. Although these new mills spun yarn in a wide range of numbers, they focused on the lower numbers, precisely the coarser yarns that had become the hand producer's last stronghold. By the turn of the century, in an atmosphere of increasingly intense international competition and falling yarn prices, matters had become very grim for these Ottoman hand spinners.

Events at Maraş in 1904 illustrate the competition between European and Ottoman mechanized spinners and between them and the hand spinners. In that city, Nr. 20 Adana undyed yarn sold for some 7 percent less than the equivalent Nr. 20 English yarn. But the cheapest yarn at Maraş was hand spun, selling for 10 percent less than the lowest-priced yarn, Nr. 4, produced at Adana. And, this home-spun was one-half the price of the lowest-numbered European yarn (Nr. 16) available in Maraş. When the mechanized spinning mills of Italy and India entered the fray, prices for the coarser yarns fell still further.[76]

Mechanized factories to spin cotton yarn were few and far between in the Ottoman lands. Except for those established to fill government needs, Ottoman mills were founded at the end of the nineteenth century and later. In 1904, they provided some 13 percent of all mechanically spun yarn used within the empire and, within a decade, had increased their share to about one-quarter of the total.[77]

The founding of cotton yarn factories occurred at two distinctively different periods. The first group emerged during the 1870s and 1880s during the Great Depression. Since European loans for additional Ottoman imports were more difficult to obtain, local production of consumer goods became more important. Also, the depression pushed down raw material prices, an advantage for most Ottoman mills that were located very close to raw cotton supplies. And, third, depressed agricultural prices meant decreased earnings for cultivators, the major market for Ottoman textile producers. Hence, the need for cheaper goods. The second cluster of factory foundings came in quite different circumstances, after 1896, when agricultural commodity prices were rising. This upward trend favored local capital accumulation and triggered the expansion of internal markets for cloth, in turn prompting demand for yarn, both foreign and domestic. Further, the rise of Ottoman yarn manufacturing was part of the global diffusion of mechanized production. In Europe, two trends had been favoring Ottoman yarn factory formation during the post-1870 era. First, the wages of European workers had risen, thanks to their comparatively successful mobilization and, overall, standards of living improved in many West European countries. Thus, production costs relatively became higher and the prices of some goods rose to levels that permitted competition, for the first time since the rise of British yarn-making hegemony. Also, the mature European industrial economies were de-emphasizing the export of textiles and light consumer goods and focusing on the shipment of capital equipment. The export of machinery had emerged as an important part of British business, in contrast to earlier decades, when the British government routinely had prohibited the export of textile machinery.[78] Hence the growth of Ottoman, as well as Indian and Italian yarn manufacturing in the later nineteenth century. By the end of the 1890s,

owing to the facilities enjoyed by these [Ottoman] factories, to the cheapness of labour, and to the privilege they enjoy of importing raw materials duty free, it is found that foreign cottons cannot compete with them in the coarser numbers (3s to 14s) of unbleached yarns.[79]

There were a few mills at widely scattered locations. The earliest privately owned yarn factory probably was at Harput, that worked as early as 1864. It used European machinery to make cotton thread (as well as silk cloth and cotton fabrics) and the yarn was well regarded. Although equipment difficulties restrained production, cotton spinning continued until the end of the period.[80] Much later, in 1899, the state awarded a concession to open a yarn factory, steam or water-powered, in the province of Sivas or Ankara.[81] There was a successful mill at Elazığ, established in *c.* 1903 and one at Gallipoli, founded sometime before 1913. A Muslim founded the first mill at Manisa before 1910 and a British subject established another there in 1911. Beyond the fact of their existence, we have no information on these mills at present.[82] The vast majority of Ottoman yarn factories were located in just a few areas, notably İzmir, Adana, Salonica and, to a lesser extent, İstanbul.

Mechanized spinning

İstanbul

An English–French family, Eastfarre, that had resided at İzmir since the eighteenth century, founded the yarn spinning mill at Yedikule in the capital. Family members won the concession for a spinning mill in 1886 and opened it about two years later.[83] The mill enjoyed early successes thanks to cheap labor and the erasure of internal tariffs. In 1890, the factory spun *c.* 1.1 million kg. (240,000 packets) of yarn and, by 1897, successfully competed with England in the low numbers. Its 9,000 spindles made yarn in the 3–8 number range while sometimes shifting to 2–14 yarns, to meet the demands of its Ottoman customers. It found significant export markets in Bulgaria, Egypt, India and even the United States.[84] For a time, it supplied much of the yarn for a state textile factory (*basmahane*).[85] In May 1900, however, the mill operated only two days a week but, in 1901, production boomed, to a record 2.2 million kg. (500,000 packets worth some 7 million piasters).[86]

İzmir

A French family at İzmir founded a steam-powered spinning mill, Cousinery *et fils*, in 1892 and its production immediately cut into foreign yarn imports. In

1901, annually using as much as one million kg. of local cotton on its 8,000 spindles, the mill sold coarse yarns, Nrs. 8–14, in İzmir, the hinterland and the archipelago. By then, it was offering serious competition to the Italian yarns in Nrs. 8–10. Its yarn exports totalled 307,000 kg. in 1900, while, several years later, daily production equalled 3,000 kg. per day.[87] A Belgian stock company bought the firm in 1903 and, later in the decade, exported part of its output to Bulgaria under a special low tariff. Producing the coarse numbers, 4–16, the mill spun about 10 percent of all yarn used locally.[88] In 1912, when it was joined by a second mill at İzmir, its output had risen 20–40 percent over the past decade. As World War I began, the two mills together operated 28,000 active spindles.[89]

The Adana region

Despite severe labor shortages, the Adana region rose to occupy the second rank among mechanized Ottoman yarn producers. By World War I, it possessed an impressive industrial complex, with over 40,000 active spindles, located in the heart of the greatest cotton-producing region in the Middle East outside of Egypt.[90] Nomadic tribes from the mountains supplied most of the labor for the cotton harvest, that increased 2.5 times in the early twentieth century. Each week, employers obtained the laborers in the markets of Tarsus and Adana, negotiating with the headman chosen by each gang. The cotton was ginned, but some hand removal of the seeds was required in addition. In 1907, workers typically received meals and 1.2–4.0 piasters per six-day week.[91] The total number of gins rose from 550 to 1,000 during the first decade of the century, concentrated in at least 22 ginning factories. Adana alone contained 600 gins, Tarsus another 300 while only a handful were located in small villages.[92] A few of the gins worked for wage hire but most belonged to the various spinning mills.

The Mavrumati family, owners of a 60-gin operation, founded the first spinning mill as early as 1878. Located at Tarsus, it was water-powered and produced Nr. 4–18 yarns on 2,700 spindles. In the early 1890s, it annually spun about one million kg. of yarn. By 1900, the Tripani brothers had founded a second steam-powered mill, at Adana. Together, the two mills daily produced *c.* 8,100 kg. of yarn. Regional yarn exports by sea from Mersin then averaged *c.* 3.5 million piasters while caravans carried an approximately equal amount into the Anatolian interior.[93] The two mills prospered and, in 1902, were unable to fill the orders being received, reportedly using an extraordinary 10,000 bales of local cotton. But the cotton shortages in Europe during 1903 doubled the prices of local cotton and sent it to the West. Mill operators cut back operations, reducing the regular workforce by half.[94] By 1907, markets again had been restored. There now were three spinning mills. Cosma Simyonoğlu owned the most recent one, also at Adana, that contained 3,500 spindles.[95] The three mills now held 16,000 spindles, with an annual productive capacity of *c.* 1.6 million kg. of yarn. Rasim Dokur, a Muslim Turk from Egypt, founded the last spinning mill at Tarsus in 1911; three years later, it contained some 10,800 spindles.[96]

Cotton textile production in the Adana area expanded substantially in the years immediately prior to World War I. Two, or perhaps three, of the spinning mills integrated vertically, acquiring important weaving capabilities, while expanding their spinning capacities as well.[97] One mill at Adana expanded to 10,000 spindles, producing *c.* 4,000 kg. (800–1,000 bundles) of Nrs. 10–12 yarn per 12-hour day.

In 1914, the spinning and weaving mills in Tarsus and Adana contained an aggregate 42,000 spindles, that used 10,000 bales of local cotton.[98] Yarns up to Nr. 20 could be made, but the focus was on Nrs. 0–14. In good years, the four mills together consumed 40 percent of the local cotton crop and daily produced some 72,000 kg. of yarn.[99] This represented a nine-fold increase over the output of the two regional mills back in 1900. But they competed with difficulty even in their own backyard since hand looms in the area used both "native and foreign yarns, especially Italian yarns" to make napkins and sheets.[100] Italian competition prevented the mills from expanding further, even though they did profit from the Tripolitanian war and the temporary break in commerce with Italy.[101]

Adana yarns were sold "all over Turkey," a commercial network encompassing coastal and interior regions as disparate as Silifke, Anamur and Antalya as well as Konya, Karaman and Maraş. The mills also supplied a small quantity of yarn to Aleppo weavers who used it for the weft. They annually furnished the Mardin district with some 22,500 kg. of yarn, only 5 percent of its total needs,[102] but supplied 40 percent of the urban market in the Harput area. Sivas weavers of *manusa* cloth sometimes used local hand-spun but had come to rely primarily on Adana yarns.[103] As early as 1898, Adana mills controlled 10 percent of the Diyarbakır market while, at Konya, in the next decade, Tarsus supplied one-quarter of its Nr. 6–24 yarns.[104]

Salonica and the Macedonian interior

Macedonia held the densest concentration of spinning mills, a network lost to the Ottoman economy just before World War I. The oldest mill, at Niausta, dated back to the mid-1870s while five others were established after 1900. Two of the smaller mills annually spun 364,000 kg. of yarn. The two mills in the city of Salonica emerged between 1878 and 1885 and, at the latter date, annually produced 540,000 kg. of yarn. Managed by Englishmen, the two mills earned 25 percent per year in the 1880s, helped by government duty exemptions on intra-empire shipments.[105] In *c.* 1906, the Macedonian yarn mills contained 42,900 spindles and annually produced 2.9 million kg. of yarn. By 1909, the number of spindles had risen to 60,000 and, four years later, some 70,000 spindles (28,000 more than in the Adana area *c.* 1914) were working in ten mills, located at Salonica, Niausta, Karaferia and Wodena.

Not counting the Salonica mills, the Macedonian factories consumed 2–3 million kg. of raw cotton. Most mills obtained cotton from local cotton gins; for example, there were some 100 in the district (*sancak*) of Serez. These gin operators provided cultivators with cash advances, obtained the cotton at harvest, and negotiated directly with mill owners. Although cotton cultivation in Macedonia had increased because of the mills, it was not enough to meet the rising demand. And so, the mills bought some cotton from İzmir, Adana and even Aleppo. In 1904, for example, Syria shipped 900,000 kg. of raw cotton to the Salonica and Niausta mills. A general lack of investment capital meant that each of the mills was owned jointly. Ottoman Jews owned two mills, both in Salonica, while Ottoman Greeks owned the remaining eight spinning factories.

The mills supplied one quarter of local yarn requirements and shipped to other markets as well. Villagers near the two smaller Niausta mills, for example, bought the yarn, made into 4.5 kg. bundles, for home weaving.[106] In common with other Ottoman mills, the Macedonian factories produced mainly coarser yarns, Nrs. 4–12, although some of the newer mills produced Nrs. 16–24 and even up to 32. By 1900, the Salonica mills were competing against Italian (and English) yarn in the lower, 4–10, numbers. The two Salonica mills shipped one-third of their production to Macedonia and Albania and exported the rest to Bulgaria, Serbia, Anatolia and the archipelago.[107] When Bulgaria declared its independence from the Ottoman Empire in 1908, the Salonica mills lost an important market; thereafter, most sales were in Macedonia and Albania. Already in the mid-1880s, the Salonica mills supplied İzmir with important quantities of yarn, for the "shirtings used by both sexes in the interior of Anatolia."[108] They also supplied Bursa with cotton thread, perhaps one-fifth of its total consumption, in the lower price qualities.[109] Commercial weavers at Edirne generally used thread from Salonica, that sold for one-third less than the British equivalent while Edirne cultivators used thread made in Salonica as well as in İstanbul and İzmir.[110]

The mills at Salonica, well-placed at the waterside with good rail links to the hinterland, initially enjoyed a number of advantages over rival mills in the Macedonian interior. But, by 1900, the Salonica mills found it difficult to survive and one of them shut down for seven years.[111] There were several problems, beginning with crop failures in the 1880s that had interrupted cotton supplies in the nearby Vardar river valley. In the early twentieth century, the Salonica mills suffered from the booming demand for tobacco as many cotton growers switched to tobacco, thus undermining the proximity advantage to the cotton fields. Also, the Salonica mills had higher production costs, land values and overheads than their inland competitors. These mills used coal to run steam engines while the competing mills at Karaferia, Niausta and Wodena instead employed water power. This might condemn the factories to seasonal closing as the water sources froze in winter or dried up in summer; but their operational costs were lower. Also, mill operators at Niausta and Karaferia further reduced overhead costs by milling flour as a sideline enterprise. The Wodena mill, largest of the Macedonian mills with its 16,000 spindles, attempted vertical integration, by producing cotton cloth. In the early twentieth century, six of the mills outside Salonica combined into two syndicates, controlling some 41,500 spindles. This was part of an overall pattern as Ottoman yarn manufacturers sought to form cartels in response to global cotton shortages. In 1900, the larger mills at İstanbul, İzmir, Salonica and Tarsus had tried but failed to effect such a consolidation.[112] The six mills attempted to control access to Macedonian cotton, reduce production costs, and further rationalize marketing procedures. And they adopted a division of labor, agreeing that a particular factory would produce only a certain yarn number.

Generally, however, there were few other wage-earning jobs near the mills of interior Macedonia and so the operators could rely on cultivators who were available seasonally. During the summer harvest, the numbers of workers did fall sharply. But, since they had few other opportunities to earn cash wages, their labor remained cheap and available for the yarn factories of the Macedonian interior.

The full potential of these few mechanized yarn factories in the Ottoman Empire remained unrealized, in part because of foreign competitors, including the new producers such as India and Italy. Also, the development of Ottoman yarn manufacturing was disrupted by the diversion of raw cotton supplies at the beginning of the twentieth century, when world-wide shortages caused European buyers bid up raw cotton prices.[113] Local mills, therefore, had to cut back production just as their operations were gaining real momentum.

Contemporaries liked to blame the mills' relative lack of success on the workers, specifically, on labor turnover. Since the young girls who formed the bulk of the labor force did not remain long on the job, it was said, much time and capital was lost in training new hands. Because they lacked skilled labor, the argument continued, Ottoman mills were unable to make the finer numbers.[114] Hence, Ottoman industrial development was retarded. But, this logic seems flawed. European and American mills also relied on young girls and certainly were familiar with the turnover problem, and these competed successfully. In fact, the Ottoman focus on coarse yarns derived from the nature of local raw cotton on which they depended, that was suitable for only these lower number yarns.

The Ottoman experiences with privately owned factories in some respects parallels that of Egypt during the later nineteenth century. In both instances, the textile and other industries remained very small in scale. In Egypt, at the very end of the period, only 4 percent of industrial enterprises employed more than nine workers while another 8 percent had between five and nine workers. Also, mechanized textile factories similarly came very late in Egypt. In the

Egyptian case, the dismantling of Mohammed Ali's industrialization efforts early in the century had been followed by decades of hiatus. Private textile factories appeared only in 1899, even later than many Ottoman enterprises. Moreover, the two big privately owned textile mills in Egypt proved particularly unprofitable, generating little profit and no dividends: one went bankrupt and the other only staggered along.[115] Some Ottoman textile mills also went under and many did poorly. But others turned decent-enough profits and paid dividends to their shareholders. During the first decade of the twentieth century, for example, one textile mill in İstanbul often paid 2 or 4 percent dividends while another in Salonica averaged 4–5 percent.[116]

The workforce of the spinning mills

In the Salonica regions, and probably elsewhere, many members of the owners' families worked in the mills, in managerial and, sometimes, production jobs. Everywhere, young girls and women formed the vast majority of the work force although there is little specific information about their numbers and the conditions of labor. Approximately 300 women and children were working in the İstanbul spinning factory, c. 1902, each daily earning between 2.5 and 10 piasters.[117] In the Adana area, the Mavrumati mill in the early 1890s employed c. 300 workers, also usually women and children.[118] At one of the combined spinning and weaving mills at Adana in c. 1907, the spinning section employed 550 persons, who averaged 5 piasters silver per day of 12 hours. The headman earned 15–20 piasters. Overall, weekly wages in the spinning department totalled 20,000 piasters. Female and child labor also was common at the cotton gins scattered throughout the area. Labor was particularly scarce in this southeastern region and the mill owners were in the process of building houses to attract Armenian workers from Hacın, Zeytun and Aintab. This particular mill ultimately planned to employ 1,500 persons, who would work on 22,000 spindles and 400 looms.[119]

There is more detailed information, but still very incomplete, about the Macedonian mill workers. Just after its founding in the 1870s, the first mill in Niausta employed 250 young women and 50 males, all Jews.[120] Females, mostly girls as young as six years of age, were three-quarters of all Macedonian spinning mill workers who, c. 1906, numbered some 1,570 persons. Among the mills of the Macedonian interior, that is, away from Salonica, the workers usually were Greeks, except at Wodena, where most were Bulgarians. During the 1890s, Macedonian mill workers daily labored 15 hours in summer and 10 hours in winter, with a 35-minute break for dinner and none for breakfast. At Salonica, in 1885, the two mills together employed 800 workers, while in the early 1890s, they employed 160 men and boys and 480 girls, 12–18 years of age. All were Jews, reflecting Jewish demographic preponderance in the city. The wages of men were two and three times those that the boys received and girls' starting wages were 50 percent lower than the boys'.

The Jewish girls are very skilful; they work til they marry, which at Salonica takes place from the age of 15 and upwards, or as soon as they raise by their savings a small dowry ... besides the necessary clothing.[121]

Tobacco processing (and the diversity of the Salonica economy) competed for workers in the Salonica yarn mills, draining away the reservoir of cheap female labor. As the tobacco industry expanded rapidly and offered high wages and as the general business climate in Salonica improved, wages in the city rose to a level that prevented the Salonica mills from meeting the prices of their inland competitors. By 1913, Salonica mill workers were earning up to three times the wages of their sisters inland. In the Macedonian interior, labor generally remained abundant and available for mill work, especially at Karaferia and Niausta. In these more rural regions, mill workers more often also were cultivators and hence less dependent on wage work. Thus, the dependence of the Macedonian mills on seasonally available water power fit well with the character of the local work force. At Wodena, silk raising drew away workers from the two large cotton spinning mills. In the summer season, the labor-intensive demands of silk raising reduced the work force available for cotton spinning by more than 50 percent. And so, like the Adana entrepreneurs, Wodena mill operators attracted the workforce from more distant areas – this time Karaferia and Niausta – by offering housing and other incentives. Thus, they built barracks while one factory operator opened a kitchen offering cheap, hot meals.[122]

2 Trends in cloth production in the Ottoman lands from Salonica to Aleppo

The following chapter adopts a geographical approach in narrating the story of nineteenth-century Ottoman cloth making. The focus usually is upon cotton textiles, but there is discussion of wool, linen and cotton-silk textiles as well. It first focuses on those Balkan areas that remained Ottoman throughout the nineteenth century and then moves eastward from region to region, to İstanbul, west, west-central and then the Black Sea region and its hinterland. The final section studies east-central, east and southeast Anatolia and the region of north Syria, dominated by the great production center of Aleppo.

The result is not entirely satisfactory. The rapid change in locations can be bewildering. Overall, there is not enough information on the industry of any single area while, at the same time, there is too much stress on the later period and not enough on the early years of the nineteenth century. These lacunae reflect the Ottoman and European sources, primary and secondary, consulted for the present study. But this chapter is an overview of Ottoman textile production that has been unavailable until now. By outlining the activities of producers in these various locations and showing the many different kinds of enterprises, it forever destroys the clichés about moribund Ottoman industry. And it points the way to the monographic research that many industries clearly deserve but whose very existence had not been considered before – e.g., those of Arapkir and Gürün or Buldan and Kadıköy or Diyarbakır and Aintab.

The European provinces, İstanbul, West- and West-Central Anatolia

The European provinces

Coarse-wool cloth production easily dominated the textile industry of this region although other textiles also were woven. Thanks to this regional speciality, most local producers avoided confrontations in cotton cloth making, the competitive industry *par excellence* of the age. In the Edirne region, wool cloth manufacture of the coarse *aba* and the finer *şayak* maintained a high volume of production, especially for shipment to distant markets, throughout the century. In villages of the districts (*sancak*s) of Gömülcine and Dedeağaç, *c.* 1902,

49

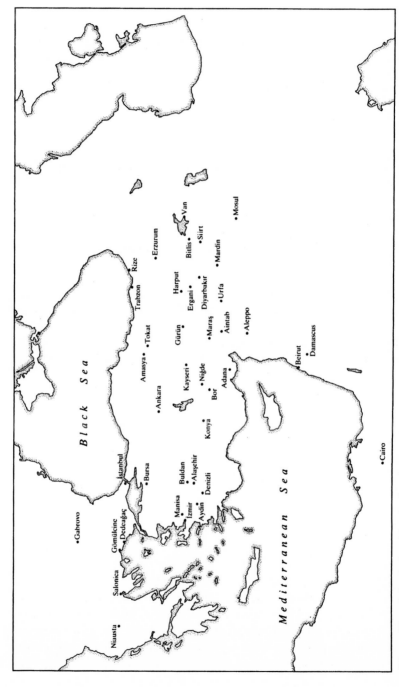

Map 2. Trends in clothmaking in the nineteenth century

cottage industry workers produced about 250,000 meters of the coarse and fine wool cloth (*aba* and *şayak*), for the lower end of the local market and for shipment to Anatolia. In addition, the Edirne area produced important quantities of wool cloth for the Ottoman military, that also bought from other producers in the European provinces.[1]

In Ottoman Bulgaria, wool cloth production thrived until the end of Ottoman domination (also see chapter 3).[2] On the north slope of the Balkan Mountains, at Gabrovo, some 1,000 looms annually produced 10,000 pieces of cloth, selling mainly to the army but also to local and Anatolian peasants.[3] In 1867, the Plovdiv region produced and consumed some 4.0 million piasters worth of the coarse cloth; about ten years later, shipments to Anatolia reportedly were twice that amount.[4]

In Salonica province, despite the grave losses represented by the collapse of international sales and the destruction of the Janissary Corps, commercial textile production retained considerable importance during the subsequent decades. After maintaining comparatively stable levels, cloth production began to increase substantially in the late 1880s. As the boom began, the province, by one count, held some 7,470 full-time artisans who commercially wove on 4,500 looms. (These figures do not include those weaving for home use or part-time workers.) Some of the vitality derived from the adoption of imported yarn as a replacement for homespun; in the 1840s, cheap British yarn brought a new textile activity as local residents began to wear cotton stockings. In the 1880s, cotton cloth producers shifted over to yarn from Ottoman factories, supplemented by smaller amounts of handspun. By the 1890s, Drama and Demir Hisar had emerged as commercially important centers of stocking production, some 300,000 pairs/year.[5]

The weaving of coarse wool cloth remained important around Salonica and in the Macedonian countryside but there is little direct evidence in the form of statistics concerning numbers of weavers, looms or output levels. Coarse-wool cloth production, often based on cottage industry, probably increased in the Salonica area during the century. Local weavers, *c.* 1800, had used *c.* 295,000 kg. of raw wool to make the coarse wool cloth while, in the mid-1890s, they consumed some 350,000 kg.[6] At this later date, the three leading coarse-wool cloth centers were the regions of Nevrokop, Niausta and Mayada, that altogether contained some 2,125 looms.[7] During the late 1830s and early 1840s, the town of Mayada annually had marketed some 300,000 pieces of the cloth and, for decades after, remained a major center. In the Crimean War, for example, it furnished cloth for the Ottoman and British troops and ranked first among cloth producers in the European provinces.[8] Following the slight increase between *c.* 1800 and 1890 that was noted above, wool cloth production in the Salonica region rose sharply. The export of raw wool from Salonica decreased between 1880 and 1895 because of "the extension of native industries for the manufacture of coarse cloth for the army" and "the growing local consumption caused by the expansion of native industries."[9] Salonica now was importing significant quantities of raw wool (in one case 120,000 kg. from the Edirne area for army cloth production) to supply this growing industry.[10] At this point, mechanized looms located in a number of factories helped to push local cloth output still higher (chapter 3). Thus, textile output in these European provinces began increasing sharply during the 1880s, in the middle of the price depression and well before the general price rises of the post-1896 era.

The continued survival of coarse-wool cloth manufacturers in the European provinces derived from their production of a textile at the very bottom of the market, a rough cloth that was very cheap in price and had a vast clientele. Competition with European wool cloth producers was not as severe as in cotton textiles because there had not been as many innovations driving down prices. Natural advantage played a larger role in the Ottoman wool cloth industry and survival was somewhat easier. In addition, the weavers benefitted significantly from a captive market – sales to the Ottoman military – a factor that should not be underestimated. The gendarmerie and regular military forces stationed in the province remained the most important consumers of this cloth. The cloth also was worn by vast numbers of Ottoman peasants all over the empire. Despite competition from Austrian, German and British manufacturers, the European provinces (as well as formerly Ottoman Bulgaria and Serbia) maintained significant sales in a very broad market area that reached into most corners of the empire outside of Iraq and the Arabian peninsula.[11]

İstanbul

Guild manufacturing

İstanbul is the attractive trap from which Ottoman economic history must escape.[12] The trap lies in the combination of documentation availability concerning its economic activities and patterns of production and the unique place of İstanbul in the economic life of the empire. The sheer quantity of İstanbul-related documents is mind-numbing and beyond the ability of any generation of scholars to exhaust. Because of this ready availability, scholars have tended to focus on İstanbul and use its history, usually implicitly, to illustrate the economic activities and patterns of production for the Ottoman Empire as a whole. In many respects, however, İstanbul is not the norm but its opposite. Because it was the capital, it had become a huge city and had very special requirements that make its economic history unique. In regards to manufacturing, the guilds in the capital were more important and more regulated than elsewhere because they directly supplied the needs of the imperial bureaucracy and military, both for day-to-day and wartime use. Throughout the Ottoman centuries, these requirements played a key role in the economic life of the empire. The city remained the greatest urban center of the eastern Mediterranean until the end of the empire. Its estimated one million inhabitants, including the central bureaucracy and imperial court, drew on the resources of the entire empire for their food, clothing and shelter needs. To meet these demands, the state had erected a formidable, complex and changing provisioning system that funnelled products as dissimilar as wheat and shoe leather to residents of the capital. For example, grain from Egypt, Rumania, Bulgaria, the Marmara and the north Anatolian shores poured in, by camelback, wagon, ship and, late in the century, by railroad, to make the city's bread. In the capital itself, a rich and variegated artisanal and commercial infra-structure processed, re-worked and/or distributed the goods. İstanbul, with some exceptions, was not a major manufacturing center, in the sense of supplying quantities of finished goods to the rest of the empire. But the incredible size of the population assured that it was the seat of important industrial activities keyed to furnishing local needs.

These economic workings and the provisioning and supply mechanisms are relatively well-known for the pre-1800 period.[13] How these activities and mechanisms changed during the nineteenth century, however, is not understood clearly. There certainly is super-abundant archival evidence concerning state-run industrial activities in the capital. More nineteenth-century documentation *presently* is available on the various imperial factories in İstanbul – e.g., the Tophane or the Tersane complexes that respectively made guns and ships – than on whole Ottoman towns that were important manufacturing centers, for example Tokat or Diyarbakır.[14]

İstanbul possessed more mechanized factories than anywhere else in the empire (see factory section). Nonetheless, small-scale manufacturing predominated in the city although we know still less about such production than about the factories. Ongoing research by twentieth-century anthropologists is demonstrating that whole quarters of the modern city are teeming with small-scale manufactories that still account for a considerable output. These surely were present 100 years ago but the records of their activities need to be located and explored.[15]

This book is about manufacturing in an empire and not just its capital; it does not pretend to exhaustively exploit the sources relating to manufacturing in nineteenth-century İstanbul. This would entail another, probably several books. Instead, it focuses on two issues that seem to encapsulate textile production in the city, themes directly tied to the momentous changes occurring as free trade encroached on autarchy. Thus, we first examine several İstanbul guilds and their fates during the liberalization of the Tanzimat reforms and then the phenomenon of expanding industrial sectors with very cheap, highly exploited labor that seems characteristic of the subsequent era.

The Tanzimat changes assaulting monopolies inaugurated an intense struggle among textile-making guilds in various quarters of the city. Some guilds wished to maintain monopolies while others welcomed the chance to break them. The quarrel shows up clearly in a series of petitions from cloth printers in the Üsküdar workshop (*basmahane*) and from those in the Yeni Kapı and Ahmediyye quarters on the other (European) side of the city.

These and other groups, in *c.* 1813, had worked out an uneasy agreement that permitted each to monopolize the production of a certain textile. The cloth printers in an area of Üsküdar had possessed monopoly rights to make a certain cloth (*hassa yemeni*) with cochineal.[16] The Tanzimat regulations, however, snapped this arrangement and a quarrel erupted with cloth printers on the European side of the city, in the Yeni Kapı and Fazil Pasha neighborhoods. The Yeni Kapı group, that represented some 100 masters, journeymen and apprentices – both Muslim and non-Muslim – petitioned the government and received permission to make the special cloth that had been the monopoly of the Üsküdar printers. It also retained the right to continue making a coarse, logwood-dyed cloth (*yemeni*). Working outside the new gate (Yeni Kapı), the group then established a great factory (*bir fabrika-i cesime*) and began making the cloth with cochineal.[17] The aggrieved guild members in Üsküdar admitted that the new factory did not violate Tanzimat principles (of free commerce), but warned that it would ruin them. In repeated petitions, they asked the government to restore their monopoly (that they implicitly admitted no longer had legal force). Just as persistently, the Yeni Kapı group defended itself by appealing to the Tanzimat decree and other imperial orders, that now prohibited monopolies, and to the recent imperial permission that allowed them to make the special cloth.[18] After much hesitation and indecision, the government resolved the issue by coming down against exclusivity and permitting both the Üsküdar and the Yeni Kapı groups to dye in colors that the other once had held as monopoly right.[19]

In this struggle, the state withdrew its protection for monopolies, thus destroying a guild's privileged status and exposing it to unaccustomed open competition.[20] Within scarcely a decade of these quarrels, monopolies in cloth printing at İstanbul vanished altogether. The rival guild printing factories in the Üsküdar, Yeni Kapı and Ahmediyye quarters shared a common fate as the total number of guildsmen employed in all of them reportedly fell by 95 percent, from 130 to only 6 persons. The latter two guilds consolidated into a single group, but in the early 1850s, the guild factories in both European and Asian İstanbul reportedly closed down. The guilds had declined precipitously as new centers of production arose in the Tanzimat era. But, if these guilds were vanishing, the cloth printing industry in the capital flourished: at least 8–10 new printing factories began operations during the 1840s.[21]

The news of the printing guilds' deaths, however, was greatly exaggerated. In the 1880s, the guilds of the printing houses at Üsküdar and of the consolidated Yeni Kapı and Ahmediyye printing factories still existed. When the state reviewed its industrial tax rates in 1887, it listed the former and new taxes for 287 İstanbul guilds. The survey is important here because it noted the continued presence of the two groups of cloth printers who had been in such desperate straits a few decades earlier. The enumeration, however, is not very helpful for understanding the actual condition of the two groups, beyond the fact of their legal existence. The masters, journeymen and apprentices of the two guilds paid taxes that placed them in the upper one-third of the 287 guilds listed. The new taxes that the journeymen and apprentices of both guilds paid rose in about the same proportions as in the other guilds while those of the guild masters fell somewhat, an unusual pattern in this enumeration. These changing tax burdens, however, probably say nothing about guild prosperity or poverty but speak of government needs for more revenue.[22]

If the government threw the cloth printers into the free market, it simultaneously defended the monopolies of other guilds engaged in textile making. In *c*. 1841, a group of Muslim and non-Muslim workers challenged the monopoly rights of the fez dyeing guild and requested permission to open competing retail shops. The affronted guildsmen pointed to prior certification (in the form of *gediks* from the *evkaf-ı hûmayun*) that, they claimed, bestowed monopoly rights. The would-be competitors, it turns out, originally were fez repairers who had worked in the fez-making factory (*feshane*), had become redundant through mechanization, and lost their jobs. A high official council (the *Meclis-i Vâlâ*), maintained the rights of the fez dyers and forbade the former fez repairers to compete with them.[23] Two decades later, the fez dyers' guild reappeared before the council, complaining of improper competition from other guilds. The certificates (35 *gediks*) in their possession, they asserted, had become a bad investment because of illegal dyeing and thus largely had gone unrented and unused. As earlier, the government, in 1862, upheld the fez dyers' right to the monopoly.[24]

In sum, the state supported particular guilds' privileges while withdrawing them from others. In the examples given here, it upheld monopolies for the fez dyers. But it denied the validity of such restrictions among cloth printers.

Non-guild manufacturing

İstanbul participated in the general revival of Ottoman manufacturing that took place during the final quarter of the nineteenth century. As elsewhere, the willingness of workers to accept very low wages played an important role. In İstanbul, this willingness was especially keen because, during the later nineteenth century, Muslim refugees from the Balkans poured into the city in vast numbers, to stay permanently or on their way to new homes in the Anatolian and Arab provinces. These urban migrants thus offered a large and cheap labor pool. This new labor force combined with excellent transportation and communication linkages and a large merchant community to make İstanbul particularly suitable for the emerging low-wage industries of the late nineteenth century. Home industries and sweatshops played a vital role in the manufacturing life of the city. Commercial lacemaking, for example, caught on among many Ottoman women and girls working at home. Some labored full-time, for example, the 200 young Jewish girls at nearby Silivri, but others made lace in their spare hours. İstanbul merchants supplied imported thread and picked up the finished product for export to France, Germany and other European locations. This became an important industry, providing the equivalent of over 7,000 full-time jobs by *c.* 1900.[25] Similarly, large numbers of Turkish women in Bosphorus villages near İstanbul worked at home, decorating veils and headcloths for sale in Anatolia and Persia (see chapter 3).[26]

The rising availability of the sewing machine played an important role in the emergence and expansion of several sweatshop industries, including the manufacture of umbrellas, ready-made clothing and shoes. Invented in the 1840s, sewing machines did not appear in significant numbers on the Ottoman scene until the end of the century when the Singer Sewing Machine Company began its Middle East operations.[27] This American company sold pedal-driven machines to full-time manufacturers for one-half the price of the English, German and French machines. And, it offered a still cheaper hand-driven machine aimed at the home market. Using the system that had won it worldwide markets, the company introduced installment buying and depots with repair facilities and a ready supply of spare parts.[28] In the early twentieth century, thousands annually were imported into the empire; in 1907, for example, total sales exceeded 11,000 sewing machines.[29]

The once-considerable trade in imported umbrellas came to a nearly complete halt at the end of the nineteenth century when the capital emerged as a major production center. The necessary fabric and metal were imported from Germany, England and Italy. Men, but also large numbers of children and women, assembled the components in workshops. The children received 10–25 piasters per work week of unspecified length and the women obtained 25–30 piasters. After assembly, the umbrellas were shipped to buyers not only in İstanbul, but also Salonica, Anatolia, İzmir and Beirut, as well as Bulgaria and Cairo. In *c.* 1902, the industry started reducing its dependence on foreign materials when a workshop in the Stambul area of the capital began manufacturing umbrella handles, cutting the sales of Viennese handles. By the early twentieth century, umbrella production in the capital totalled some 75,000–100,000 dozen pieces, valued at *c.* 13 million piasters.[30]

A ready-made garment industry similarly thrived on the combination of imported materials and cheap local labor. Large textile houses in the city directed the industry, importing foreign cloth for cutting and sewing. *Circa* 1900, sales of local ready-made clothing totalled 31 million piasters, more than the value of the imported product.[31] Final products included men's clothing as

well as women's dresses and linens. The industry produced two lines of clothing
and used sewing machines for all operations except the fastening of buttons. The
first line of goods competed directly with Austrian producers, the major source
of imports. Using fabric as good or nearly equal in quality, the İstanbul
manufacturers made a final product for a much cheaper price. They also
produced bottom-of-the-line clothing using inferior German or Austrian cloth,
employing labor of "incredible cheapness." Tailors employed their wives and
children and several other young workers, all working for piece-work wages. In
1909, the cost of the labor input in a sewn pair of trousers was 5–6 percent of the
retail selling price, an extraordinarily low figure. The final products cost
one-half or less than the imported product and were sold in Austrian-owned
stores in the capital.[32] New credit procedures boosted sales. The department
stores offered credit and installment purchases to the employees of local com-
panies. The employees who bought the clothing on time agreed to have their
company bookkeeper withhold regular payments from the paycheck. Further,
the employees agreed to be collectively responsible for the debts of all fellow
workers who entered into such arrangements.[33]

İzmir province

Unlike the wool cloth manufacturers in the Balkan regions, most textile makers
in Anatolia overall made a variety of cotton cloths, thus working in the most
competitive sector of the nineteenth-century international economy. The deep
involvement of İzmir province in commercial agriculture often caused labor
scarcities and the high wages in agriculture drew off workers from other sectors,
checking textile production.[34] And yet, the province held rich and varied
traditions of textile production, both for domestic consumption and for sale in
local and distant marketplaces.

It is not generally known that apart from the very important carpet industry a considerable domestic industry in textiles is carried on in this province, i.e., yarns for carpets, bath
towels, shawls, socks, underclothing, bed covers, material for men's suits, &c., chiefly
used by the lower classes.[35]

The textile industry in the İzmir region was on the rise in *c.* 1900, doubtlessly
helped by the positive price trends of the post-1896 era. A resurgence in local
dyeing reduced colored yarn imports while introduction of the Singer sewing
machine helped to overcome labor scarcities.[36] At this time, annual sales of these
machines at İzmir averaged some 5,000–7,000 units.[37] Provincial weavers,
c. 1900, altogether used some 30,000 bales of undyed and dyed imported yarn
and perhaps 4,000 bales from domestic spinners.
Production of the cloth *alaca*, beloved by the population and used as vests,
undergarments and bathing stuffs, alone equalled about 1.5 million pieces,

valued at 9.5 million piasters, or *c.* three-quarters of total textile output in the province. Fabric for clothing and furniture (*manusa*), as well as materials for the bath and sofa covers (*peştemal*) were among the other most common locally manufactured goods. These textiles sold well because of their strength and long-wearing qualities, and the fast colors that were lively and harmonious. Regional weavers also made pure silks, mixed silk with gold and silver thread, cotton-silk and linen-silks.[38]

The Alaçatı and Yeninahiye regions together annually produced some 10,000 meters of silk products called Ödemiş handkerchiefs (*mendil*). The town of Ödemiş, for its part, made cloth of pure silk as well as silk mixed with gold thread for *çarşafs*; the same cloth also was used for bed coverings. Three villages in the district (*kaza*) of Bozdoğan wove sacks, bags, horseblankets and saddlebags while others nearby variously made lining (*boğası*) the *alaca* fabric and cotton trouser cloth (*pantalonluk*) that women in the interior also wore.[39]

The Denizli district (*sancak*) was the most vibrant cloth production center in western Anatolia during the later nineteenth century. The town of Denizli contained 190 looms that annually produced 69,000 pieces, more than half of it the *alaca* fabric.[40] The fame of the region rested on the output of two large nearby villages, Kadıköy and Buldan. In Kadıköy, where output was rising sharply at the turn of the century, 15,000 villagers used British yarn and German dyes.[41] Some 784 looms wove 321,000 pieces of various textiles (*üstlük, bez, kuşak* and *alaca*) *c.* 1900 while, several years later, output of just the *alaca* cloth reached 300,000 pieces. Buldan, in common with Kadıköy, possessed a good water supply and was famed for its cotton-silk cloth, used chiefly for bed covers and table cloths. The townspeople wove 40,000 pieces of the *alaca* cloth and a similar number of cushion and mattress covers. Buldan weavers also produced over one-half million handkerchiefs and a large number of cotton curtains. In common with Kadıköy, output at Buldan was growing very rapidly at the end of the century, and the number of looms doubled in just a decade, to 1,500.[42] In addition to the two towns, other places in Denizli district made silk cloth, embroidered with gold thread, for furniture and clothing decoration.[43]

There also was a certain concentration of production at Alaşehir, a town of 22,000 mid-way between Manisa and Denizli/Buldan.[44] The Manisa region probably ranked second in importance to the Kadıköy and Buldan industry. Manisa weavers, who spent most of their time in agriculture, used cotton yarn from England and Greece and, to a lesser extent, from the brand-new spinning mill at İzmir. During the mid-1890s, the Manisa region annually produced *c.* 2.6 million piasters worth of textiles. This included 150,000 pieces of *alaca* cloth that alone accounted for one-half the output, 60,000 pieces of shirting, 50,000 hand towels, 40,000 sofa and mattress covers and 1,000 pairs of socks and *c.* 200,000 piasters worth of a woollen undergarment (*gömleklik*).

The great port city of İzmir not only imported substantial amounts of foreign yarn and cloth for redistribution in the Anatolian interior but also reworked considerable quantities of these imports. By 1900, according to one count, İzmir manufacturers were dyeing and printing 1.5 million pieces of imported plain cloth for women's head covering. Another estimate states that İzmir dyehouses *c.* 1900 annually dyed 100,000 pieces of cloth that then were cut up, each yielding 20 *yemeni* or *kalemkâr* headgear for a total of two million pieces. In addition, they dyed 50,000 bolts of *çember* cloth, a headcovering of very soft cotton. Each of these yielded 20 pieces for a total of one million pieces. The dyehouses were very active during the later nineteenth century in the production of various kinds of printed headgear for women and, to a much lesser extent, coloring furniture fabrics. In addition, the city held one of the more important clusters of mechanized factories for both yarn and cloth making (chapter 3).[45]

Bursa

The city of Bursa bustled as an important manufacturer of cotton cloth during the nineteenth century. Throughout the period, however, the cotton weaving industry scarcely is mentioned, overshadowed by (and sometimes part of) the famed silk industry. From the 1830s until World War I, the city consistently ranked among the leading Ottoman import centers of British cotton yarn. In 1840, for example, Bursa imported some 100,000 kg. of yarn while, in 1905, the volume equalled some 245,000 kg.[46] During the early twentieth century, about one-third of the yarn received was shipped out of the city as cloth while the balance was woven for local use. (By comparison, local consumption accounted for a full 80 percent of imports in the town of Baghdad.) Many weavers made the famed Bursa towel, of cotton and silk, and much imported yarn was used in combination with silk.[47]

Bursa weavers had been among the first to adopt British cotton yarn and, during the 1840s, its sharply increasing sale had helped locally woven cottons to displace silk cloth in the every day apparel of many Ottomans (see chapter 1).[48] During the latter 1850s, however, British cotton weaves were replacing local cloth,[49] a trend traceable to the boom in steam silk reeling (see chapter 4). This burst of factory formation placed a strain on the local labor market and temporarily gave high wages to the young girls who reeled in the new factories. Hence cotton cloth weaving declined, apparently to a new low. By 1862, only 60 looms were active in both cloth and towel weaving while 26 others made "long" dresses. Production of towels had fallen from 20,000 to 10,000 pieces as the work force gravitated towards the higher-paying new jobs. But, when the American Civil War pushed up English textile prices some 50 percent, local cotton weavers, in 1863, tripled production of towels and bath wrappers.[50] At about this time, some 60–100 looms actively were weaving towels.[51]

By the beginning of the new century, when prices finally were rising again, the number of looms weaving towels had increased quite impressively, to some 600.[52] At this time, Bursa weavers regularly were providing the İstanbul market with better qualities of mixed – cotton and silk – *çarşaf*s and sofa covers in addition to bath towels. In 1905, this aggregate production equalled some 8,700 kg. in weight, worth 1.5 million piasters. The number of active town looms, according to one count in 1906, had increased to 800 (exclusive of silk weaving), making bathhouse as well as home towels and bath materials, in addition to *çarşaf*s and sofa covers.[53] But another estimate states that, beside the 600 looms making towels, there were another 860 looms in town commercially producing textiles other than silk. Three-quarters of these wove linen cloth while the balance mostly made various kinds of coarse cloth and shirting (*kanunlu bez* and *bürümcük* and *helal bez*); 60 looms wove aprons and shawls (*futa* and *kefiye*). In addition, *c.* 1912, 700 hand looms wove silk cloth in the town (see chapter 4).[54]

Konya

The town of Bor stands out as the only textile center of any importance in this poor and thinly populated agricultural region. During the 1840s, it contained 2,000 houses, *c.* 85 percent Muslim. Artisans were engaged chiefly in the spinning, weaving and dyeing of a coarse white cotton cloth as well as a colored striped cloth (*alaca*). They spun Adana raw cotton and benefitted from abundant local supplies of madder and yellow berries. Other dyestuffs, such as indigo and cochineal, arrived from Kayseri and Konya. At the time, Bor manufacturers supplied local markets and also sent large quantities of cloth to Kayseri, and to Gümüşhane and other areas on the Black Sea coast.

These activities at Bor bustled for the remainder of the period. Production of the white cloth, now made from British yarn, continued into the twentieth century. By the early 1890s, the town had doubled its 1840s' size. *Alaca* weaving now occupied 2,250 looms in the town.[55]

Weavers in the city of Konya, 1907, supplied local residents with about one-fifth of their textile needs (recall that Bursa and Baghdad weavers supplied over two-thirds of local consumption). Worth about one million piasters and made from British and Tarsus factory yarn, locally made textiles included men and women's underwear, women's trousers and sheets and towels. Merchants bought the rest outside, *alaca* and *yazma* cloth woven in Aintab, Damascus and Isparta, and in other locations.[56]

Ankara

During the nineteenth century, the mohair yarn and cloth industry of the region collapsed (see chapter 3) but other weaving activities persisted. The district of

Yozgat further endured the Russian conquest of its markets across the Black Sea but, in 1907, still had some 600 looms, weaving ordinary cotton cloths for local use. Weavers in the Kayseri district at this time worked on 1,500 looms, mainly producing a coarse natural-colored cotton cloth, using Adana-made yarn for the woof. To a lesser extent, they produced colorful *alaca* cloth, with imported European yarn. In the prospering conditions at the turn of the century, the city of Kayseri contained a growing muslin printing industry of some importance, employing 500 workers and using 2.7 million piasters worth of English cloth.[57]

East-Central and East Anatolia

Amasya

In the 1830s, Amasya was famed for its coarse dyed and printed calicoes and for canvas used in tents and sails, spinning and weaving large quantities of Adana cotton for the purpose.[58] At the same time, artisans at nearby Vezir Köprü also spun the Adana cotton brought by Kayseri merchants and wove it, usually into striped cloths, a local speciality.[59] Both industries suffered badly from the loss of their northern markets but seem to have hung on. During the final decades of the century, cotton weavers at Amasya and some nearby towns routinely were out-competing British producers for the local market. Between 1900 and 1907, Amasya cotton textile production annually averaged 2.4 million piasters.[60] In Sivas province overall, of which Amasya was a part, manufacturers annually were using a total of 10,000 bales of Adana and Harput cotton and somewhat more British yarn (see chapter 1). In 1907, some 13,600 looms in the province were producing the *manusa* cotton fabric, one-third more than the total number of all looms just a decade before.[61]

Tokat

The town of Tokat in northern Anatolia, long famed for its dyeworks, entered the 1830s often using British rather than locally made cloth. In addition to printing British muslins, local manufacturers also found it advantageous to use British yarns to make muslin and calico.[62] At Karahisar, with a far smaller textile industry, by contrast, weavers still were using "country yarn" to weave a few calicoes. During the 1850s, Tokat produced a high quality, quite expensive fabric (*peştemal*) made of silk mixed with linen yarn.[63] Perhaps an experiment seeking to find a new market, this endeavor seems to have disappeared while that of weaving and printing cotton cloth persisted.

Called the "Manchester of Asia Minor" by one European, the town relied on good quality water and cheap labor.[64] It specialized in making a headware of light cotton material (*yemeni*). "At Tokat there is a considerable trade in stamping patterns in colour on white Manchester cotton." Large pieces of the cloth first were printed with black patterns and then dyed with the desired basic color. Artisans then hand stamped patterns in three to six colors. The printers annually imported, *c.* 1907, 4.3 million piasters worth of cloth from Manchester, sent to Tokat by their brothers or associates, without the more costly intervention of outside middlemen.[65] In addition, some 600 looms wove *manusa* cloth, yearly worth some 2.7 million piasters. Except for red fast yarns from Germany and Switzerland, they used mainly British yarn and dyed it on the spot.[66]

Gürün

Unusually for Anatolia, wool cloth dominated the textile industry at Gürün. The textile industry at this town, located roughly midway between Sivas and Malatya, was thriving during the early part of the nineteenth century. This prosperity, in large measure, was thanks to nomadic Kurds and Turkmen who wintered near Ankara, returned to Syria in the spring and spent much time in the pastures around the town. During the 1830s, some 1,800 families, in approximately equal numbers of Muslims and Christians, lived in Gürün; since the agricultural base was poor, they had come to rely on these tribal migrations. Gürün merchants furnished the tribes with supplies, including the textiles of Damascus and Aleppo and the linens of Rize, received payment in wool, and then distributed much of it for spinning and weaving. In the 1830s, Gürün merchants also annually were importing some 3,000 pieces of British calico, dyeing it blue and then re-shipping the entire lot.[67] Thus, Gürün then was important both for its wool cloth weaving and its cotton cloth dyeing.

A half century later, Gürün's wool weavers continued to thrive. Some 500 looms in the town and the villages of the district (*kaza*) wove shawls, trousers and jackets from wool (as well as some light silk fabrics). Some of the wool yarn still was home-spun, from local sources, but most now came from Britain, preferred for its strength.[68] Besides fine shawls and men's clothing, Gürün produced coarse wool (*aba*) cloth for the army as well as the finer *şayak* cloth.[69]

Buoyed up by the rising prices of the early twentieth century, Gürün's market grew noticeably. Diyarbakır consumers began buying Gürün goods for the first time in 1907, followed by the entry of Egyptian purchasers in 1910.[70] At this time there seems to have been a shift from weaving pure wool textiles to also making a cotton and wool cloth. Production of both textiles was climbing sharply.[71] In 1907, the total number of looms in the town reached 2,000, perhaps four times as many as during the previous decade.[72] Just a few years later, in 1911, there were 3,500 looms, using wool and cotton yarns from Manchester. Weavers now made a wider variety of textiles including cloth, covers, curtains, and cushions in either pure wool or a wool and cotton mix. The town had emerged as the leading textile center in Sivas province: annual cloth production totalled some 13.2 million piasters, triple the average levels of the preceding decade.[73]

Trabzon

In *c.* 1860, the city and its hinterland contained a mixed textile-making sector that included the manufacture of silk veils, linen and cotton shirting, sheets and towels, cotton and wool braids and socks, woolen aprons for women, and "a common rugging." Local artisans then were printing European muslins for head dresses. White calicoes similarly were imported and dyed blue, very popular as the chief clothing of the town's "lower classes." Many of these weaving, dyeing and printing industries fought with foreign and Ottoman producers to serve the local market (see chapter 3). At the turn of the century, the production of silk cloth enjoyed a certain revival that absorbed some of the workers who were losing their jobs weaving the *peştemal* fabrics. The best and most favored silk weave was the local copy of the Persian silk *çarşaf*; this garment (*keşan*) had become very fashionable, thanks to a 50 percent drop in its sale price during the prior half decade. A full one-half of local women reportedly wore a silk *çarşaf* of one style or another, depending on their religious affiliations. These particular tastes gave local weavers protection from outside competition as well as securing them a strong regional market, reaching from Samsun to the Russian border on the coast and south to Erzurum in the interior. Imported factory-made *çarşafs*, by contrast, generally were of cotton and scarcely in demand. For less-expensive *çarşafs* from cotton, the weavers dyed their own yarns, in red and other colors as well, particularly in indigo. They also dyed yarn and wove colored silk cloth for clothing, mainly for Muslims, and for bedcovers and upholstery. Production of these last items were extremely restricted, perhaps 12,000 piasters per year, because of competition from other Ottoman producers.[74]

Rize

The town of Rize on the eastern Black Sea coast is situated on stony soil, in mountainous terrain that rises 2,000 meters in fewer than twenty kilometers. In the nineteenth century, it was not really an urban center but rather hundreds of houses dispersed among gardens that offered a verdant, picturesque appearance.[75] Agriculture was marginal, affording subsistence only and the inhabitants had developed a variety of textile manufacturing activities, notably linen cloth production.[76] This Rize cloth (*bez*) was beloved throughout the empire for its "remarkable" lightness, a real advantage in the heat.[77]

Over the century, Rize linen production increased impressively in volume but perhaps not in value. Annual production averaged 75,000 pieces, of all qualities, during the mid-1830s. By the 1890s, the volume of output had doubled and then rose again (by *c.* 8 percent) during the next decade. Production of the finest grades in the early twentieth century totalled some 12,500 pieces, each selling for 40–100 piasters while output of the second quality equalled 150,000 pieces, costing 11–12 piasters.[78] Despite the uniqueness of their linen product, Rize weavers (in common with other Ottoman textile producers) competed by lowering prices. Between *c.* 1896 and 1910, the unit price of the best quality Rize linen dropped nearly two-thirds,[79] during a period when prices generally were increasing. Rize weavers therefore suffered considerable losses in real income during the final Ottoman decade.

Bitlis

The town of Bitlis remained a comparatively important textile producer throughout the period. In 1839, it was celebrated for its bright red and coarse cotton cloth. Local artisans obtained some plain cloth from Van weavers but wove most of it themselves with raw cotton from adjacent regions to its south and west and from Khvoy in Persia. The Persian city of Shirvan at that time provided the madder root while, several decades later, the Bitlis industry relied on Siirt and Diyarbakır for these supplies. In the late 1830s, Bitlis annually shipped several hundred thousand pieces of the cloth to "distant parts of the country." During the 1860s, it sold 2,094 bales of its red-dyed cloth at Erzurum in a good year but only one-half that amount in a bad year.[80] Bitlis was still a significant commercial textile producer in the twentieth century. In 1901, the town sent 1.5 million yards each of the red and of white canvas cloths; these were worth nearly 2.0 million piasters and formed up to 50 percent of the value of all goods sent from Bitlis province.[81] But in years of political instability and crop shortfalls, such as 1908 and 1909, textile shipments could fall by one-third.[82]

Van

Textile production in the town of Van similarly showed considerable continuity over the century. Local weavers not only made a coarse calico from Persian

Table 2.1. *Textile shipments from the town of Bitlis, 1896–1905 (in piasters).*

year	red cotton cloth	natural-colored
1896	108,000	n/a
1901	982,800	982,800
1903	756,000	756,000
1905	216,000	356,000

Source: Buhi 9, 8/20/1907, 703. Converted from marks at 5.4 ptrs./mark.

cotton but also, unusually, they wove a raingear made from goathair.[83] A half-century later, in the 1880s, some 200 houses in the town annually wove 50,000–60,000 pieces of cotton cloth for sale at Başkale, Ercis and locally. The mohair *aba* cloth still was being made commercially, in another 67 houses in the town. In addition, seven so-called factories at Van and another 60 at nearby Çatak produced a fine-textured mohair cloth (*şal*) used for men's tunics and women's dresses.[84]

The Harput region

The industry at Arapkir is perhaps the clearest example of an Ottoman hand-weaving industry born of the European Industrial Revolution. Producers in the town adopted British yarn during the early 1830s; for the rest of the nineteenth century, Arapkir remained the most important production center, probably, in Harput province (see chapter 3).

The looms at Malatya in the 1830s produced large quantities of "striped nankeens, cotton cloths, picture and plain silks," mainly for sale in Erzurum (200 bales in volume) and to Russia. Imports of British textiles then were very limited: in the towns of Harput and Malatya, British yarn formed the weft and local silk the warp of the silk cloth while artisans dyed and stamped the plain imported shirtings with local patterns.[85]

When local manufacturing again is visible, in the mid-1880s, the production of cotton cloth, prints, handkerchiefs and of coarse woollens in the Harput region had increased considerably.[86] The introduction of cotton gins during the late 1880s improved efficiency and quality, certainly helping to promote this upwards trend.[87] As prices fell in the depression, imports of some textiles were reduced sharply; those of Swiss handkerchiefs, for example, declined by four-fifths. Manufacturers in Harput province, during the late 1890s, annually shipped an average of *c.* 150,000 pieces of silk and cotton cloths. This production continued to rise during the 1890s. In addition to using 2,500 bales of imported cotton yarn, more than twice the levels of the previous decade, the weavers also consumed three-quarters of the local cotton harvest. Production levels during the 1890s were perhaps more than ten times greater than during the 1830s.[88] In part, the increase derived from the emergence of a new industry, the manufacture of red prints using Austrian-made alizarin, just around the time of the Armenian massacres. This was a shift away from the earlier emphasis on silk-cotton cloth and focused on the lower end of the market (see table 2.2).

At the end of the century, the quantity of total cloth shipments outside of Harput province apparently was greater than at any point during the past 15 years (table 2.2). But, their value was at a new low, reflecting the declining importance of the more expensive silk-cotton cloths and their replacement by the cheaper cotton textiles. In 1898, Harput province shipped record amounts,

Table 2.2. *Shipment of various cloths from Harput province, 1884–1910*

	qty. (pcs)	value	bales used	
		(piasters)	of imported yarn	types of cloth
1884	125,000	1,650,000		silk-cotton
1885	125,000	1,650,000	1,082	"
1886	172,000	2,310,000	1,786	"
1887		2,640,000		"
1888		2,475,000		"
1889		1,980,000		"
1890		1,650,000		"
1891		1,705,000	2,500	"
1898	130,000	910,000		*manusa*
1898	90,000	450,000		red cloth and print
1906		704,000		*manusa*
1907		0		"
1909		136,000		"
1910		"a boom year"		

Source: FO 195, various reports, often by Boyajian, for Harput province, 1886–1911. Converted from pounds sterling at 110 ptrs./£S except for 1898, which originally was given in Ottoman pounds, converted at 100 ptrs./£T.

220,000 pieces, of *manusa* cotton cloth and red prints (to Erzurum, Trabzon, Sivas, Bitlis and Diyarbakır) but their value was less than the smaller quantities of silk-cotton textiles sent during the previous decade (table 2.2).

In the early twentieth century, Harput province held some 5,000 looms for *manusa* weaving including 1,200 at Arapkir (see below), 1,000 at Malatya and its environs, and 300 at Eğin.[89] Shipments to neighboring provinces fluctuated very sharply during these years, sometimes dropping to zero and in other years booming (table 2.2).[90] During these last years, silk and cotton-silk production seems to have resumed greater importance, in part thanks to rising prices. In this more positive atmosphere, several factories were established in the region, at Harput and Mezre (see chapter 3). Thus, atypically (but in common with the introduction of jacquard looms at Diyarbakır, see below), mechanization played a role in the revitalization of weaving.

Diyarbakır

Despite the loss of its international markets during the eighteenth century (see chapter 3), the Diyarbakır region continued as one of the most important Ottoman textile production centers. Diyarbakır weavers, by the mid-1830s, were focused on the domestic Ottoman market and had accepted some British-made cotton yarn. There was another change as well. The industry once had relied on external sources for all of its raw silk needs, both for the pure silk and

Table 2.3. *Textile shops in the town of Diyarbakır in 1857 and 1864*

	1857	1864
calico handkerchief printers	14	
red thread makers	7	4
red thread sellers		6
loom makers	9	
silk and cotton goods	150	
cloth and linen sellers		180
felt makers	14	15
linen drapers	4	
silk fringe makers	34	40
silk winders	10	6
pattern setters for silk goods		7
tailors		50
hair cloth and thread makers	9	
horsecloth makers	27	
dyers	8	10
retail cotton dealers	55	
cotton sellers and cleaners		14
sellers of fancy silk, chintzes and cloth		26
weavers	311	320
Total	652	678

Source: FO 195/459, Holmes at Diarbekir, 3/31/1857; FO 195/799, Taylor at Diarbekir, 3/31/1864.

Table 2.4. *Production and shipment of cloth at Diyarbakır in 1857 and 1863*

1857 production	1863 export
15,000 pcs cotton-silk (*kutni*)	
15,000 pcs cotton-silk brocade (*çitari*)	40,800 yds.
25,000 pcs cotton-silk, 50/50 (*gazliye*)	
40,000 yards silk (*canfez*)	15,300 pcs.

Sources: various FO reports, including those in table 2.3.

silk-cotton cloths. But, about a decade after local workers had accepted British yarn, they began raising silkworms locally. On the average, during the early 1860s, the town workshops annually consumed 15,000 kg. of silk and 340 bales of British cotton yarn.[91] When they worked with British yarn, Diyarbakır-area weavers named it the devil's cloth (*şeytan bezi*). But homespun yarn remained a vital part of the industry and when it was used, the end product simply was called cloth (*bez*). Often the yarn was obtained through the system, described earlier, of picking cotton and exchanging the spun yarn for more raw cotton for subsequent spinning (see chapter 1). In the 1850s, this picking-spinning-exchanging-spinning method provided enough yarn to weave some 100,000 pieces of coarse cotton cloth (*bez*) for shipment outside the province. This alone accounted for one-third of total Diyarbakır textile shipments. By contrast, rural weavers then used British yarn to produce about 5,000 pieces of *şeytan bezi*, only *c.* 5 percent of the cloth sent from the area. Diyarbakır urban and rural producers also wove important quantities of handkerchiefs (*mendil*) and *çarşaf*s.[92]

At "Redhwan," they made a high-quality linen for sale in Bitlis while in the towns of "Deh" and Eruh, Christians monopolized the manufacture of *şal* cloth on 600 looms. They produced a high quality product of unique and varied patterns that was so preferred by local Kurdish buyers that the English product had vanished from the local market. In the Mardin district, there were important manufacturing activities in several locations. Workers at Cebel Tur and Mardin specialized in making woollen cloth (*aba*) and their annual production during the 1860s was devoted in equal measure for local use and shipment to the northern part of the province, to be worn in winter or rainy weather.[93]

Not later than the beginning of the 1870s, the Diyarbakır region was experiencing a "great manufacturing revival." This upward trend in part derived from shifts in the international economy, namely, the price depression of 1873–96 that sharply reduced Ottoman cultivators' purchasing power and placed many imported goods outside their reach. The revival at Diyarbakır, however, had begun at least several years before the start of the depression and was said to be underway in November 1872. It seems closely connected to a sharp rise in the use of imported materials, practices that continued cost-cutting techniques begun decades earlier at Diyarbakır, notably the adoption of British yarn and inauguration of silk raising. To minimize costs, artisans imported "plain and red cotton and wollen yarns, [and] plain shirtings" and then wove or stamped the cloths with local labor.[94]

The precise magnitude, pattern and nature of the upward trend after 1872 is uncertain. The narrative sources present a dramatic picture of positive change but the competitive struggle must have been grim as prices of foodstuffs, raw materials and manufactured goods fell. During the mid-1880s, the sale price of Diyarbakır and Mardin *manusa* cloth overnight fell by one-half as producers sought to maintain their sales outside the province (shipping some 20,000 pieces of the cloth to Erzurum). At this time, the volume of Diyarbakır sales of cotton-silk specialities reportedly doubled. The revival faltered temporarily when drought and crop failures in the late 1880s afflicted the industry's Anatolian customers.

During this crisis, Diyarbakır shipments of the cheaper cotton cloths actually increased but "that of [more expensive] silk stuffs fell off considerably," throwing many town artisans out of work. When the crop failures ended, production of the mixed cotton-silk cloth quickly bounced back. Thereafter, until 1914, overall textile output in the town and the region seems to have climbed steadily, for customers in Bitlis, Van, Harput, Erzurum, and Baghdad as well as in the

Table 2.5. *Production of textiles in Diyarbakır province, 1884–1903*

	Diyarbakır district		Mardin district		Ergani district	
	1884	*1903*	*1884*	*1903*	*1884*	*1903*
çitari#	16,000	17,500				
kutni#	3,000	3,200				
gazliye#	24,000	25,000	20,000	20,000		
white *bez#*			16,000	16,000	26,000	28,200
red *bez#*			8,000	8,000		
red yarn	15,000#	16,000#	6,000*			
white yarn*			8,000			
manusa#	30,000	32,400				
yerli basma#	20,000	21,500				
çarşaf						
ipleği#	3,000	3,400				
mendil@		2,000	10,000	10,000		
şal aba@	4,000	4,700	10,000	11,000		
yün aba			5,000	5,000		
çorap pr.	30,000	35,000		16,000		
külah@	11,000	11,000		5,000		
canfez	30,000	2,000				

Units of measure: # = *top*/piece; @ = each; * = *kiyye*/weight

Sources: Diyarbakır vs 1302/1884–5, pp. 98–100, 131, 153; Diyarbakır vs 1321/1903, pp. 194–6, 204, 212.

local area. The narrative testimony to "revival" and strong growth indicate that within the town of Diyarbakır itself, the volume of textile manufacturing reached levels that were higher in *c.* 1908 than at any point during the previous one-half century. At Mardin, a new manufacturing activity – cotton weaving – emerged to supplement the woollen cloak (*aba*) industry.[95] In the region overall, the use of British yarn quadrupled or quintupled between the 1860s and late 1880s and, by the mid-1890s, had doubled again. Diyarbakır weavers in 1895 employed more than eight times (340 vs. 3,000 bales) as much British yarn as they had in the 1860s![96]

In addition to the production of various cloths, the town and region of Diyarbakır at the end of the nineteenth century possessed a thriving export business in raw silk and cocoons. These were activities particularly reliant on very cheap labor (see chapter 4). At the end of the period, raw silk and cocoon shipments from Diyarbakır exceeded, by 25 percent, those of mixed cloth.[97] By this measure, the cheap and comparatively unskilled jobs in the silk industry had become more important to the Diyarbakır economy than the skilled tasks involved in making the famed cotton-silk cloths. Reduced wages and low material costs played an indispensable role in the industrial life of this community.

The few statistical tables on textile production have been assembled for

Table 2.6. *Textile production in Diyarbakır region, 1863–1903*

	1863	1884	1903
çitari	10,000	16,000	17,500
kutni	21,000	3,000	3,200
gazliye	4,000	44,000	45,000
canfez	15,000 yds	30,000	2,000
bez	107,000	50,000	52,200
manusa	no mention	30,000	32,400
yerli			
basma	"	20,000	21,500
çarşaf	3,500	3,000	3,400
aba	15,000	19,000	20,700
"el medeen"	5,000	no mention	
çiçekli	800		"
mendil	5,000	10,000	12,000
misc.	20,000		
TOTAL	206,300	225,000	209,900

Sources: derived from tables 2.4, 2.5; units of measure and sources as cited therein.

comparison of trends between the 1860s and the twentieth century (see table 2.6). This comparison does *not* bear out the argument of growth, that contemporary witnesses attest was taking place; but, rather, it gives the impression of stagnating production levels. The assembled data argue that aggregate textile production around Diyarbakır was stable, at *c.* 200,000 pieces, between the 1860s and 1903. Decreases in output of one kind of textile were offset by increases in other varieties.[98]

Comparing the data delineates several trends in Diyarbakır production. There was an important shift in the relative market shares held by local and more distant buyers. The local market annually accounted for less than one-fifth of all textiles produced in the Diyarbakır region in 1864 and 1889 but one-half of all textiles sold in 1884 and 1903.[99] Generally, local buyers were more important for the cotton cloth industry and those at a distance played a greater role in the sale of the other textiles. Production of more costly textiles seems to have been decreasing in favor of cheaper materials, at least until the opening of the twentieth century. Hence, the tables show the decline in the production of pure silk *canfez* cloth and the stagnation of mixed cotton-silk fabrics while the output of simple cotton textiles clearly was on the rise, for example, the emergence of a new cotton cloth industry at Mardin. This pattern, however, shifted in the final years before World War I. Entrepreneurs moved to take advantage of rising prices and introduced jacquard looms into the silk cloth industry at Diyarbakır. These looms allowed good quality production of cloth on a small scale, thus enabling local weavers to compete more effectively. Thereafter, the production of silk and mixed cotton-silk cloths increased, surely at lower unit costs than before.

Mosul

Mosul textile production remained very active and (see chapter 1), homespun played a major role even at the end of the period.[100] By the 1890s, however, coarse cloth weaving, once the local speciality, had fallen sharply in importance, accounting for only one-quarter of the 785 looms counted in the town. Aniline dyes came late, in the 1890s, but then were widely adopted. Natural indigo, imported from India, remained important but major changes occurred in the structure of the local dyeing industry. As elsewhere, the dyers' monopoly was broken by around the mid-century.[101] Indigo dyeing then spread out from the three dyehouses that had controlled the craft to dyers who also worked in other colors. During the early twentieth century, the textile industry at Mosul supplied local markets as well as buyers in Bitlis, Siirt, Trabzon and Persia.

Overall export and production trends at Mosul are difficult to determine. The industry clearly was vibrant and busy at the end of the period. The number of looms in the town equalled perhaps 1,000, by 1910, when a roughly equal number were working in the villages of the province. The quantity of indigo imports and the value of yarn imports rose very sharply during the early twentieth century. Those of indigo increased by 70 percent while the value of yarn imports and their share of all textile imports fully doubled. Thus, it seems likely that Mosul participated in the increases that occurred in many Ottoman manufacturing areas during the latter part of the period.

Aleppo and northern Syria

Introduction

In the world that existed before the Great Powers partitioned the Middle East, Aleppo and the line of cities to its immediate north formed an inter-dependent economic region located in northern Syria. With the final collapse of the Ottoman universe, however, Aleppo became part of the modern Syrian state while the other cities and towns – Urfa, Maraş, Kilis and Aintab – were incorporated into the Turkish nation state. In this work, they are discussed together, as the economic unit they once were.

Stripped of its international markets by *c.* 1800 (see chapter 3), Aleppo remained one of the most important centers of Ottoman textile production, vying with Damascus for first place among regional textile producers. The adoption of British yarn was credited with reviving a decaying industry (see below) but local spinning remained common enough. In the 1840s, large numbers of children and women spun while, during the late 1850s, some 400 shops with 6,000 urban workers similarly were employed. Hand spinning hardly had died out.[102]

During the first half of the century, Aleppo textiles were traded especially actively in north Anatolian towns such as Samsun, Bafra, Merzifon, Amasya and Sivas and at the great annual fairs at Zile and Yapraklı.[103] In *c.* 1860, during the peak of the destruction brought by European competition, the "lower classes" in Urfa, Diyarbakır, Mosul, Baghdad and their hinterlands bought important quantities of indigo-dyed coarse cotton cloths from Aleppo. Aleppo merchants also exported a small quantity to Persia. Silver-embroidered Aleppo silk cloth covered the Kaaba in the Holy City of Mecca. In the 1860s, the manufacturing center of Gürün obtained undyed cotton cloth from Aleppo while customers in Egypt, the Iraqi provinces, İstanbul and İzmir bought a variety of its textiles.[104] Buyers "eagerly attended" the Yaprakli fair in 1871 in order to buy Aleppo cottons while, in the following year, Egypt alone bought about one-quarter of the city's total production.[105] Because of their cheapness and strength, substantial quantities of Aleppo (and Damascus) cottons and colored half-silks were sold at İzmir, *c.* 4.5 million piasters' worth during the early 1870s.[106] Salonica and Macedonia first are mentioned as markets for the higher-quality textiles during the early twentieth century, when generally rising prices were bringing prosperity to many manufacturers. Thus, the industry was expanding its market nexus at the end of the period.[107] The city then possessed an impressive range of outlets for its textile production, including the Sudan as well as the Persian frontier provinces.

The changing textile mix

Already in the 1830s, the richer fabrics were "not manufactured to nearly the extent that they once were, but the cheaper stuffs are decidedly increasing in consumption ..."[108] At the bottom end of the market were muslin cloths; next were the silk-cotton cloths costing four times more and at the top were the luxury cloths, for women, selling for fifteen times the price of a simple cotton fabric. A full one-half of all active looms during the 1830s wove cotton cloth; about 40 percent worked up the famed mixed cotton and silk cloths and fewer than ten percent manufactured the luxury cloths of silk and gold and silver thread.[109] These relative proportions remained approximately the same into the mid-1850s, when a detailed enumeration of these looms and their products was offered.[110]

During the early 1860s, cotton cloth formed one-half of total textile production but its share of operating looms was only 33 percent. This slump, however, surely was a function of the U.S. Civil War and global shortages of cotton. Various kinds of silk and cotton goods, notably *kutni*, *alaca* and *gazel* on silk/*harir*, totalled 46 percent of output and used 56 percent of the looms. Silk and cotton goods then cost about six times more than plain cotton textiles; thus the differential was greater than in the late 1830s (see table 2.7).

Table 2.7. *Types of cloth woven at Aleppo, 1830–1900 (in percent of total active looms and value of production)*

| type of cloth | 1830s | | 1860s | | 1871 | | 1900 | 1907 |
	looms	prod.	looms	prod.	looms	prod.	prod.	looms
cotton	50	43	34	50	80	66	75	82
cotton-silk	43	53	56	46			24	17
silk	8	4	10	4			1–2	2
Price (index)		1830s		1860				
cotton		100		100				
cotton-silk		400		600				
silk		1,500		4,600				

Sources: Bowring (1840), p. 84; FO 195/741, 6/5/1862 for 1861; A&P 1872, 57, 3575, Skene for Aleppo, 12/31/1871; Buhi III, 10, 1/22/1902, Aleppo; Buhi, 9, 8/20/1907. Prices: in each time period, the cotton cloth price is the basis of comparison among the various cloths and is assigned an index number of 100. The prices in the two time periods are *not* to be compared.

Pure silk products continued to account for *c.* 10 percent of the looms in operation and some of the pure silks (for example, *canfez*) cost over forty times plain cotton cloths. In 1871, 80 percent of all looms working in the city made winter and summer cloth, presumably all cotton, for the "lower orders" of the people.[111] At about this time, in 1875, the industry consumed some 82,000 kg. of raw silk, three-quarters of it from Europe, India and Iran and the balance from a variety of Ottoman locations, including Mt. Lebanon and Tripoli.[112] In the early twentieth century, cottons accounted for some three-quarters of total textile output. Mixed silks accounted for most of the balance and pure silks scarcely were present.[113] Another early twentieth-century estimate states that two-thirds of all Aleppo looms wove cotton and the remaining made wool, silk and mixed fabrics.[114] Thus, these statistics show a sharp rise in the relative importance of cotton cloth weaving over the period (if we ignore the artificial low in the early 1860s), from about one-half to two-thirds and more of all looms in the city. Pure silk cloth production sharply declined while the relative importance of cotton-silk fabrics also fell, but less drastically.

Some of the city's favorite textiles, moreover, had changed composition over the course of the century. In the 1850s through the 1870s, the cloth called *alaca* had been a mixed silk and cotton fabric: it contained a "little" cotton in the mid-1850s and was still one-half silk in the 1870s.[115] The shift to a completely cotton fabric began in response to the import of all-cotton *alaca* cloth, that first reached Syria in the late 1860s or early 1870s.[116] During the early twentieth century, Aleppo weavers made the cotton *alaca* cloth using British yarn for the weft and Adana or Indian yarn for the warp.[117]

Factors influencing Aleppo textile production

As seen earlier, changes in tariffs and taxes played an important role in the evolution of the Aleppo textile industry and merchants of the city had been particularly active in seeking to overturn government policies that they felt were detrimental to the health of local industry. Abolition of several duties, including that on the water transport of goods within the empire, certainly had a positive impact on textile production. We also have seen the effects wrought by the falling prices of the 1873–1896 depression and the subsequently positive price trends that continued until World War I. A wide variety of other more specific factors, ranging from rebellious pashas against the Ottoman state to Confederate generals fighting the authority of Washington, also affected the Aleppo industry. During the 1820s, Egyptian factories and Mohammed Ali's monopoly system hurt Aleppo weavers by drawing away raw materials and closing access to a major market. In 1850, a taxpayers' revolt in the city resulted in 500 pillaged houses and 400 destroyed manufactories. Some 450 silk and cotton weavers, using British cotton yarn, were thrown out of work.[118] But Aleppo weavers could benefit when disorders occurred elsewhere. When the riots of 1860 destroyed silk-weaving factories at Deir el Kammar and Damascus, the number of active Aleppo looms immediately rose from 4,000 to 6,000 in order to supply Egyptian buyers.[119] As the American Civil War began, raw cotton prices skyrocketed and first affected British textile prices, temporarily creating a price advantage for Middle Eastern fabrics. Seeing the opportunity, Aleppo manufacturers jumped in and seized the British T-cloth market in Diyarbakır and Baghdad. By the end of 1861, however, local raw cotton prices also had risen enormously and they abandoned the effort. The great if emphemeral prosperity that the Civil War brought to the Egyptian peasants substantially increased their purchases of Aleppo textiles.[120]

Bumper crop conditions around Aleppo could boost agricultural production in ways that were disadvantageous to weavers. In 1867, local food prices fell with a good harvest and no means of export. The low price of food in turn depressed the price of local manufacturing labor, making Aleppo textiles more competitive but, at the same time, reducing the local cultivators' purchasing power. At the beginning of the year, a mere 800 looms reportedly were operating. The very low number of active looms and the reported drop in wages also may be attributable to the post-Civil War slump in Egypt, when the price of cotton collapsed. But the lowered wages at Aleppo and the end of the cotton bust meant that some 3,000 looms were "rapidly weaving" for the Egyptian market by 1867.[121] The Egyptian market continued to boom until 1872, consuming one-quarter of total Aleppo textile production. At least 1,000 more families were "supported by weaving than in 1871."[122] This seems to have been a particularly active period; 8,000 and sometimes as many as 11,000 looms reportedly were "at work."

The bubble of activity then burst in 1873–74, when the last killing famine of the century struck Anatolia, a major market of Aleppo. Drought combined with harsh winters destroyed crops and livestock and brought exceptional devastation. Sales collapsed; for example, Trabzon buyers abandoned Aleppo textiles for British yarn that they then wove themselves. Aleppo weavers put away their looms and took on other jobs; "most of that class are emigrating to other provinces where they can find work."[123] Despite the government's 1874 abolition of most internal tariffs (see above), the crisis continued. Without work in 1876, weavers either had found new jobs "or have emigrated to Egypt."[124] The number of active looms reached a new low, of 700. Political upheavals in the Sudan – the wars of the Mahdi and later of the Khalifa – damaged sales beginning in the mid-1880s. Several years later, crop failures and drought again struck in Anatolia as well as in the Aleppo region itself. In 1887, Trabzon, for example, reduced its imports of *manusa*, *gezi* and *"ghontin"* cloth from Aleppo in favor of cheaper goods from Russia.[125] Wages in textile making correspondingly fell; cotton weavers continued to work, but "for 12 hours a day for a pittance ..." By later 1889, however, exports to Anatolia were seen as particularly active, a trend that carried into the following years. Cocoon exports dropped as local weavers needed increased quantities of the raw material.[126]

Textile shipments halted only briefly with the Armenian massacres of 1894–95.[127] But there were other economic consequences. Armenian weavers at Aintab and Maraş emigrated to Europe, whether permanently or not is unknown.[128] Many other Armenian weavers and merchants migrated to Egypt and set up their looms to serve the local market.[129] During the new century, the loss of artisans mounted with additional migrations to Egypt, there weaving *alaca* cloth to meet Egyptian and Sudanese demand.[130] Production in the other urban centers of northern Syria outside the city and environs of Aleppo was increasing substantially, partially because of these migrations and, perhaps, rising wages at Aleppo (see below).

Other factors affecting textile production included a local crop failure in 1898 that triggered a bread riot at Aleppo[131] and a bad harvest in Aydin province, "one of the chief markets," during the next year.[132] The Young Turk Revolution and the 1909 conscription law that rendered Ottoman non-Muslims eligible for military service affected the industry in several, quite different, ways. During the first year of the new law, 10,000 young men, of Armenian and Syrian Christian origins, reportedly left from Aleppo alone, mostly bound for the United States.[133] Their departure may have hurt output but the resulting reduction of the labor pool could have raised weavers' wages. The conscription law gave new life to an already impressive wave of Syro-Lebanese migration, in motion since the 1860s. These immigrant workers had an additional economic importance, besides remittances and investments by returnees. Homesick and with high wages, they provided new markets for Aleppo textiles. Living in Great

Table 2.8. *Looms in Aleppo and adjacent areas, 1800–1914*

	Aleppo	Aintab	Urfa	Maraş	Kilis	Total North Syria
1820s*	25,000					
1829*	6,000					
1838*	4,000					
1838a	2,800					
1845*	1,500					
1846b	800					
1848*	5,000					
1850*	10,000					
1852c	10,000					
1855*	5,560					
1856*	10,000					
1856*	5,500					
1858*	1,400					
1859*	10,000					
1859d	4,000					
1850s*	3,500					
1860e	6,000					
1861f*	10,000					
1862g	3,650					
1862*	4,000					
1868h	800					
1868i	3,000					
1871j*	5,000					
1872*	6,000					
1872k	6,400					
early 1870s	8,000					
1874*	5,000					
1875m	4,900					
1875*	2,400					
1876	700					
1879*	3,000					
1889	3,610	2,500	2,000			
1891*	5,884					
1893	3,610	2,500	2,000	(per a 1902 source)		
1896	(per a 1902 source)					3–3,500
1897*	3,000					
1899	2,915					
1900		900				
1901	2,915					
1901–2			2,900			
1902			2,500			
1904	4,200	5,500		1,500		+ 800 more
1906			14,000			
1907	9,000 in city					
1907	5,735	3,726	1,150	2,090	115	12,816
1907			12,000			

Sources: * from Issawi (1988), table on p. 374.
a – FO 195/741, Aleppo, 6/5/1862; b – BBA Cev Ikt 1024, 11 X 1262/October 1846; c – FO 195/741, Aleppo, 6/5/1862, certainly Skene; d – FO 195/700, Skene, Aleppo, 12/31/1860; e – FO 195/700, Skene, Aleppo, 12/312/1860; f – A&P 1872, LVII, 3565, Skene, Aleppo, 12/31/1871; g – FO 195/741, Aleppo, 6/5/1862, certainly Skene; h – FO 195/802, Skene, Aleppo, 4/2/1868; i – ibid.; j – A&P 1872, LVII, 3565, Skene, Aleppo, 12/31/1871; k – A&P 1873, 64, Skene, North Syria for 1872; l – A&P 1876, 75, 3925, Skene, Aleppo, 12/31/1875; m – BBA I MM 2276, 28 III 1292 /May 1875. After 1875, see various A&P reports from Aleppo.

Britain and the United States, the migrants avidly bought Aleppo embroideries, silk embroidering on Manchester cloth, used for wall and table coverings and other purposes.[134]

The fictitious decline of Aleppo textile production

In the introduction of this book, beliefs in Islamic civilizational and industrial decline were said to have blinded us to the realities present. Aleppo is an excellent case in point since it incessantly has been cited in Ottoman historiographical literature as a major example of Ottoman industrial decline. Its decline, however, truly was in the eyes of the beholders rather than real. Consider the data given in table 2.8, stating the number of looms in Aleppo and the Aleppo region. In particular, note the varying number of looms during the period from the 1820s through 1871. The 25,000 and 10,000 loom figures stand out in the table as anomalies. In every example but one, the figures derive from a *later* source reporting on the production levels of a preceding period. In each case, the observer has established the decline of Aleppo industry in his own day by comparing its output with production levels in the past. The 1850 and 1852 figures thus are respectively from an 1862 book and an 1862 consular report; the 1861 figure, for its part, is from an 1871 report. The 1862 consul proved the manufacturing decline in the city by comparing the 3,650 looms of his own day with the 10,000 looms that he said were present just ten years earlier. But the consular official in 1871 used the 1860s for the mythic past. He proved the sharp decline of the Aleppo industry by comparing the 5,000 looms then operating, in 1871, with the 10,000 looms that he said had been present ten years before![135]

Rather than declining, the nineteenth-century Aleppo textile industry encountered constantly changing conditions. As seen, wars, political instability, international crises or crop failures affecting peasant customers might depress output and cause many weavers to put away their looms, waiting for better times. A return to normal conditions, or bumper crops stimulating cultivator demands for textiles, or the misfortunes of competitors, brought Aleppo weavers back to the looms. Thus, the statistics in table 2.8 do not show decline; but they do reflect widely fluctuating market opportunities. In most years, between 3,000 and 6,000 looms actively wove but the number often fell below 3,000, sometimes to 1,500 and less. On several occasions, lows of 800 and 700 were met, due to particularly unfavorable combinations of events. The number of active looms generally continued to fluctuate within the 3,000–6,000 range until World War I, although there are indications of real production increases at Aleppo after 1907. More certainly, the number of active looms in Northern Syria generally increased very dramatically in just a few years during the early twentieth century.

Other statistics besides the number of active looms argue strongly against the notion of decline in the Aleppo textile industry. The output of gold and silver thread, important in the luxury silk textiles, indicate the health of that particular branch of textile making. In 1838, Aleppo held 15 manufactories making the gold and silver thread; these employed 60 workers while, in 1902, the workers numbered 70 persons. Thus, apparently, the making of gold and silver thread did not decline during the period as a whole even though luxury cloth lost in *relative* significance in Aleppo textile production.[136] Also, the number of dye-houses in Aleppo remained steady and probably increased over the nineteenth century. In *c.* 1838, there were perhaps 100 dyeshops (and printshops) in the city, employing 1,500 workers. In 1868, the city contained 89 dyehouses while, in 1899, there were 129 of them operating, together with 27 printing factories.[137] In 1901, approximately 100 dyehouses worked in indigo alone; about 10 percent of these dyemasters worked with two helpers and the rest worked alone or with children. By 1907, the number of dyehouses had increased substantially, to 120, using both synthetic and natural indigo.[138] Contemporary foreign observers fundamentally misunderstood the meaning of these increases in indigo dyeing and the quickness with which Aleppo dyers adopted the new synthetic; and they refused to acknowledge the dyers' actions as rational efforts to remain competitive. Instead, they insisted that the prosperity of indigo dyeing proved the progressive impoverishment of the region; they saw increasing output in the craft only as an effort to serve the poorer classes that were becoming ever larger.[139]

Trends in the use of domestic and imported cotton yarn and in the production of cloth reflect similar patterns of resiliency and then growth. Between the mid-1850s and early 1870s, the levels of thread usage, both foreign and domestic, and cotton cloth production were at least stable, at *c.* 900,000 kg. and two million pieces respectively.[140] In 1900, Aleppo imported 7.1 million kg. of cotton yarn while in 1905, yarn imports were given at 3.5 million kg.[141] Even the lower figure shows very substantial growth in Aleppo's cotton yarn usage since the 1850s–1870s. By the early twentieth century, the total volume of all yarns used, Ottoman and imported, had increased at least four times at Aleppo.

There is another, less direct, suggestion of rising prosperity in the industry during the early twentieth century. In 1903 and 1904, weavers and dyers in Aleppo successfully struck. They won very impressive wage increases, some 20 percent, while the wages of embroiderers doubled. Wage increases of this magnitude do not occur in moribund or stagnating industries: they show that profits or market conditions were sufficiently attractive so that merchants were willing to pay higher wages to maintain production.[142]

Textile exports from Aleppo bear out and support the argument for stable and then increased textile production during the period *c.* 1830s–1914 (see table 2.9). Textiles from Aleppo and other North Syrian centers exited at the port of Alexandretta for shipment to İstanbul, İzmir and the European provinces and,

Table 2.9. *Textile exports from Alexandretta, 1880–1911*

	quantity (tons)	value (pounds sterling)
1880		218,000
1881		159,000
1882		129,000
1883		92,000
1884		92,000
1886		133,000
1887		113,000
1888		104,000
1889	235	99,000
1890	363	113,000
1891	326	132,000
1892	365	138,000
1893	353	135,000
1894	378	145,000
1895	297	113,000
1896	353	134,000
1897	503	178,000
1898	504	190,000
1899	438	165,000
1900		176,000
1901	525	197,000
1902	541	202,000
1903	587	256,000
1904	596	262,000
1905	562	247,000
1906	589	258,000
1907	649	285,000
1908	319	147,000
1909	390	170,000
1910	427	194,000
1911	360	163,000

Sources: 1880–89, 1900 – Firro Kais, "Alep, une ville traditionnele face à l'impact de l'Europe, 1830–1914," *Cahiers de la Méditerranée, Actes du Colloque* (Décembre 1987–Juin 1988), p. 143, based on FO reports, British consular reports, 1889–99, 1901–11.

c. 1900, these seaborne exports represented about one-half of total textile output. Generally, their value remained approximately steady from the early 1880s through *c.* 1900. (More specifically, the value of the sea-exports fell in the late 1880s, regained the lost ground and then rose fractionally in the 1890s.) Thereafter, and until the Young Turk Revolution, textile exports via Alexandretta jumped more than 50 percent in value. Similarly, the volume of these exports rose 17 percent during the 1890s and increased by another 38 percent during the twentieth-century years before the Revolution. The instability of the post-revolutionary period then took its toll and exports slipped, but only back to the levels of the later 1890s.

3 Patterns of cloth production in the Ottoman lands from Salonica to Aleppo

Introduction

The previous narrative account of cloth production outlined output trends over the course of the period. This history of cloth production revealed the broad range of responses in the various regions to changes in the domestic and international economy. The present chapter offers information, culled from these narrative histories, relating to a number of topics such as the workforce and the organization of production in Ottoman home, workshop and factory. In addition, this chapter traces the markets that artisans in the various regions served as well as the struggles among and between foreign and domestic producers for the Ottoman market.

The workforce

The Ottoman textile workforce in home, workshop and factory was diverse in its gender, ethnic and religious makeup. Depending on time, place and market, men and/or women of Muslim, Christian and/or, occasionally, Jewish origins dominated textile production. In their ethnicity, the workers were Arabs, Armenians, Turks and Bulgarians; they also were Kurds, Laz, Greeks and Persians. But scarcely any details are available concerning the size, ethnic and gender composition of the workforce making textiles. Only occasionally do we learn anything about the people who were weaving and printing cloth, in whatever location. Given the preoccupation of the nineteenth-century Great Powers with the well-being of the Ottoman Christian community, the absence of information on the workers' religion and ethnicity is somewhat surprising; but, given the social composition of the consuls, perhaps it is not. The unconcern about gender is predictable. In the sources, therefore, they usually are merely workers, of undetermined ethnicity, religion and gender. The historical sources most commonly reveal the identity of products but not producers.

Very few occupations relating to cloth production were the sole prerogative of either men or women. An exception seems to have been embroidering both for personal use and for sale, that everywhere exclusively was a female occupation.

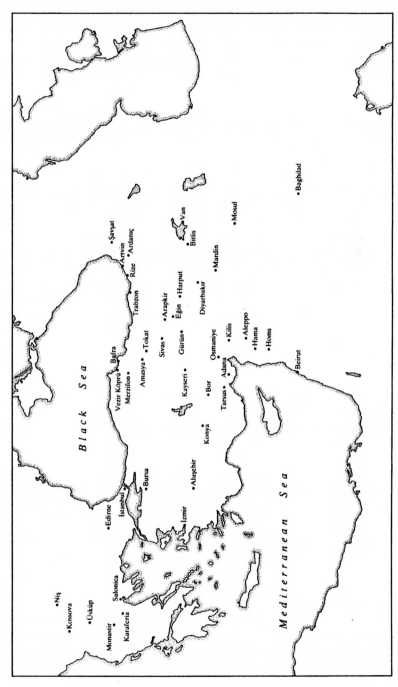

Map 3. Patterns of clothmaking in the nineteenth century.

In reportedly every village of İzmir province, for example, young girls embroidered, most using threads of silk and gold that were made at İstanbul. Otherwise, there was considerable crossing of gender lines, in spinning and weaving alike as well as in the silk reeling and carpetmaking industries (see chapters 4 and 5 for more details). Both women and men, here meaning females and males of any age group, wove and printed, to meet subsistence and market needs. While there does not appear to have been a rigid gender division of weaving labor, the sources more frequently do mention women as the subsistence workers and men as the commercial, often town-based, weavers of cotton, wool, mohair and other textiles. Further, there is more discussion of women working in the home and men weaving in work places outside the home. Within the framework of this generalization, however, there is a rich variety – given the very limited discussion in the sources on these questions – of local patterns.

During the 1890s, women in their homes wove most of the cloth in the greater İzmir region, both for subsistence and sale. At this time, women and children in the Sivas region, working at home, wove a coarse cloth, both from yarn they themselves had spun and from British yarn. Elsewhere, around Ankara during the 1830s, in reportedly every surrounding town and village, women not only spun wool yarn and wove shirts but also made trousers, *çarşafs* and felt hats.[1] Near the end of the century, in the Davas district of İzmir province, both men and women commercially wove: 143 young girls and women and 43 males made 15,000 pieces of cloth, mainly lining (*boğası*) and the *alaca* fabric.[2] Much further east, during the 1830s, in the small town of Hinis, family labor working on 120 looms wove a coarse cotton cloth for sale in adjacent and regional markets. At a nearby town, Palu, families used local cotton to spin and weave.[3] Thus, as some of these examples demonstrate, women wove commercially.

The pattern of men dominating the commercial production of cloth is broken further by the following example of women weavers who annually worked for up to three months. During the 1830s, these Muslim women participated in a home industry network in the far eastern Anatolian towns of Artvin, Ardanıç, Şavşat, and "Saded" and commercially wove both linen and cotton cloth at home.[4] In the city of Trabzon, most nineteenth-century linen weavers were women, who worked at home. There, during the 1870s, Muslim women also printed British muslins for use as head-dress handkerchiefs.[5] At the turn of the century, Trabzon women involved in some 20 home-industry networks wove *peştemal* cotton cloth at home for sale. Working for piece-work wages, they made three large or four small pieces daily, earning between five and nine piasters.[6]

In the most important textile producing centers, and in many cities, men were predominant in the commercial weaving workforce. Men worked the 1,000 looms operating at Baghdad in *c.* 1907. In the great production center of Diyarbakır, during the 1850s, 1,500 Armenian men and boys worked on 1,200 looms, located in over 300 shops.[7] They annually averaged between 200 and 290 workdays, depending on the textile. This continued an eighteenth-century pattern in which Armenians wove the cotton "chafarcanis" cloth and handled their international shipment as well.[8] At Aleppo, male artisans exclusively, it seems, wove. During the eighteenth and throughout the nineteenth century, women provided them with the spun cotton and silk. These women, during the middle and end of the nineteenth century, were assisted by "a considerable number of children." This is an example of the more general pattern in which guilds of male weavers used female labor to supply them with materials, particularly yarn. Thus, women spun for the famed Ankara mohair weavers until the industry vanished *c.* 1850. In Trabzon, Armenian shopowners worked together with a putting-out network of female workers to provide the *yazma* cloth.[9]

In some places, such as Aleppo, Diyarbakır and Baghdad, weaving was a more or less year-round occupation. But this was not everywhere or always the case. Even in textile centers with comparatively significant output levels, weaving often was seasonal work. Take, for example, the Manisa area, that was one of the leading textile producers in İzmir province. There, weavers in urban workshops worked only in the winter, hiring themselves out for more lucrative agricultural tasks during the other seasons.[10] Even in the most important centers, weaving families often had ties to the countryside. The food and livelihoods provided by such links (as we shall see) sustained many weavers in the highly competitive conditions that prevailed during the nineteenth century.

Overall, there probably was a correlation between agricultural fertility and patterns of weaving, particularly of cotton. Generally, the richer the agriculture of a region, the less likely peasants were to commit time to commercial manufacturing and the more likely it was that cotton weaving would be an urban, comparatively full-time occupation. Thus, in richer areas, there was a more rigid division of labor between town and country. In poorer areas, cotton weaving tended to center on the countryside, where households engaged in a combination of agriculture and manufacturing. Silk weaving generally tended to be urban based regardless of agricultural fertility. Wool weaving, at least in the Balkans, had been more urban-based but largely occurred in the countryside during the later nineteenth century.

The labor force in the silk reeling and weaving and carpet making industries examined later in this study displays similar patterns of gender and ethnic/religious variety. Armenian, Greek and other Christian groups dominated the silk industry, but many Muslims and some Jews were present. In the carpet industry, Muslims formed the original and large nucleus of the workforce while Christians were in the majority of those who came into the industry after *c.* 1870. In the silk industry, men wove at the important production centers at Bursa and Diyarbakır. But at Trabzon, of far lesser importance in the industry, silk weaving was a female occupation, done by Muslims and Christians who, working at home, first dyed the individual silk threads brought from Bursa, Bafra and Amasya. It may have been the nature of the fabric that determined the gender of the weavers but this point is speculative. Both men and women spun silk at home, in many districts. But, once mechanized factories were established, only women spun (while men carried out the machine maintenance tasks). In the important carpetmaking industry, there were some male knotters to break the general pattern of female labor. Yarn spinning in this industry in some areas was a female domain but elsewhere the task of both men and women.

Organization of home and workshop production

General

According to observers, every or nearly every home in many regions held a loom. While this might have been an exaggeration, the number of looms in the late Ottoman Empire was considerable. Thus, the Sivas region held some 10,000 looms during the 1890s while İzmir province had a similar number. There were nearly 12,000 in the Harput-Erzurum region during the 1870s. In *c.* 1900, Harput province contained 5,000, just for cotton *manusa*, while the north Syrian region held as many as 12,000. This partial enumeration totals nearly 50,000 and surely the regions not mentioned here contained looms as well. According to other estimates, all of Syria in 1909 held 20,000 looms while, in Egypt at this time, there were 45,000 weavers.[11]

The concentration of looms varied considerably, regionally and within a particular area of a region. Take, for example, the province of Diyarbakır: the district (*sancak*) of Diyarbakır averaged one loom for every twelve houses while the district of Siirt, with ten sub-districts (*kazas*), contained one loom for every 27 houses and Mardin district maintained a ratio of 1:16. Beneath these district averages there were still more local variations. One sub-district in the district of Siirt, for example, contained but one loom for every 100 houses. It was quite otherwise in two other sub-districts of the same administrative unit, where every fourth and seventh house respectively held a loom.[12]

Whatever the exact home to loom ratios, it is clear that weaving (and spinning) were every-day and familiar tasks. Very large numbers of women, children and men worked at home, producing coarse cloths, often of cotton that was more workable than wool or silk, for family needs. Looms that wove mainly for household use help account for the majority of the tens of thousands of "rude" looms working.

Many of the looms located in households also wove for sale, either at the independent initiative of the urban or rural weaver, or as part of merchant-organized production networks. It seems impossible to estimate whether weaving for subsistence or for the market, under whichever system, was in the majority at a particular time and place. In some places, commercial weaving was rare. In the city of Sivas, for example, women at home throughout the nineteenth century used homespun cotton or wool to weave for family needs only, usually the strong coarse cotton cloth called *donluk* or sometimes *bez*. Similarly, weavers in the Adana region between the 1840s and 1870s were engaged in the "insignificant" manufacture of some coarse cotton cloth and hairsacks, almost exclusively for home production.[13] By contrast, commercial weaving dominated life in some towns. At Rize, on the Black Sea, footlooms that were located in most homes of the town during the 1830s manufactured the "linen used for the shirts worn throughout Turkey, which is taken to Trebizond for sale." In the town of Bor in south central Anatolia, there may have been as many as one commercial loom for every two homes.[14]

Vast and well-organized putting-out networks located in the European provinces controlled the production of coarse wool cloth for sale in other regions of the empire. Through the 1870s, commercial weavers on the Gallipoli peninsula at the entrance to the Dardanelles were producing considerable quantities of wool cloth (*aba*), totalling several thousand bales per year.[15] In Ottoman Bulgaria, villagers at mid-century were working with urban guilds in Plovdiv to make the coarse fabric. The artisans then travelled, for a month or more, to their customers in Anatolia, Syria and elsewhere, selling finished goods and making clothing to order for customers.[16] Such patterns probably prevailed around Salonica, but details are lacking. In the Edirne area, village-based cottage industries produced the wool cloth, compressing it at small mills and then selling to merchants in the larger towns.[17]

Similarly impressive home industry networks existed early in the century, south of the Black Sea littoral in Anatolia where Kayseri merchants supplied raw cotton from Adana for spinning and weaving. In this system, that European competition may have destroyed by *c.* 1850, the merchants then arranged for the weaving of the newly produced yarn, either on the spot or at other locations in northern Anatolia or southern Russia. Merchants in the town of Gürün during the 1830s distributed raw wool locally and to residents of "the cities around" for spinning. The merchants then gave the yarn to weavers in these surrounding towns and unloaded any surplus on Gürün workers who, apparently, made cloth only for their own use.[18]

Foreign missionaries in the Ottoman Empire played an interesting, if minor, role as organizing merchants in their own, unique, putting-out networks. In the textile center of Arapkir as well as at nearby Eğin, they intervened in local manufacturing after the massacres of 1895–6 and provided Armenian weavers with looms and imported thread. Whether this was an effort to restore an existing activity to previous levels or begin a new industry is uncertain. An 1836 account relates that Armenians were the majority of the weavers but an 1880s' report says only that most residents of Arapkir wove. A year after the massacres,

Arapkir exports of its main product – *manusa* cloth – were back to normal. This rapid recovery from the turmoil suggests either that many weavers were Muslim after all or that few Armenian weavers had been killed, displaced, or disrupted in their work.[19] British and American missionaries also were active in the Adana area and there organized many hundreds of Armenians to weave coarse cotton cloth, as well as rugs, carpets and curtains. Centered at the Hacın orphanage, the industry employed "many of the orphans and poorer inhabitants."[20] A "new" commercial industry, embroidering, also emerged in the Aintab area under the direction of women at the local American mission. Using "cambric, silk or the finest linen from Belfast," women made "ladies handkerchiefs, doyleys, table centres, collars and scarves".[21] By 1911, the agent of an Irish firm employed several hundred girls and women to make linen handkerchiefs and lacework, mostly for export to the United States. To capture some of this thriving business, a number of local entrepreneurs established their own networks, manufacturing the hankies and lacework for direct export to America.[22]

Elsewhere, home industry produced a wide variety of textiles for sale but the details often are absent. In the town of Mosul in the 1820s, for example, most commercial weavers worked at home, in houses that were "half subterranean," for piece-work wages. They made mostly coarse cotton cloth (*ham* or *çit*) and *alaca* cloth as well. They also wove fabrics for men's robes, for women's coverings, and the wool *aba* cloth.[23]

Workshops – separate labor sites located apart from the home – typically were small, often with one or two workers, were very common in towns and cities, and regionally often coexisted with putting out networks located in Ottoman towns as well as country. At Edirne, at the beginning of the twentieth century, wool weaving workshops were concentrated in one quarter while commercial production also was taking place in private homes elsewhere in the city. In Salonica, until *c*. 1850, workshops of guildsmen wove both wool and cotton cloths but only cotton at Karaferia. At Alaşehir, in western Anatolia *c*. 1900, some 250 workshops with a "great number of workers," wove cottons for sale.[24] Small shops perhaps made most of the cotton as well as silk cloth at the important center of Bursa and had employed the majority of workers in the Ankara mohair cloth industry. In the town of Bor, the textile center of the Konya region, some shops were comparatively large: 26 workshops in 1908 were said to hold 2,250 cotton looms.[25] During the 1860s, the town of Bitlis held some 500 weaving shops, usually with one and not more than three looms; these worked nearly year-round, cooperating with 50 dyehouses to make its bright and coarse red cloth. Nearby, during the 1830s, 500 commercial looms in the town of Van spun and wove a coarse calico, sending it to Bitlis for dyeing, and a special coarse wool cloth from goat's hair, that produced a strong and nearly waterproof garment.[26] Whether the looms were located in homes or shops is not certain but, fifty years later, nearly 300 home-situated looms were weaving the same two textiles.[27]

Dyehouses on the average held more workers than the typical weaving work-shop but still tended to be small in size. In İzmir, up to 1,000 workers in these dyehouses dyed yarn and printed thin cotton cloths while at Kayseri, *c.* 1900, 15 dyehouses working in cotton cloth each employed an average of 20 workers.[28] At the important center of Tokat, during the 1830s, there were "two extensive dyeing establishments" that printed cotton cloth. But there must have been many others, far smaller in size. In the early twentieth century, 150 dyeing and printing workshops in Tokat employed 1,800 workers, an average of 12 workers per shop.[29] At Trabzon in the late 1860s, similarly, these kinds of workshops averaged *c.* 10 workers while, *c.* 1900, there were a number of larger houses as well.[30]

Sometimes the typically silent sources speak but are confusing and misleading about the organization of production. At Kayseri, a single enterprise is said to have occupied 250 workers. These may have worked under a single roof, but it also is possible that they were scattered about in private homes, working on behalf of a single merchant firm.[31] At the town of Arapkir in the eastern Harput region, large workshops may have accounted for the bulk of its *manusa* cotton cloth. But the character of the worksite is not altogether certain. One account states that 1,000 commercial looms in Arapkir were weaving cotton cloth while another states that 15 manufactories were producing the cloth. Were the 1,000 looms in these 15 locations? These latter might well have been dyehouses working cloth produced on home industry looms.[32]

Home and workshop production at Trabzon, Diyarbakır and Aleppo

There is a relatively large amount of information on the organization of pro-duction in these three Ottoman cities. The patterns of production differ from one another and, altogether, probably display the range that was extant in the late Ottoman economy.

Trabzon

The port city of Trabzon was not a major textile producer and yet the local organization of labor at first glance seems unique in its exquisite variety. This quality, however, probably is apparent rather than real, stemming from the simple fact that the activities of this particular port city were heavily documen-ted in the sources consulted for this study. Home weavers commercially made silk cloth, after dyeing threads that merchants likely provided. Less formally, peddlers regularly toured linen-weaving neighborhoods and bought the surplus for sale in other areas. In cotton textiles during the 1870s, merchants operated a production nexus that included urban workshops and home weavers in the hinterland, making *manusa* cloth.[33] At the end of the century, the workers in urban workshops were weaving on consignment for merchants who provided the yarns needed.[34] In 1912, independent workshop weavers of the cotton *peştemal* fabric accounted for one-third of the looms in the city while home industry producers made up the balance, selling to merchants by the piece.

In addition, *c.* 1900, a number of large and small Trabzon dyehouses cut, dyed and printed imported cloths for use as women's head gear. They imported both coarse and fine cotton cloth from England and used mainly German dyes. At the worksite, they cut up the bolt of cloth into approximately 25 pieces (of either *çember* or *yazma*). Persians operated the large shops and were seen as more skilled, printing in all colors and marketing their own products (*çember*) in the retail trade. The Armenians (*yazmacıs*) were small shop owners who first printed the black background color of the *yazma* cloth and then gave it to Turkish women who worked at home tracing out in color the general patterns, copied from İstanbul, of the head dress. Using woodblocks sent from the capital, they then stamped in patterns with the traced colors. In addition, they printed various kinds of turbans (*sarık*), made from Manchester cloth, and produced the *abani* type, worked with yellow silk, as well. The women dyer/printers received payment by the piece; in contrast, only men worked in the dyehouses and they received wages, of 5–6 piasters a day.[35]

Overall, the impression is that centralized textile production at Trabzon gradually declined while household production was able to compete more successfully. By 1900, putting out networks and household production dominated textile manufacturing in Trabzon far more than at any time in the preceding century.

Diyarbakır

The town of Diyarbakır and its surrounding villages contained one of the densest concentrations of looms in eastern Anatolia. In the 1850s, the town of Diyarbakır held some 300 weaving establishments controlled by 200 masters who directed some 1,500 men and boys. Unusually for the Erzurum-Harput-Diyarbakır region as a whole, most looms – approximately 86 percent – in the local area of Diyarbakır were urban based. This urban concentration probably derived from Diyarbakır weavers' focus on silk cloth making, a more highly skilled activity that typically occurred in towns rather than the countryside. Town weavers specialized in silk and cotton-silk textiles, including red and white-thread *kutni* and *çitari* cloths as well as silk cloth (*canfez*). Paid by the piece, silk weavers in town then annually earned 50 percent more than the cotton weavers. Workers owned their looms, either for silk or cotton, that cost up to one-third of an annual wage.[36]

In the surrounding rural districts, most weavers focused on the production of cotton cloth. Commercial and subsistence weaving was scattered throughout these rural areas.[37] This pattern owed much to the poor agriculture of the Diyarbakır region, that encouraged peasants to weave as a means of insuring survival.

Aleppo

There are three snapshots, sometimes giving a detailed look, of the organization of production at this major textile center. Taken together, they suggest a certain continuity over the period *c.* 1800–1900. At the end of the eighteenth century, large factories with numerous looms under one roof produced silk and cotton textiles at the same time that a large number of (male) artisans with one or two looms worked in their own homes. Women, working part-time in their homes, spun most of the silk and cotton, probably for piece-work wages, for the master artisan who gave them the raw materials.[38] In 1777 and 1786, the workers – Muslim and Christian, master and worker alike – who fulled these textiles petitioned to eliminate wage differences among them.[39] In *c.* 1840, weavers similarly were working in large shops for particular manufacturers and received piece-work wages. The weavers owned their looms but the masters provided the materials.[40] In *c.* 1900, a small number of merchants dominated the industry, then characterized by a very minute division of labor. There were independent weaving masters with one, two and up to five looms, and some of them prepared warp and weft. Sometimes, two to four independent master weavers worked side by side, so they could divide the labor, employing a few helpers and apprentices, usually women and children. But, as before, merchants controlled almost the whole industry, about 100 cloth-making enterprises, mostly located in homes, and focused on the export trade.[41] The larger ones each employed 5–15 intermediary masters (*Zwischen-meister*), supplied the artisans with yarn and other materials and paid them piece wages.[42] (These may be the large factories mentioned in the earlier reports.) The merchant bought the yarn and then gave it either to his own dyers or to independent waged dyers. Local spinners still made the yarn for the indigo-dyed cotton cloth marketed among the bedouin. The merchant then distributed the variously dyed yarns to the warp maker and frequently to yet another master for preparation of the weft thread. The prepared yarn then was delivered to weavers. They, generally, gave the woven cloth to finishers who returned the completed product to the merchants who originally had bought the yarn. The merchants then sold the cloth to middlemen or shopkeepers. Thus, the organization of production in 1800 and 1900 are similar in their general outline but it is unclear if the minute division of labor was a recent innovation or a long-standing pattern simply not mentioned in the earlier reports.[43]

Over the period, however, there may have been a somewhat greater physical diffusion of looms in the Aleppo area. It might be that some of the production was transferred from specialized workshops to private homes in an effort to reduce prices. In this view, workshops remained predominant but household production was present and increased somewhat in importance.[44]

Organization of production in privately owned mechanized weaving factories

Most privately owned factories opened very late in the Ottoman period and concentrated in a few regions, notably in the Balkan provinces, the cities of İstanbul and İzmir and in the Adana region of southeastern Anatolia. Factories were particularly scarce in the Syrian lands, Damascus as well as Aleppo.[45] Those in the Balkan provinces often worked on military contracts while the others, to a significant degree, satisfied local demand. Many, as we shall see, were situated in the port cities that were growing disproportionately fast during the nineteenth century.

The entrepreneur Yorgi Sirandi operated a small factory at Edirne in the early 1890s, supplementing the output of hand weavers of wool flannel. But it employed just four workers and monthly produced only 400 meters of cloth.[46] The city contained two or three other small mechanized factories, with mainly Manchester machinery, making cheap, coarse stockings that supplied virtually the entire local market. The largest factory, *c.* 1905, employed 40 workers and daily produced up to 500 pairs. In 1911, two more opened, partially directed towards İstanbul buyers. All these small factories, that used thread from İstanbul and Italy, also produced coarse wool flannel underwear.

During the early twentieth century, a few other mechanized wool cloth factories emerged to augment hand weaving in the Balkan provinces. Some, however, required finer grades of foreign wool and depended on imported raw material.[47] The first significant mechanized cloth factory in the region, located at Niausta, became operational in 1908, joining two small factories with manually operated looms. Possessing a 200-horsepower engine driven by water, it contained 19 looms that annually produced 300,000 kg. of cloth. The factory employed 80–90 young women and 60–70 male workers, numbers that declined in the summer season, respectively paying them 3–7 and 5–9 piasters per day. They chiefly made khaki-colored wool cloth (*şayak*) for the military contracts that were its mainstay. A small factory, with five Bielefeld looms, opened in 1908 at Salonica, to dye and finish fine wool cloth (*şayak*) for the Ottoman administration.[48] Another Salonica mechanized wool cloth factory opened in 1911, a joint stock company financed primarily by local Jews and equipped with 30 looms. This effort, however, failed almost immediately. At Salonica, several large ateliers produced textiles such as knitted goods and flannel shirts. The city also contained a jute weaving mill, opened by the Torres family in 1906, that burned in 1908 and was rebuilt with better equipment in 1909. Containing 60 looms, the mill had a daily capacity of 10,000 meters, mainly sacking for the booming tobacco industry.[49]

The region around Monastır contained one large and numerous small enterprises, making wool yarn and cloth. The Casazis factory at Dichovo operated for a few years but closed with the owner's death. It had possessed both steam and water power, making its own yarn and weaving on four mechanical and 28 manual looms, annually consuming *c.* 65,000 kg. of wool, mostly from Edirne. The smaller establishments in the early twentieth century began using a steadily increasing number of wool carding machines. Averaging around 20 looms each, these small mills operated around Monastır and Üsküp and wove bordering, some of it for merchants who provided the wool and paid cash wages.

In the imperial capital, most textile factories were state-owned and served the needs of the palace and the Ottoman military. Among the earliest were those to produce the fez and to print cloth. Outside the city proper, the Hereke factory complex initially wove cotton cloth before converting to silk weaving for the palace.[50] Later in the century, a number of privately owned cloth factories emerged, for example, the Yedikule mill in the 1880s that wove cloth as well as spinning yarn (see chapter 1). An immigrant Bosnian, *c.* 1900, received state subsidies and manufactured cloth at Karamürsel, primarily for the military. His factory, commercially tied to the capital by steamship, employed some 500 male workers, mainly fellow countrymen.[51] A new Imperial Ottoman Cloth and Material Factory at Eyüp, on the Golden Horn, was established at about this same time and employed some 600 workers, both males and females.[52] While each of these must have made an important impact on local neighborhoods, there is little information currently available on this subject or on working conditions within the factories.

Several mechanical weaving mills for both cotton and wool cloth opened in İzmir just before World War I, thanks largely to the prospering rug industry (see chapter 5). The Ottoman Cloth Company, set up by the Oriental Carpet Manufacturers Ltd. in 1911, used wool remnants from carpet production to produce the finer *şayak* wool cloth as well as coarse military cloth. Utilizing English equipment, the mill employed 300 workers.[53] A sister enterprise (*Société anonyme Ottomane de manufacture de coton de Smyrne*) also opened in 1911 and employed 400 workers to weave cabot cloth.[54] At the same time, the former Cousinery spinning mill (see chapter 1) was expanded to include a cabot weaving operation.[55]

In the early 1860s, the city of Harput already possessed a factory with European spinning and weaving equipment. Probably set up by an Armenian emigrant who had returned home from Europe, the factory produced dyed cotton and silk cloths (as well as cotton thread). In *c.* 1900, a second factory opened in nearby Mezre, thanks to an Ottoman Armenian who had worked in American and English silk-reeling factories. Concerned about obtaining replacement parts in this central Anatolian town, the entrepreneur substituted steam with human power and most of the metal machinery pieces with wood parts. But, a few years later, this Mezre factory had mechanized in the more usual sense of the word and possessed a 40 ps petroleum engine and modern equipment to spin and weave cotton and silk cloths.[56]

In the Adana area, a number of the cotton spinning factories also had mechanized looms. The presence of the mills had given a sharp stimulus to hand weaving that, in 1902, consumed one-quarter of the yarn spun in the local mills.[57] In 1908, one spinning mill at Adana also contained a weaving department with 180 mechanized looms that employed 280 workers, earning 25,000 piasters per week. They made cabot cloth, up to 180 pieces daily, using *c.* 1,600 kg. of their own thread. By 1912, daily output had increased to 250 pieces of cabot and a second Adana mill had opened, with 50 looms daily producing 50–100 pieces.[58] A factory at Tarsus, that had planned to run 400 looms, daily made only 50 pieces of cabot in 1912. Other weaving activities in Adana included fifteen new hand looms for napkins and cloth, using local and Italian yarns. In addition to these operations, there were some 30 German knitting machines in Adana, Hacın and Osmaniye; these used mainly local yarn to make socks, up to 900 pairs daily.[59]

The fall of international markets

By the middle of the nineteenth century, almost all Ottoman producers of cotton, mohair and wool cloth had lost their western and central European markets. If anywhere, the truth of the "decline of manufacturing" argument lies here, in the disappearance of these foreign markets for Ottoman textiles.

In *c.* 1800, the textile manufacturers of Salonica presided over a vast international export industry. The famed Jewish wool cloth makers exported to Italy and France and also shipped a fine-grade wool cloth made from Morean wool. In villages around the city, workers annually wove some 80,000 pieces of wool cloth for export to Livorno, Genoa, Venice, Messina, Malta, Ancona, France and Holland as well as to İzmir. At one point, France annually bought up to 8,000 pieces for its black slaves in the Antilles. But English and continental wool weavers then undercut the Salonica industry and its markets in Western Europe vanished forever.

The mohair yarn and cloth industry of Ankara once had been among the most successful in Ottoman manufacturing. A unique product, Angora mohair textiles had enjoyed international markets that annually bought 20,000 pieces.[60] In *c.* 1800, this industry was giving steady employ to between 1,000 and 2,000 looms in and around the city. Some 10,000 persons worked, both the women who spun the yarn and the guildsmen who wove the cloth (*sof* and *şal*).[61] By the middle of the nineteenth century, this industry too had collapsed and virtually disappeared. A combination of factors was involved, ranging from European purchases of the raw materials to fashion shifts among Ottoman consumers. The decline seems to have become visible in the early 1820s, when English demand for the raw mohair wool increased sharply. By 1840, the international market for cloth was gone and only "a little yarn" was being exported to Europe.[62] Thereafter, just the raw wool was sent, to be spun and woven in Europe.[63] Yarn and cloth manufacturing in small quantities hung on in a few spots, such as in Ankara itself where women knitted gloves and socks. In the early twentieth century, the city still made mohair stockings for women and men, as well as jackets for women and children, for domestic customers.[64] The only other remaining center of any significance was the village of Stanos that, *c.* 1903, annually produced 1,500 pieces of mohair shawls and clerical apparel.[65]

Diyarbakır similarly had a rich tradition of providing major quantities of textiles for European markets. Chief among foreign exports back in the eighteenth century were the "chafarcanis," a well-made, double-bordered cotton cloth with red and violet background. Produced in imitation of an Indian textile, annual exports to Marseilles averaged around 30,000 pieces during the 1750s–80s.[66] Diyarbakır producers, in common with those elsewhere in the empire, suffered losses with the collapse of French trade at the end of the eighteenth century.[67] In 1805, in response to these deteriorating conditions, workers at Diyarbakır sought to control more closely Ottoman textile production. All of the weavers' guilds at Diyarbakır and a large number of other textile centers pledged to bring their goods to single centralized locations (*mengenehane*) in each place for finishing (*perdaht*). To enforce this pledge, they transferred all their finishing tools and implements to this single location.[68] But the measure failed to restore the lost foreign markets.

Aleppo also entered the nineteenth century with a long-standing but tarnished reputation as a commercial and industrial center. Harmed by the commercial rise of İstanbul and İzmir and the global shifts in trade away from the axis of India–Europe to that of the Atlantic, the city in 1800 was still a formidable industrial producer. A major pillar of its international fame had rested on indigo-dyed blue textiles, made from bleached cotton cloth woven in the city and surrounding villages. In earlier times and until the eighteenth century, indigo-dyed cotton cloths formed nearly all of its cloth exports to France. More generally, Aleppo dyed large quantities of the raw and bleached cloths made in northern Syria and southeast Anatolia and then exported them abroad. But with the development of New World indigo sources, the rising importance of the Atlantic trade and increasing European demand for bleached cloth, eighteenth-century French merchants at Aleppo shifted over to buying only bleached or raw cloth. Indigo dyeing in the city for the export trade thus declined in importance.[69]

Ottoman manufacturers also lost markets when border changes transformed fellow Ottoman subjects into inaccessible foreign consumers. Cloth makers in northern Anatolia – the Black Sea hinterland – were particularly hurt by Ottoman military defeats and territorial withdrawals, that may have caused as much or more harm as the competition from European producers. Many of these manufacturing centers had depended heavily on their shipments of cotton and wool yarn and cloth to the Crimea and Georgia (Taganrog and Abaza). In the early nineteenth century, Trabzon, the main outlet for these producers, maintained a substantial trade with the Crimea and with Abaza, carrying salt, sulphur, lead, "and considerable quantities of the manufactures of Turkey." But, in 1832, the Russian government blockaded Abaza, placed extremely high duties on all non-Russian goods seeking entry into Georgia and halted the flow of Ottoman and other foreign products. By 1836, Trabzon exports to the Crimea and to Abaza had been "annihilated."[70]

These injuries to local manufacturers were compounded by the defensive actions of Ottoman merchants who frantically sought new commercial ventures to make up for the lost business. In compensation, they turned to importing British goods from İstanbul, hastening the confrontation between European and Ottoman manufacturers. "Before 1830 there was scarcely to be found in the Bazars a piece of European manufacture."[71] In 1836, however, beleaguered Ottoman merchants at Trabzon had opened a "hundred" shops filled with Western manufactures.[72]

Although many markets thus were lost either because of foreign competition or Ottoman territorial shrinkage, there were a few gains in sales for the international market (also see chapters 4 and 5). Lacemaking became a comparatively large export industry. Based in İstanbul homes, in missionary-run workshops and in putting out networks organized by European merchants, lacemakers produced important quantities for west European consumers (see chapter 2). In *c.* 1900, Bursa cloth – often a combination of silk and cotton – again was selling abroad because of "a good reputation ... even beyond the boundaries of the Empire."[73]

Russia reemerged as an important customer for some Ottoman textile producers of the Black Sea hinterland who had been harmed by earlier Czarist interdictions. In the late 1860s, notably, Tokat again was exporting its wares to Russia.[74] Further away, Malatya shipped important quantities of both cotton and silk textiles to Russia after the border changes of the 1830s while Arapkir, in the 1860s, exported to it "large quantities" of cotton cloths.[75]

Persia remained an important consumer of Ottoman textiles although it rarely was discussed specifically. In the early twentieth century, Mosul textiles were flowing there in large quantities. Throughout the nineteenth century, the city of Erzurum, a great transit point in the trade with Persia, constantly was mentioned as the destination for impressive quantities of textiles from a host of different production centers. On arrival in Erzurum, some of these goods without question were transshipped to Persia.

Domestic markets

General

Ottoman textile manufacturers sold their goods to the peasantry, townspeople and tribal population, a vast and expanding internal market that sustained them throughout the period. Most Ottoman textiles were made for subsistence needs or for consumers in the immediate or adjacent neighborhoods. Many textile producers served a peasant society and depended heavily on successful crops and good prices. Prosperous peasants bought yarn and cloth in good years and withdrew their purchases in less successful times. The peasant market provided the economic underpinnings for the Ottoman towns and cities that manufactured or marketed textiles. The populations of the port cities, for their part, were among the heaviest *per capita* consumers of foreign textiles and other goods.

Tribes played an important role in the vitality of many textile production centers, providing materials as well as markets for their finished goods. They furnished the raw cotton or wool and, sometimes, spun yarn for sale as well. Without such supplies, whole industries would have foundered. Tribes' clothing demands, for generic materials as well as for very specific patterns, fueled the textile industry of many areas. It seems certain that some of the commerce passing through Erzurum, for example, ended in the hands of the Kurdish, and perhaps the Arab, tribes of the Ottoman east and southeast. The merchants and townspeople of Gürün depended heavily on the surrounding tribes for supplies and for markets. Elsewhere, at Mosul, Aleppo and Aintab, neighboring tribes continued to form a major market for manufacturers.

Production for long-distance and interregional trade

In a few locations, producers wove and printed for buyers in distant, widely scattered, areas of the empire and, sometimes, for those beyond the imperial frontiers. These included the Balkan wool and cloth weavers, and the textile makers at Aleppo, İstanbul, Diyarbakır and Rize. The weavers of both the coarse and finer wool cloths in the Ottoman Balkans typically worked for the medium to long-distance trade, for customers in Anatolia as well as Syria, in addition to buyers in the independent states of Serbia and Bulgaria. Rize similarly sold its linen over a vast area; its customers included the residents of Anatolia, Syria, Egypt, the Yemen and the Hejaz, as well as Basra, Baghdad and Persia.[76] Aleppo sold its textiles in a very broad market that fluctuated in scope (see chapter 2) but usually included most of Anatolia, as well as Iraq, the Arabian peninsula and Egypt. In the early 1870s, for example, three-quarters of its cotton cloth production went to buyers in Anatolia and Egypt. More generally, Syrian manufacturers at Damascus, Homs and Hama as well as Aleppo routinely shipped the majority of their various cloths to Anatolia and Egypt, in about equal shares. Similarly, in the 1880s, all but one-fourth of Beirut's textile output went to the Ottoman capital, western Anatolia and Egypt.[77] İstanbul producers of various textiles (and umbrellas) typically shipped their wares to Egypt, to Aden, Beirut and Cairo. Diyarbakır sent most of its production out of the immediate area, to buyers in Anatolia, Syria and Iraq. İzmir cloth printers sold their thin cotton textiles very widely throughout the empire. The towels and bath house materials of Bursa, for their part, enjoyed similarly wide, if fluctuating, sales throughout the period. Tokat merchants sent some of their printed cloth to the Mediterranean, presumably for shipment to the Arab provinces. The city of Sivas sent its wool stockings (but little else) far and wide, all the way to İstanbul. Preferring them for their color and warmth "from olden times," the Armenian porters of the capital would wear no other.[78] In contrast to such well-established networks, Gürün textile makers were aggressively expanding their markets at the end of the period and, in 1910, were selling in Egypt for the first time.

Struggles for the internal market against foreign competitors

Introduction
As the examples of Ambelakia red yarn, Salonica wool cloth and Ankara mohair cloth and yarn make clear, Ottoman textile manufacturers frequently failed in their struggles for the international market (but see chapters 4 and 5). It is a similarly familiar story that many lost their domestic market to these foreign manufacturers. Thus, for example, the sail cloth industry on the Gallipoli peninsula was in difficulty during the 1860s because of competition from European factories and probably collapsed shortly thereafter. The decline occurred despite government exemptions from customs' duties that regularly had been granted and continued to be offered into the 1890s.[79] Similarly, consider the decline of the cotton cloth weavers who had been famed for their towels and apparel for the public bath, an early nineteenth-century speciality of Karaferia and Salonica weavers. In 1805, guild members in the two cities manufactured more than 25 different kinds of these towels and robes.[80] During the late 1840s, local producers were using British yarn to make bath cloths that were still "much esteemed all over Turkey."[81] But, by the end of the century, European competition sharply had reduced production at Salonica and had annihilated the industry at Karaferia where, in one quarter of the town, only 50 looms remained.[82]

Also, for example, take the weavers in the village of Darağaç in İzmir province who held out until the 1890s. These workers specialized in making a cotton trouser cloth (*pantalonluk*), that women in the interior also wore. Annual production averaged 300,000 piasters in *c.* 1890 but then was encountering grave competition from Italy and Germany in the better qualities.[83] Other incidents of this sort could be recounted here, but the point seems clear enough.

This, decline, part of the tale certainly is important. But, as stated before, there is more to the story, namely, the continuing competition for the nineteenth-century domestic Ottoman market. First, there are the means that Ottoman producers employed to successfully compete with imported textiles. And, second, we must consider the rivalries among Ottoman manufacturers for control of the domestic market.

Successes against foreign competitors

Inexpensive yarn, as seen, played a vital role in the ability of Ottoman weavers to compete and, at the end of the century, many were using machine-made yarn from Ottoman factories. The city of Edirne and its surrounding districts, for example, remained a center of cloth weaving to meet the textile needs of local residents and surrounding villagers. These urban workshop and home weavers used thread made in the Salonica spinning mills, that cost one-third less than the same size thread manufactured in England. They wove a thin fabric, dyed green (*etamin*) that Muslim peasant women used for their outer garments (*ferace*) and they also wove important quantities of a coarse dark cloth specific to the Edirne region. In addition, they made men's trousers and children's clothing, as well as coarse bed coverings, towels, napkins and upholstery covers.

At the end of the century, Kadıköy villagers in İzmir province wove a strong cloth and, thanks to very low wages and a good water supply, undersold their European competitors.[84] In the town of Manisa, similarly, urban workshop weavers wove a very high quality cloth that overcame foreign competition, despite its low price.[85]

One of the great success stories in reversing the initially successful inroads of foreign manufacturers is that of the very thin cotton cloth (known in its various forms as *yemeni*, *kalemkâr*, *çember* and *yazma*), used as head coverings. The weaving and decorating of these coverings had been an important activity in a number of locations, including İzmir and İstanbul. In the 1850s, the industry was in severe difficulties everywhere in the Ottoman lands. At the port city of İzmir, for example, scarcely 10 percent of these factories were still operating.[86] At İstanbul, similarly, the guilds involved in this industry had fallen into disarray by *c.* 1850 (see chapter 2). By the early 1870s, however, the manufacturers at İzmir and İstanbul had turned the situation around and were competing successfully with Swiss and British producers. In İzmir (and in Menemen), producers imported plain cotton cloth from Manchester and, in small dyehouses, dyed and printed it locally to yield a carefully made product that was cheaper than either the British or Swiss equivalent. At İstanbul, the guilds had fallen away, replaced by a number of non-guild printing factories (see chapter 2).

In addition, Armenian merchants at İstanbul organized a putting out network among Turkish women who lived in villages along the Bosphorus. These workers received the imported *kalemkâr* cloth from Manchester and decorated it in their homes.[87] At Trabzon, *c.* 1900, all of the three or four large dyeing establishments and numerous smaller ones worked in dyeing and printing women's head gear, locally called *çember* and *yazma*.

As a result of such adaptive responses by local manufacturers, Ottoman imports of the Swiss printed *yazma* textiles fell sharply, from previous annual levels of 1.5 million to 200,000 piasters in *c.* 1873. Instead, İstanbul shipped some two million piasters' worth of the material to Aden while İzmir manufacturers sold a similar amount in other locations.[88] By 1900, the dyehouses at İzmir produced between 1.5 and 3.0 million pieces of headgear of various sorts.[89] At Trabzon, at about this time, annual local output of the two kinds of head gear totalled about 1.5 million pieces. The large establishments there cut, dyed and printed about 750,000 *çembers* while the small shops dyed and printed about the same number of *yazma* cloths.

Unlike the situation a half century before, when finished and printed cloth arrived from abroad, Ottoman artisans now provided the labor for the dyeing and printing. The value added by such labor annually equalled at least *c.* 15 million piasters, if we include the head gear being made at İstanbul, İzmir and Trabzon.[90]

Another success story is that of weavers in some north Anatolian towns (once a part of the network that Kayseri merchants had organized) who made a comeback during the 1870s. At this time, when British manufacturers sought to maintain sales by producing for the very bottom of the market, we read that they were underbid by weavers from Merzifon, Amasya and "Uzzak" (?), who enjoyed a gradual revival in cotton textile production. During the 1870s, these three towns used 5,000–6,000 bales of British yarn and wove cloth that won preference over "the very inferior qualities of British cotton goods" then flooding the market.[91] Similarly, Aleppo cottons during the early 1870s were driving foreign competitors from the marketplaces of many areas. For example, buyers "eagerly attended" the Yapraklı fair in 1871 to buy these textiles.[92] Two decades later, Amasya weavers along with those from Beirut and İzmir were increasing their sales in the city of Trabzon, undercutting their British competitors at this seaport community.[93] At the turn of the century, cotton textile production from Amasya and Zile was increasing (but that of Merzifon fell, since it was judged not solid enough).[94]

In the Diyarbakır region, artisans responded to foreign (and domestic) competitors by accepting declining wages and gave momentum to the "revival" that was underway in late 1872.[95] At the wool weaving center of Gürün, weavers imitated competitors, specializing in light weaves that were used for summer clothing. They made shawls that imitated Iranian and Indian patterns while the other wool textiles often were copies of European patterns, aimed at the men's clothing market.[96]

Arapkir – a mid-size town northwest of Harput with houses nestled in mountainous terrain, surrounded by vineyards and fruit orchards – was the site of a fascinating story of rising textile imports and industrial growth. Until *c.* 1830, there had been a few looms, using locally made yarn, weaving only to meet subsistence needs. But then the townspeople adopted British yarn and began to weave commercially. Here might be the hand of Trabzon merchants seeking new markets to replace those being lost on the other side of the Black Sea. That is, cut off from Abaza and Tagonrog, the merchants found new buyers, this time of British yarn. This new cotton weaving industry at Arapkir was not an ephemeral burst of activity, but rather an industry that maintained itself throughout the century. Because the Arapkir cloth was cheaper and more durable, British cloth (nankeens) quickly disappeared from the market. The number of looms at Arapkir expanded and, within a half-decade, annually required some 95,000 kg. of imported yarn. In 1836, "some 1,000 looms" in Arapkir busily were weaving cotton goods from British yarn.[97] For several decades after, production was at least stable and the industry was shipping "large quantities" of nankeens and other cotton cloths, mainly to Russia and to Erzurum.[98] Arapkir in the 1880s held 4,800 Muslim and 1,200 Armenian homes, with a total population of about 29,000 persons, who "chiefly" wove coarse cotton cloth on 1,000 looms.[99] In 1885, output reached 120,000 pieces, valued at 1.2 million piasters, double the level of the preceding year.[100] Durability and color fastness of the locally made *manusa* textile retained the competitive position despite the very low price of Manchester prints, then selling for as little as 26 *para*s per *arşın* of 26 inches.[101] The industry at Arapkir continued to prosper and, by 1907, the number of looms had risen to 1,200.

In addition to the Arapkir weavers, there were other new industries that emerged in the intensely competitive struggle for the Ottoman domestic market. At Mardin, for example, 600 looms became active in the early 1890s, weaving cotton cloth although "nothing of the sort" had existed there previously.[102]

Domestic competition for domestic markets

Introduction
Success against foreign competitors, however, was no assurance that a textile producer would survive. For example, consider the makers of women's headgear at İstanbul, İzmir and Trabzon, who used imported cloth (and dyes sometimes) in combination with local labor, and drove out foreign producers of the thin printed cloth. In Trabzon, as we will see shortly, manufacturers who overcame the obstacle of foreign competitors succumbed later on to domestic rivals and quit the business. Often these domestic rivalries led to a division of labor. In

essence, the competing groups segmented the market and specialized. Thus, Aintab and Aleppo weavers fought head to head for a time until the latter withdrew from the production of one particular textile, leaving that activity to the Aintab producers (see below). Similarly, Trabzon linen weavers specialized in making the coarser grades of linen for shipment out of the region.[103] At Rize, typically, weavers manufactured the higher quality grades, of such quality that they won first prize in the Paris World Exhibition of 1855. The cloth, made on foot looms, came in numerous qualities and was sold in bundles of five pieces each.[104] There were some 40 different kinds and the best quality, called *altınbaş*, sold for 17 times the unit price of the cheapest grades made in the town.[105]

The Trabzon market

The story of the Trabzon textile makers provides a window through which to view the struggle for the internal Ottoman textile market in unusually close detail, surely relevant to the general story of Ottoman manufacturing. The close-up view is fascinating because it reveals manufacturers who adapted by shifting from one to another activity. Trabzon's tale also shows that the greatest enemy of local artisans sometimes was not Manchester but other Ottoman manufacturers. In fact, Manchester and Elberfeld often appear as allies of Trabzon weavers in the fascinating interplay of competition among local, foreign and other Ottoman textile producers.

Trabzon's printers of women's head gear (*yazma* and *çember*) competed with one another in the local marketplace that they had divided between them, using radically different production techniques for each of the two types of cloth. The Persians (*çemberci*) operated large dyehouses and were considered the more accomplished. Nonetheless, between 1892 and 1902, their workshops had declined to three in number because of competition from Ottoman producers outside the city. The dyer/printers in Trabzon and its hinterland competed at a disadvantage with producers at Tokat and İstanbul. Trabzon dyeing was considered inferior in part due to poor quality water and because the locally humid weather retarded proper drying of the printed cloth. The Tokat dyers were the strongest factor in the Trabzon market area and annually sold about 1.5 million piasters of *çember* head gear, perhaps seven times the value of the locally made product. The colors and patterns from Tokat, that seem to have served the lower end of the market, were considered superior to the Trabzon manufacture although they also were cheaper. Better quality head dress goods, both dyed and printed, also came from İstanbul, in quantities rivalling the total output of all Trabzon producers. The few workshops at Trabzon survived by undercutting the Tokat producers in making the very cheapest qualities.[106]

A new manufacturing activity emerged at Trabzon when the widespread Anatolian famine of 1873–74 reduced incomes. To capture this impoverished market, local weavers began using British yarn to make *manusa* textiles instead of importing them from Aleppo.[107]

In the 1880s and 1890s, Trabzon weavers and printers waged a sharp battle for local markets with foreign and rival Ottoman weavers. In the end, they won against their foreign competitors but were vanquished by their fellow subjects. In 1886, Trabzon linen weavers suffered as their customers bought "the cheaper and inferior stuffs of Europe."[108] Local production of the *manusa* and *peştemal* fabrics, as well as of mixed linen-cotton goods, also declined. During 1887 and 1888, cheaper cloth from Western Europe and from Russia replaced both locally made cloth and that from Aleppo, Merzifon and other Anatolian production centers.[109] But weavers at Trabzon accepted lower wages and, in 1889, increased their production of cheap cloth, made with imported yarn.[110] When Trabzon residents purchased cheap red cloths and prints from France and Germany in 1891, they threatened manufacturers in Aleppo, İzmir and Sivas, but the situation again quickly reversed itself.[111] For, in both 1892 and 1895, rising sales of cheaper *manusa* textiles from Beirut, Amasya and İzmir diminished European imports.[112] The weaving of *manusa* cloth at Trabzon was said to be in considerable decline at the end of the nineteenth century, despite their ability, when the local harvest was good, to drive English *dokuma* cloth and Swiss *alaca* cloth completely from the market. But they could not meet the competition from other Ottoman producers. This failure to compete with producers at Eğin, Merzifon and Aleppo – where textile makers had adopted European machinery that gave a higher luster – perhaps lay behind the emigration of Armenian weavers to Russia in the 1890s. And so, more and more of the Trabzon-made *manusa* cloth was used for lining and underclothing or not sold at all. Total production dropped nearly 50 percent between 1895 and 1902, at a time when textile production in many Ottoman regions was rising sharply.[113] After these reversals, *manusa* weaving recovered somewhat during the Young Turk period. *Manusa* output at Trabzon in 1910 had risen to 60,000 pieces, a six-fold increase over the nadir levels of 1902 and triple the output levels of the mid-1890s.[114]

Trabzon weavers of the *peştemal* fabric competed in the early twentieth century by mixing imported, usually British and Italian, with Ottoman yarns.[115] Household weavers fared much better than those in workshops. The former made and sold the *peştemal* fabric to merchants and overall, in 1902, were said to be holding their own against foreign competition. These weavers abandoned the locally dyed red yarn because it was too dark for changing local tastes and instead had come to rely on imported red yarn for the favored light and bright background.[116] But other Ottoman producers, as well as foreign competitors, were making cheaper *peştemal* fabrics and continued to drive the Trabzon makers from the field. Some 300 looms had been active in 1906 but, by 1912, only 75 *peştemal* looms mainly in private homes, remained operating.[117]

Aleppo and its north Syrian rivals

Throughout the century, Aleppo competed with Damascus for the first rank among textile makers in the eastern Ottoman lands. In certain years, output levels in the two cities were nearly identical while, on other occasions, one surpassed the other by several orders of magnitude.[118] Variously, the producers in one city rose to the top as their rivals endured some political or natural misfortune, only later to be struck down themselves. In north Syria, Aleppo was the first among a number of rival textile centers; others included Aintab, Maraş, Urfa and, to a lesser extent, Kilis. Competition among them dated back to the early eighteenth century and well before. Over the period, one or another of the centers had risen to pre-eminence, only to lose out to an emergent rival, a pattern of fluctuating fortunes that continued into the twentieth century.

Cotton cloth weaving for export at Kilis had been significant at several points in the eighteenth century. But, subsequently, its cloth production, whether for foreign or domestic sale, fell to unimportant levels. During the late nineteenth century, when north Syrian cloth-making boomed, this town's output becomes only faintly visible in the sources (see table 2.8). The town of Urfa, on the other hand, had been far less important than Kilis in the eighteenth-century export trade. But, the fortunes of Kilis faded and those of Urfa comparatively prospered until the early 1890s, when there were some 2,000 active looms. Urfa textile output then suffered, however (see table 2.8), probably because many of its Armenian weavers emigrated.[119]

At Maraş, during the later 1850s, weavers concentrated exclusively on a coarse-striped cloth of cotton or wool. About 1,000 predominantly Muslim "workmen" wove on 300 looms, making a cheap and durable product that made the city "a provincial celebrity." They recently had adopted Manchester yarn, almost totally abandoning the hand-made twist and causing local cultivators to give up cotton growing.[120] During the early twentieth century, Maraş weavers annually used 292,000 kg. of imported white and red thread and 46,000 kg. of the locally spun product. The number of active looms had risen very impressively, five to seven times since the 1850s, and exceeded 2,000 in 1907.[121]

Although the international export trade of Aintab had fallen away at the end of the eighteenth century, the city's textile industry remained prominent, now focused on the Ottoman market. In the later 1850s, a great number of Aintab inhabitants worked in weaving, dyeing as well as leather tanning.

The native hand looms supply the middle and the lower class of the population, with the striped woollen garments universally worn in the East; whilst the richer inhabitants have contracted a taste for the finer textures of Europe.[122]

In addition, local weavers used *c.* 500 bales of British yarn in cotton weaving, perhaps the *adjami* or *toiles larges* cloths.[123] By then, local Christians had taken over the import trade from British merchants and had cut out the Aleppo middlemen; they lowered the price of imports on the local market and enabled manufacturers to ship directly to the coast. The cheapness of imports must have harmed local textile producers but manufacturing in the town was said to be prospering in the late 1870s. Its looms reportedly were fully occupied in making cotton and woolen textiles and its streets "thronged" with laden camels and mules.[124] At the end of the century, consumers in many regions purchased Aintab cloth. It was important at Van, driving out locally made cloth; sales were increasing at Bitlis[125] and, similarly, Konya residents bought important quantities of Aintab *alaca* cloth.[126] Generally, by 1900, Aintab "ordinary" *alaca* cloth (presumably all cotton) had replaced that of Aleppo provenance in Ottoman markets. And finally, for what it is worth, the figures in table 2.8 indicate a doubling in the number of looms active in Aintab between 1893 and 1904. Altogether, the various statements and bits of data collectively affirm that real growth had taken place in textile production at Aintab around the turn of the century, mainly producing inexpensive red cotton cloth.

Until *c.* 1875, Aleppo had dominated regional textile production, accounting for two-thirds to three-quarters of aggregate output in north Syria. At the turn of the century, its own cloth output likely was rising. At the same time, textile production in many other locations increased sharply – at Aintab, Maraş, Urfa, and Diyarbakır (as well as Amasya, Gürün and many other locations) – and stripped markets from Aleppo, creating a new division of labor among Ottoman textile producers. Some former markets for Aleppo cotton cloth became self-sufficient, for example, Urfa and Maraş. Other producers, such as those at Aintab, Diyarbakır and Mardin, began competing in markets that Aleppo once had dominated, thanks to the lower wages that they were willing to accept.[127] Aleppo manufacturers surrendered supremacy, it seems, in two kinds of textiles. Its red cotton cloth industry was surpassed by Aintab makers while its colored printed cloth fell behind production at Mardin, Diyarbakır and Urfa.[128]

Struggling with domestic and foreign competitors, these manufacturers adopted a number of different stratagems. Earlier in the century, many had abandoned homespun in favor of British yarn. In the early twentieth century, they would seek out still-cheaper yarn – Indian Grey Twist and mercerized Italian yarn – as replacements for the British product.[129]

A particularly sharp rivalry developed between Aintab and Aleppo producers and, in the end, Aleppo lost markets. The successful wage strikes of 1903 and 1904 perhaps help explain these defeats.[130] If they were confined to Aleppo, relative labor costs there would have risen, rendering producers more vulnerable to competition from Aintab and other weavers. But the differential in wages at Aleppo and its rivals already had existed for some three decades before these strikes.[131] The new dyeing technologies played a vital role both in the development of the struggle and its outcome. When, during the 1880s, Aintab began to cut deeply into Aleppo markets by producing a red cloth from imported yarn,

Aleppo producers countered by importing synthetic dyes, both high quality alizarin and the cheaper but photo-sensitive aniline dyes, and white yarn as well. Since European labor costs were higher, dyeing the yarn locally dropped the final yarn cost a full 10 percent as compared to red yarn imported from Germany or Switzerland.[132] In the early 1890s, the import of undyed yarn

largely increased, to the detriment of red yarns, native manufacturers finding it to their advantage to dye imported white yarns by the aniline dyes brought from Europe, and are thus by degrees dispensing altogether with European red yarns.[133]

But the gamble failed as even the alizarin red faded, creating disgruntled customers. Blame was placed on the travelling salesman who allegedly had not offered proper instruction in handling the dyes. And so, after 1899, the Aleppo weavers abandoned the experiment and resumed their imports of red yarn.[134] In just a few years, Aleppo was importing 1,500 bales of red yarn, mainly from Switzerland and Germany.[135] Except for indigo blue, as seen, local dyeing became unimportant.[136]

But while producers in Aleppo abandoned local red dyeing in favor of importing red yarn, those in Aintab adopted precisely the opposite tactic. In the summer of 1904, Aintab dyers and weavers, who had been boycotting European-dyed yarn, finally reached an agreement with the municipal administration. Thereafter, they would use only yarn dyed in the city, thus halving the final costs.[137] The cloth produced was not as color fast as the European, but it was cheaper and satisfied its peasant buyers.[138] At about this time, Aintab dyers adopted parinitralin, a new dyestuff. While not quite as color fast as alizarin, it was comparable to the fastness of Indian yarns. Aintab dyers preferred the new dye because it was considerably cheaper, helping them to underbid Aleppo (and other) competitors.[139] Thus, Aintab cornered part of the lower end of the market formerly held by Aleppo, specializing in red dyeing and red cloth production, while Aleppo continued its tradition of excellence in indigo dyeing, now using synthetic as well as natural indigo. The quality of dyeing in both cities was considered to be very good, even by European observers.[140]

Plate 1. Women sorting large piles of silk cocoons, Antioch, Syria.

Plate 2. "Making costly Persian rugs by hand in a Persian carpet factory," Anatolia.

Plate 3. Bursa silk mill interior, 1980s. The equipment is probably early twentieth century.

Plate 4. Silkworkers, *c.* 1892. *Servet-i-fünun* no. 101, 4 Şubat 1308.

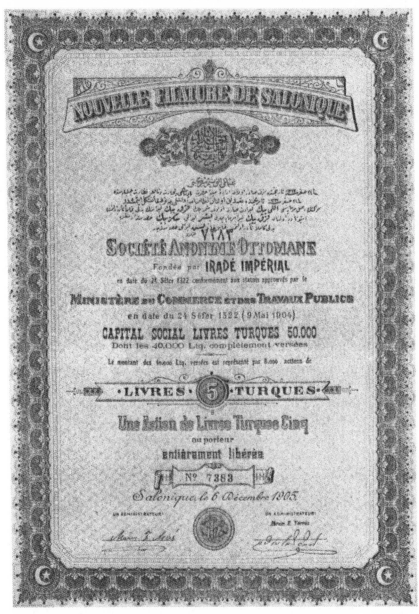

Plate 5. Bond certificate, for Salonica spinning mill, 1905.

PART II Manufacturing for the international market

4 Silk cloth and raw silk production

Introduction

Ottoman silk production has received comparatively great attention from scholars during the past several decades.[1] In part, the attention derives from the romance of this fabled textile whose Middle East origins lay in the medieval smuggling of silkworm eggs from the Orient. In equal measure, however, the emphasis derives from relatively rich documentation that reflects, in turn, the industry's importance as a provider of tax revenues and then as a furnisher of raw materials needed by Europe. In early modern times, the Ottoman state lavished its attention on an industry that provided easily collected taxes as well as rich cloths and textiles for the sultans and their courts and gifts for foreign royalty and visitors. To these continuing state concerns we can add, in the nineteenth century, the records of the resident and touring Westerners who devoted whole reports, chapters and even books to a changing industry that was restructured to provide European factories with needed materials for weaving. Was their attention and this separate chapter on silk justified? Other industries not discussed in this book, such as food processing, clearly were more important and employed more workers than raw silk and silk cloth production. But, silk production was a significant economic activity. At the end of the nineteenth century the industry in all its forms and in the various locations employed large numbers of people. In the Bursa area, *c.* 1900, some 150,000 persons worked full- and part-time while approximately the same number labored in the Lebanon region. To these workers we must add the silk weavers of Aleppo and Diyarbakır as well as the spinners of Edirne, Salonica and other areas. Altogether, certainly, more than 400,000 Ottoman subjects worked in the industry. The significance of the silk industry example, however, is not just in the number of workers. The manner in which the industry evolved in the nineteenth century reveals a great deal about the vitality of Ottoman manufacturing and about the interaction of the Western and Middle Eastern economies. The resiliency of the weavers and the expansion of nineteenth-century Ottoman silk cloth production (described in the sections on Aleppo and Diyarbakır in chapter 2) illustrate the falsity of assumptions concerning the moribund state of Ottoman manufacturing.

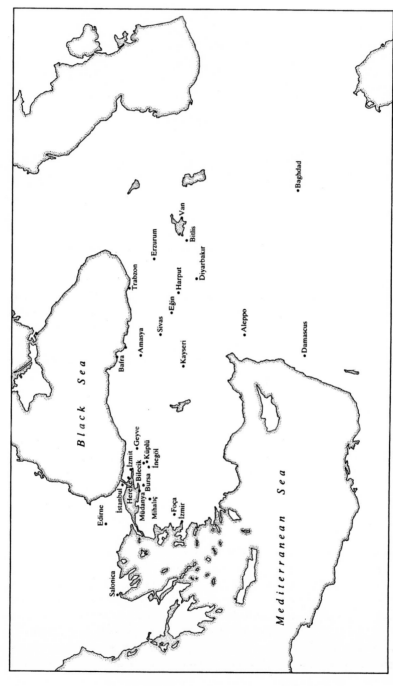

Map 4. Silk cloth and raw silk production, c. 1800–1914.

The story of raw silk reeling, for its part, exemplifies the conditions under which Ottoman manufacturers competed in the international export markets.

The silk cloth industry

Patterns and trends in production

A sharp and multi-faceted struggle raged within an Ottoman silk industry that was expanding during the early decades of the nineteenth century, as guild monopolies generally were being eroded. In part, the struggle was a domestic one among weavers in the various production centers – Bursa, İstanbul, Damascus, Aleppo, Diyarbakır, İzmir, Edirne and Salonica – to dominate the industry in a period of rising cloth production. In 1797, some members of an İstanbul silkweaving guild (*kemhacı esnafı*) had sought to increase the number of shops.[2] A similar case appeared a decade later, involving another guild (*sandalcı ve bezzaz esnafı*). The guild masters worried about the rising wages of the workers and journeymen (*amele, kalfa*) and their impact on silk cloth prices. These masters, with shops in three different areas of the capital (Stambul, Eyüp and Üsküdar), had increased the number of workshops from 1,350 to 1,500 and proposed to train more journeymen and apprentices. But they wanted to prevent any more shops from opening, beyond these 1,500 and another 1,023 (already working under the auspices of the *vakf-ı hümayun*). Their actions, and complaints about others who wanted to open additional workshops, made clear that silk cloth production was expanding at the time.

The state incidentally, refused to impose limits on the number of those who would weave silk and allowed the industry to expand at will.[3] In 1802, similarly, the state had abolished the monopoly of the silk spinners at İzmir and permitted anyone there to perform the work.[4] Thus, at the turn of the century, the state was not limiting the number of persons in the silk weaving industry.[5]

The early nineteenth-century growth in Ottoman silk weaving derived from a combination of factors. First, the Napoleonic wars gave Ottoman producers a respite from foreigners who had been buying up cocoons and raw silk and from the competition of European manufacturers. Second, new clothing fashions had emerged and were adopted by Ottoman weavers at the end of the eighteenth century. For a full century, Ottoman consumers had preferred the light and fantasy weaves of European silk cloth to the heavier and more expensive Ottoman patterns (also, see below). In response, Ottoman weavers began to imitate these fashions and, by 1800, the industry had revived and again could compete, if only for the local market.[6] And third, there was a technological breakthrough in silk cloth finishing that took place just a little later, around the turn of the century. The technological innovation involved replacing the so-called fire-finishing process with stone-finishing. The stone-finishing process produced silk cloth with a higher gloss, that was better, more brilliant and much cheaper than cloth finished using fire. The innovation first was employed in the Ottoman Empire at İstanbul, at the pious foundations around Mahmud Pasha, where a silkmakers' guild (*sandalcı esnafı*) had enjoyed a monopoly for some years. Elsewhere in the capital, and at the weaving centers of Damascus, Aleppo, Diyarbakır, İzmir, Edirne, Bursa and Salonica, the less-desirable fire method persisted. Under pressure, the state then allowed stone-finishing at Bursa and Diyarbakır, permission it quickly revoked when the İstanbul industry applied counter-pressure. A Bursa group, led by one Seyyid Halil and his partners, pleaded for reinstatement of the stone-finishing method. Since the Bursa cloth guild (*akmişe esnafı*) was only a production guild (and not also a retailers'), they said, its very existence was threatened by continued use of the uncompetitive fire method. So the state broke the İstanbul guild's monopoly and permitted silk-makers elsewhere to use stone finishing. At Bursa, the cloth makers' guild seized on the opportunity and financed the construction of seven new stone-finishing installations in the local district (*kaza*), with monopoly rights in the region. This profoundly changed the relationship between silkmakers in Bursa and İstanbul. The Bursa guild previously had sent its (Duke Zashurus/Jashuru?) fabric to the İstanbul group for finishing but ceased to do so with the opening of the stone-finishing installations at Bursa. There, the Bursa cloth makers were able to produce a better cloth and undersell their İstanbul competitors who had been accustomed to selling at monopoly prices. Bursa makers, for example, offered vermilion cloth for 10 percent less than the İstanbul cloth.[7]

During the 1810s and 1820s, thanks to the three factors mentioned above and to the lingering effects of the Napoleonic wars and Continental Blockade that reduced imports, Bursa silk and mixed-silk cloth production probably reached record levels for the period *c.* 1750–1850, perhaps as much as 100,000 pieces of all types. The absence of good data makes it difficult to measure changes in silk cloth production during the first half of the nineteenth century. From the mid-eighteenth century until *c.* 1808, indirect measurements suggest that Bursa silk cloth production had remained relatively steady. But then, between 1811 and 1833, with the new technology and construction of the finishing facilities, the taxable value of Bursa silk cloth output rose about 25 percent. In 1840 (with the arrival of the British consul Sandison), a consistent data series began that continued into the early 1860s. These reports show that between 1840 and 1857, Bursa annually produced 12,000–20,000 pieces of silk-cotton cloth for dresses (*hakir, kutni, kaftan*), plus other products such as silk handkerchiefs (see table 4.1).

Thus, it appears that Bursa silk cloth production levels rose sharply in the 1810s and 1820s and then fell back down during the 1830s and 1840s, to levels approximately equal to those prevailing during the late eighteenth century.[8] As a result of the post-1820s slump, some Bursa facilities in cloth making were

Table 4.1. *Bursa-area silk cloth production, 1840–1912*

date	pieces	item	number of looms
1840	18,000	*hakir, kutni*	130 silk and cotton
			200 "
1840	10,000	silk-cotton for dresses	city only
1841	9,000	*hakir, kutni, kaftan*	
1844	20,000	@ 5.5 yards "Brussa stuffs"	
1845	15,000	"Brussa stuffs"	400 all kinds
1846	13,000	"	
1847	14,000	"	400
1851	15,000	"	
1852	12,000	"	
1853	10,000	"Brussa stuff for dresses"	
1854	14,500	"	
1857	20,000	"	
	100	*peştemal*	
	800	silk hankies	
	2,000	silk gauze, fancy	
	300	silk gauze, plain	
1860	2,400	@ 7 yards "Brussa stuffs"	42 silk and cotton
	(plus 20,000	cotton bath wrappers)	100 cotton
1862	1,300	silk and silk and cotton dresses	26 silk and cotton
	2,000	silk hankies	60 cotton
1863	3,000	silk and cotton (*kutni*)	
	400	gauze for dresses	
	5,000	silk hankies	
	(plus 30,000	towels of cotton)	
1896	40,000	silk and silk and cotton	500
1908			700–800
1912			700

Sources: 1896 – AE, CC Turquie, Brousse, 5/29/1897; 1847 looms – USNA Film T194, R. 2, 10/10/1847, Schwaabe; GB FO and A&P reports of British consul Sandison at Bursa. *Statesman's Yearbook*; k und k Brussa, 1912.

neglected; in 1845, for example, the cloth press (*akmişe-i mengene*) in the district (*kaza*) of Bursa reportedly lay in ruins. On the other hand, the successful demand of the silk makers' guilds (*sandalcı esnafı*) for its repair indicates some continued vitality in weaving at Bursa.[9]

If the Bursa weavers enjoyed successes against their domestic rivals, all Ottoman silk weavers were suffering from developments in Europe, trends underway since *c.* 1750 but interrupted by the Napoleonic wars. Ottoman weavers already had lost their export markets to European rivals and once-common Middle East silk textiles had vanished from Western markets. By 1800, these weavers were on the defensive in their own backyards, despite successes in imitating foreign styles.[10]

The weaving industry also suffered from supply problems. Silk cloth production depended on a steady supply of raw and semi-processed materials, cocoons and raw silk (the latter in the form of both *meşdûd* and *ipek*). Some Ottoman cloth production centers, notably Bursa, were self-sufficient, obtaining supplies locally. Others depended on a mix of local and distant sources; Aleppo, for example, obtained some raw silk from Bursa and Amasya, as well as from Diyarbakır. The capital city, for its part, depended completely on others, notably Bursa but also regions such as Amasya. These deliveries were in jeopardy in several different ways. When the set price (*narh*) was too low, as in 1810, the women and men spinners hid it from the authorities.[11] Or, weavers in areas that usually supplied raw materials to other centers simply hoarded supplies in times of scarcity. Foreign merchants also were anxious to buy up and redirect these supplies of *meşdûd* and raw silk abroad, for the booming silk cloth industries of the continent, particularly England, France and the Italian peninsula. European merchants in İstanbul, Bursa and Aleppo paid premium prices and drained away Bursa raw silk. They either purchased it after the harvest or gave substantial cash advances to silk raisers in return for later delivery.[12] Between 1802 and 1839, the sultan sought to protect the Ottoman silk cloth industry with repeated proclamations. Legislation dated 1810 and 1815 and of uncertain age, for example, required Bursa producers first of all to supply the capital with specified amounts of *meşdûd* raw silk at a fixed price.[13] The next priority was given to supplying Aleppo cloth weavers, who also received raw silk from Amasya. Other decrees prohibited foreigners from making cash advances and ordered that all silk be brought to the official scales at Bursa for weighing and sale. They stated that no Ottoman subject or foreigner be permitted to buy Bursa raw silk (*meşdûd* or *ipek*) until the needs of İstanbul and other specified Ottoman markets were satisfied.[14]

The acute nature of the supply crisis is underscored by a very unusual action of the silk cloth makers' guild (*sandalcılar*) in the Stambul and Üsküdar sections of İstanbul. To relieve the shortage caused by domestic competitors and foreign buyers, the guild in 1810 obtained legal permission to open 70 *meşdûd* spinning shops in the two sections of the city (a decision that the Bursa judge opposed). In exchange, the guild pledged to reduce the price of raw silk (*meşdûd*) and of the cloth being produced.[15] This step challenged the centuries-long relationship in which the silk industry of Bursa supplied that of İstanbul.

The mounting competitiveness of European silk cloth makers and their rising purchases of Ottoman raw silk (*ipek* and *meşdûd*) coincided with the global sea-change taking place in textile consumption and production. The rise of mechanized British cotton yarn production meant the replacement of silk by cotton cloth. Momentous consequences ensued in the Ottoman silk industry. Silk cloth had played a role in dressing customs and habits that is hard to imagine today, when silk is associated with high luxury. In the Ottoman world, most strata of society except the lowest commonly wore and used silk, for elegance but also as a part of everyday living. As one observer in the early 1830s put it, "there was no individual who did not wear some article of silk."[16] Sumptuary laws had dictated the clothing that the various ethnic, official and labor groups could wear and these regulations had given a central place to silk cloth in its various forms. During the later eighteenth and early nineteenth centuries, however, fashion changes from above began to push silk from its customary pride of place, out of the forefront in dressing styles. In Europe, just as the mechanized cotton spinning technology was coming into its own, Marie Antoinette and her court set a new trend by wearing cotton instead of silk dresses.[17] In the Ottoman world, official decrees of the early Tanzimat abolished the sumptuary laws and accelerated the shift to cotton cloth. During the 1830s, this change was underway but hardly completed.[18] Behind these fashion trends lay the greatest technological success of the early industrial revolution, the machine spinning of cotton yarn (see chapter 1).

Articles similar to silk fabrics but made of machine-spun cotton yarn presented Ottoman consumers with substitute textiles at sharply lower prices. In this early period, Ottoman weavers struggled to retain domestic sales while foreign producers fought with one another for the favor of Middle East consumers. The new fabrics poured in from several foreign locations. For several decades early in the century, weavers in German Saxony successfully competed with the British in the Ottoman marketplace. Saxon textile makers imported British yarn and wove imitations of Bursa and Syrian silk-cotton cloth for dresses. In 1840, they were enjoying enormous successes by producing a "sound and durable fabric" at low cost.[19] Within just a few years, Saxon cotton cloth imports were on the increase, replacing the "formerly ... very considerable" consumption of Bursa silk and silk-cotton textiles. But the Saxon weavers then abandoned the field, leaving the British alone to compete with Ottoman weavers. The initial inroads of "cheap and durable" Saxon substitutes were lost because their quality declined, making them uncompetitive with the products of Syria and Bursa. This Saxon competition is important from several different perspectives. First of all, it, it shows how the Saxon weavers (like the Ottoman) adopted British yarn to reduce production costs and compete in the Middle Eastern markets that were so important during this early phase of European industrial development. And, this Saxon production, aimed at the lower end of the market, shows the rising use of cheaper cotton and cotton-silk cloth by Ottoman consumers.

Thus, the period from the end of the Napoleonic Wars until *c.* 1840 was a critical juncture, one of changing fashions and mounting imports of British machine-made cotton yarn. The Bursa region quickly became "one of the principal marts in Turkey" for British yarn, at prices that dropped sharply and steadily. In a single year, 1839, purchases of British yarn at Bursa rose 18 percent (to 128,000 kg.), while local consumption of British manufactures in general increased 20–25 percent. The number of Bursa shops selling British goods rose correspondingly: at the beginning of 1839, for example, these shops already numbered 160 and, by the year's end, had increased to 200.[20]

Bursa silk weavers fought back. For example, they adopted the machine-made yarn to make a variety of textiles once woven of pure silk or a mixture of silk and cotton. In most cases, it seems, the new product served the lower end of the market. They used British yarn as a substitute for silk and also as a replacement for homespun cotton yarn in the struggle to remain competitive. In 1840, for example, weavers utilized 6,100 kg. of British yarn to make 18,000 pieces of silk and cotton cloth. As a result, the selling price of Bursa silk-cotton cloths (*hakirs*, *kutnis* and *kaftans*) fell 8–10 percent.[21] By the 1840s, Ottoman women widely recognized the "waste of time spent in spinning cotton of native growth" and largely had switched over to British yarn to weave ordinary cloth for home use. Cotton yarn also continued to displace silk, regardless of its cheapness, "in the tissues to which it had been partly or exclusively applied."[22]

At this crucial point, a Bursa entrepreneur sought to adjust the industry to the changing technologies and fashions. During the 1830s–1840s, a local notable, one İsmet Pasha, tried to introduce mechanical looms and European styles into the local silk industry. He initially planned to exclude foreign workers and employ only skilled Bursa artisans in order to make taffeta and other silks according to European designs. Profits were to be shared 50–50 with the artisans. The İstanbul government refused to grant subsidies but it did offer a seven year monopoly, effectively blocking other entrepreneurs from entering the field. He soon completed a factory near his own residence and installed a dozen looms on the Italian model. Despite his intentions, he eventually hired an Italian weaver, but to little avail. After more than five years of experiments, his imitations of European silks remained unsuccessful.[23]

Shaken by taste and market changes, Bursa weavers received a devastating blow from nature in the 1850s. Silkworm diseases arrived from Europe and for decades, until the later 1880s, sharply reduced local supplies of cocoons and raw silk. Worse, local weavers were forced to compete for scarce resources with European buyers who were providing credit to Bursa reelers. As raw silk supplies vanished, so too did Ottoman silk cloth weaving. During the early 1860s, silk cloth production fell by as much as 90 percent when compared to the levels gained during the 1810s–1820s. The number of silk cloth looms in use similarly decreased, by as much as three-quarters (see table 4.1). For the next several decades, unfortunately, silk cloth weaving at Bursa becomes a historically-invisible activity and production levels are unknown.[24] Cloth output certainly was down in this era of disease and decline when, during the 1870s, raw silk production was an estimated fourteen percent of its 1857 peak. Statistics again become available in the mid 1890s, revealing several patterns. The amount

Table 4.2. *Consumption of raw silk in Bursa weaving, 1840–1908 (in kg.)*

date	raw silk used
1840	3,864
1896	40,000 pcs = *c.* 13,489 kg.
1897	11,751
1898	22,524
1899	19,619
1900	20,792
1901	30,752
1903	15,275
1904	35,772
1905	17,124
1906	21,601
1907	11,976
1908	35,873

Sources: RCL, 10/31/1899, p. 936; ZStA,AA 53739, Bl. 125; *Statesman's Yearbook.* FO 195/113, 2/15/1840; 1840 figure originally stated as 8,500 lb.

of raw silk used by local weavers fluctuated considerably from year to year, doubling between 1897 and 1898, falling by one-half between 1904 and 1905, and tripling between 1907 and 1908. These changes derived from shifts in total raw silk production, in international purchases of raw silk and in the purchasing power of Ottoman consumers that in turn was tied to several crop failures during these years and to generally rising agricultural prices after 1896. Despite these annual fluctuations, the statistics clearly show that cloth output by the mid 1890s and thereafter had shifted to new and higher levels when compared to those of previous decades. During the mid 1890s, weavers used 500 looms and 13,000 kg. of raw silk to make approximately 40,000 pieces of cloth, twice the average level during the 1840s and 1850s. These new levels continued throughout the subsequent decade when weavers' annual usage averaged more than 22,000 kg. of locally-produced raw silk.[25] In the decade after 1896, cloth production levels at Bursa had increased a full fifty percent and those levels in turn were approximately double the silk cloth output during the 1850s. (tables 4.1 and 4.2).

Silk cloth production received an additional and final impetus from the adoption, on a limited scale, of mechanized looms. This new weaving technology arrived quite late, during or after 1908.[26] By the beginning of the war, there were five factories containing 35 mechanized looms in the town, some of them jacquard looms. In several cases, the new looms were installed alongside hand looms. In 1910, for example, twelve local weavers banded together, rented a building, and installed 18 hand looms and six mechanized looms. These six looms alone annually utilized about 10,000 kg. of raw silk. A few years later, in

1913, the value of mechanized cloth production equalled about one-twelfth that of hand-woven cloth in the Bursa area.[27]

Events in some other weaving centers often paralleled the increased cloth production and partial mechanization that took place at Bursa from the final decades of the nineteenth century. In Trabzon, as seen, production rose but the weaving of silk fabrics remained a non-mechanized, largely household industry. There, in the 1880s, women at home commonly spun the silk – that arrived from Amasya, Bafra, Eğin and Persia – dyed and sold it at the local marketplace.[28] But at Harput, silk weaving mechanization occurred exceptionally early, during the 1860s, joined in the early twentieth century by a second mechanized factory, with twelve silk looms.[29] Initial efforts to mechanize at Aleppo failed *c.* 1900 but, by 1911, 50 jacquard looms were working, reportedly of local manufacture. At Diyarbakır, 120 imported jacquard looms were weaving silk in 1903 while 60 such looms were part of the 300 silk looms then working in the Iraqi provinces.[30] The jacquard looms at Diyarbakır joined an already-lively silk weaving industry in the basalt-walled town. During the late 1880s, 100 male weavers there worked at as many looms, making silk veils (*çarşafs*), one per person each week, mostly for export to Aleppo, Harput, Sivas, Bitlis, Van, Erzurum and Trabzon. An additional 100 looms made watered silk (*gezi*) while 30 others wove silk-cotton cloth, some of it for Harput and Sivas buyers.[31]

Conclusion

Ottoman silk cloth weavers had been profoundly affected by a complex bundle of changes in political conditions, taste, technology, disease and foreign demand. Silk cloth production in locations such as Salonica, Edirne and the İstanbul capital seems essentially to have vanished. But in this maelstrom of change, other silk weavers adapted and continued. Silk cloth weaving hung on and then increased later in the century not only at Bursa but also at Diyarbakır, Aleppo, Damascus, the Iraqi provinces and, to a lesser extent, at places such as Trabzon.[32] At Bursa, the weavers persevered and their output *c.* 1910 may well have surpassed all previous levels of the post-1750 period except those of the 1810s–20s.

The silk reeling industry

Patterns and trends in production

In a dramatic turn of events, Bursa during the nineteenth century became more famous for the reeled silk that it sent to European weavers than for the renowned silk textiles it had furnished to sultans and kings, a reversal tied to the Ottoman weavers' loss of foreign export markets, the revolution in apparel away from silk to cotton and the entry of British machine-made cotton yarn. Two secular trends coincided to prompt the rise of the export industry in raw silk. Abroad, European demand for raw silk sharply mounted as Western prosperity and per capita cloth consumption increased. On the domestic scene, Ottoman labor became available for increased raw silk production, in part because stagnating demand for silk cloth after the 1820s made some weavers redundant. More important, cheap imported cotton yarn freed erstwhile cotton hand spinners to take on silk spinning that initially was more remunerative. The community of foreign and Ottoman merchants who brought the new technologies and the necessary capital fused European demand for raw silk materials with newly available Ottoman labor supplies.

The restructuring of the Bursa raw silk industry had deep roots in the eighteenth century, as seen in the European purchases that had diverted Bursa raw silk from Ottoman weavers, its intended market. In the early nineteenth century, this process of reshaping continued and affected both the quality of the raw silk being produced as well as the organization of the labor force producing it. As they mechanized, European silk weaving factories – in France, England, the Italian peninsula and Switzerland – came to require regularly spun raw silk of very particular qualities, of the better grades. To obtain this product in the Ottoman world, representatives of European industry began more closely to regulate hand-spinning output, seeking more regular and higher qualities of raw silk. They also introduced the so-called short reel and, until the later 1850s, usually placed these in homes and small workshops. In addition, they established centralized factories and installed equipment, including short reels, that produced raw silk compatible with the needs of European weaving mills. These new factories sometimes were driven by water but steam-power became increasingly common.

Short reels were an effort to replace the so-called long reels, then the norm in the Ottoman silk industry. Silk mill operators in Europe preferred short reels because they took up less space inside the weaving mills and because the silk produced was softer and had a greater sheen. The short reels first appeared at Bursa in 1838, introduced at the request of London merchants who then were the major buyers of local raw silk.[33] Since the new method was somewhat more labor intensive, requiring more fuel and greater attention to temperature, merchants offered inducements to reelers to make the shift. In 1840, for example, Bursa merchants offered premiums ranging from 6 to 40 percent, depending on the grade of the silk. These inducements sometimes were as much as fifteen times greater than the extra costs incurred in using short reels.[34] Short reels first were used to produce raw silk of the coarsest quality, but low and medium grades quickly became more common. By 1843, short reeling had become more popular in the higher qualities as well, competing favorably in the best of the second-class categories. At the behest of the British consul at Bursa, the consular agent in the famed silk town of Mihallıç, in 1843, used the short reel to spin the very highest quality. The experiment succeeded and immediately was imitated by his fellow townsmen and by villagers nearby.[35] The price of high-quality short-reeled silk soon was nearly double that of the long-reeled.[36] Long reeling had been pushed to the margins by 1853; a few long reels continued to work, making speciality items such as the "coarse long reel silk" needed for ribbon manufacture in England. In 1860, long-reeled silk formed only 2 percent of all raw silk reeled in the region.[37]

There were considerable successes in efforts to regulate and improve hand reeling until the ascendancy of factory production in the middle 1850s. In c. 1840, the government and İstanbul merchants met to agree on measures to improve the quality of reeled silk. Subsequently, the state issued a set of regulations establishing uniform measurements for the physical size of both the short and the long reel. As a result, production costs rose 2–3 percent but silk prices increased 6–10 percent.[38] Production of the higher qualities continued to become more important among the hand reelers. In 1844, as the trend moved away from long to short reels, most short-reel production was of "superior quality."[39] A decade later, short-reeled Bursa silk had achieved an international reputation equal to that from any country and sold for 8–10 percent less than the highest quality Italian silk. Hand-reeled silk still prevailed: quotations for Bursa silk through 1853 remained based on hand-reeled silk produced in homes and workshops, not on the emergent factory-made product.[40] As late as 1856, after a boom in steam mill construction, the town of Bursa still contained some 7,000–8,000 hand reels. By the mid-1860s, however, when the Bursa product had surpassed the finest grades of raw Italian silk, factory reeling had won out.[41] Some hand reeling survived, using cocoons that the factories could not.[42]

Centralized factories to reel silk first appeared at Bursa in 1838. Founded by the French Glaizal family, whose efforts ended in failure and death by disease for two of its six members, the factory most likely was water-powered and contained short reels.[43] In a centralized-factory setting, workers could be brought outside their homes into environments where they could be controlled more readily, where merchants more easily could impose quality control standards on the reelers and obtain the higher grades wanted in Europe. Representing a Zurich firm, a Swiss merchant and Austrian consul named Falkeisen took over the failing Glaizal factory. Falkeisen cooperated with an interpreter at the British consulate, the Ottoman Armenian Taşçıyan, to found the first steam-powered mill in the Bursa area, in operation by June 1845. Established at some considerable expense for the building and machinery on the French model, its 20 reels initially produced only 5 kg. of raw silk daily. In the following year, however, its capacity was tripled. At the same time, the tax farmer of the silk duties, Gesailli, joined with fellow Italians to found the second steam-powered mill. Italian merchants also were founding small-scale model spinning mills, that probably were not steam-driven, "in each of the market towns of the silk district". By 1847, there were three mills in the town of Bursa, with 90 reels. The third mill had been founded by an Ottoman Armenian and did not employ steam power.[44] The silk mills at first reeled the same deneir but, by 1867, they were producing different thicknesses to meet varying European demands.[45]

The silk industry, however, was a precarious business and, in October 1848, all three of the new mills temporarily had halted operations. The European depression of 1846–47 and the revolutions of 1848 jolted European weaving factories and reduced their demands for raw silk. Prices fell accordingly. Beginning in 1846, farmers around Bursa reduced the size of the mulberry plantations, turning to grain and especially maize because silk prices were so low.[46] This downward trend, that ended in late 1848, is just one example of external problems that redounded harmfully on the Bursa reeling industry. Throughout its nineteenth-century life, Ottoman silk reeling would be characterized by violent swings between boom and bust. In March, 1841 for example, the villagers of Demirtaş and Geyve (Ghio, among the best of the silk producers) were abandoning their cornfields and vineyards in favor of silk production.[47] But, later that same year, declines on the London market depressed Bursa raw silk prices some 20–30 percent.[48]

Sustained by rising European demand, centralization continued and, in 1851, there were eight reeling mills in the city. These contained 650 reels, four mills possessed steam engines and the others used water. The largest in the city was an imperial mill, exclusively supplying the government silk weaving factory at Hereke. The factories now provided 9 percent of all raw silk exported from the Bursa area.[49] In 1852, Gesailli had opened his third mill and was building a fourth in a nearby town when he went bankrupt, losing his position and his properties.[50] The factory building boom continued, driven by rising European demand for the increasingly high-quality local silk. In 1854, the state sought to promote the boom and provided silk merchants with funds to send an apprentice to Paris in order to study steam-powered silk reeling.[51] In the following year, the city of Bursa held some 15 mills while the region altogether contained *c.* 2,000 reels.[52] But still, factories provided only 16 percent of total raw silk production in the Bursa area between 1846 and 1857.

Developments parallel to those in the Bursa reeling industry – the adoption of short reels and steam-powered mills to supply European buyers – simultaneously took place in many other Ottoman locations. The first short reels in the Ottoman Empire, probably, were installed at Salonica in 1820. Italians, including the director of the royal silk factory at Catania, instructed over 1,000 Ottoman reelers in their use. By 1839, when there were twelve steam silk mills, short-reeled silk accounted for one-third of total raw silk production in the area. The Salonica silk industry then expanded very rapidly; the total payroll of the silk mills, for example, rose ten-fold between 1840 and 1845 as the value of their production rose four times. By 1847, there were 25–30 mills, with 2,000 workers.[53] In the Lebanese silkreeling industry, French interests built nine mills during the 1840s.[54] At the village of Foça, four miles from İzmir, the British consul established a short-reel steam powered mill in 1845. His example quickly was followed and, within a decade, six large mills – four powered by steam – operated locally.[55] At Amasya around this same time, a Freiburg firm established a spinning mill while other European entrepreneurs shortly after-wards opened a second. Neither apparently employed steam power, however, and silk spinning here continued to be regarded as crudely done.[56] At the major silk cloth weaving center of Diyarbakır (see chapters 2 and 3), reeling remained "primitive" during these several decades of rapid technological change. And, despite some improvements in the weaving process, reeling remained so. Except for Diyarbakır, all the raw silk producing districts expanded to meet *European* demand. Atypically and for the entire period, these Diyarbakır reelers focused on the supply of Ottoman weavers, in this case primarily those at Aleppo as well as in Diyarbakır itself.[57]

At Bursa and other Ottoman reeling centers, already-impressive develop-ments in factory-based and short reel steam reeling catapulted to new heights because of silkworm disease epidemics in Europe. Appearing in France on a widespread scale as early as 1850 and spreading to Italy in 1853, the diseases wrecked havoc with European raw silk production, causing sickly worms that either died before making a cocoon or spun poor-quality cocoons. "It was said that something like cholera had attacked the worms."[58] Contemporaries at first believed that a single disease (*pebrine*) was responsible but further research also established the widespread presence of two others (*flacherie* and *muscardine*) as well. French cocoon production simply collapsed, falling from 26 to 7 million kg. between 1853 and 1856, to 4 million in 1865 and to a nadir of 3.5 million kg. in 1879.[59] The burgeoning European silk industry desperately needed raw silk as well as uninfected eggs and cocoons and was willing to pay exceptionally high prices. It found these supplies in many regions of the globe, including the Ottoman Middle East.

The crisis had important long-term effects. On the international front, the disease provided French silk raisers with the final nudge that pushed them out of the industry altogether. Thereafter, even when remedies for the diseases were devised, the French silk industry preferred to import the raw materials and concentrate on the production of cloth. Italy, by contrast, would defeat the diseases and continue to supply much of its own weaving requirements from local cocoon raising and silk reeling.[60] The disease outbreak also may have abetted the decline of Great Britain as a silk manufacturing nation. In the early 1850s, England appears to have been the major market for raw silk from the Bursa area. Not quite two decades later, France routinely was buying the lion's share, thanks in part to the premium prices it paid.[61] On the domestic front, the very high prices that the European industry offered for raw silk caused an extraordinary proliferation of reeling mills, both at Bursa and elsewhere. The profits gained by the first mills quickly attracted other investors. Even when a catastrophic earthquake in 1855 levelled Bursa, its factories and weaving shops, entrepreneurs were undaunted. They replaced the fallen mills, frantically erected new ones and, remarkably, quickly established record production levels.

At Bursa, disease in Europe, inflated cocoon prices and the rapid rise of factory reeling accelerated the abandonment of hand reeling in favor of cocoon raising by many villagers. A situation had emerged in which the cocoon prices practically equalled those of the reeled silk itself. Villagers could make nearly as much money raising eggs and cocoons as in reeling silk, a more laborious and time-consuming task. So, many gave up their hand reels and concentrated on raising silkworm eggs and cocoons.[62] A more refined division of labor emerged within the industry in the Bursa area and relatively few villagers continued both to raise eggs (or cocoons) and reel at home. Instead, families raised eggs and cocoons at home and sold them to the new reeling mills to which they sent their daughters.

Silkworm raising here constitutes essentially a family industry; there are few houses, either in Bursa or in the villages of the area, that do not practice this industry and don't engage in raising a few ounces of eggs; most frequently, the small raiser is at the same time owner of a small piece of land where he grows the necessary mulberry trees to feed the worms. For the peasant of some villages of the countryside, who live miserably on the products of the soil, the small sum which he gains from the sale of his cocoons is very often the only gold which might be given to him during the entire course of the year.[63]

At Bursa as well as at İzmir and Salonica, a variety of mechanisms brought the eggs and cocoons to market. Sometimes the peasants raised the cocoons from eggs and personally brought them to the great han at Bursa where they were graded by quality, then killed, sacked, weighed and delivered to the reeling factories.[64] But sharecropping also was common throughout the period and in the various areas. Each November, egg raisers (who usually were mill operators), placed their eggs with silkworm raisers. Since the peasants often were impoverished as the new season approached, they were vulnerable to exploitation. Sometimes they accepted the eggs without any immediate payment and kept part of the cocoon yield at harvest time. On other occasions, in exchange for a cash advance from the egg raiser/mill operator, the peasants promised delivery of the cocoons at a low price or repayment in cocoons.[65]

The abandonment of hand-reeling by Bursa-area families in favor of egg and cocoon raising had gained additional momentum in the decade after 1845; the number of reeling mills climbed steadily, from 3 to 5 to 15 and then to 29 in 1855. Then, as Ottoman and foreign merchants frantically sought to fill the

Table 4.3. *Bursa-area raw silk production (000s of kg.), 1810–1908*

	raw silk	% made in factory	Remarks
1810–1812	unknown		73 sent to İstanbul
1817	62–77		
1840	463–618		65 sent to İstanbul
1840	482		
1841	818		
1846	591		
1846*	433	– 1	
1847	598		26% from within city
1847*	458	2	
1848*	382	4	
1849*	445	7	
1850			267 exported
1850*	459	9	
1851*	407	11	
1852*	486	16	
1853*	382	22	
1854*	450	20	
1855*	216	48	
1855	509		
1856*	534	28	
1857*	366	50	
1858*	242	75	
1859*	178	80	
1860*	193	78	
1860	255		
1861*	299	79	
1861	312		
1862*	195	85	
1863*	280	65	
1864*	197	75	
1864	191		
1865*	127	100	
1866*	153	92	
1867*	165	92	
1868*	140	94	
1869*	131	93	
1870*	141	95	
1871*	153	92	
1874	100		
1876–80	85		
1881–85	140		
1886–90	186		
1891–95	264		
1896–1900	401		
1901–5	517		
1906–8	610		

Sources: 1864*–1872* – FO (1873), J. Mailing, Brussa, 10/5/1872. Various FO and A&P; RCL 10/31/1899, p. 934; 1876–1908 annual averages from Quataert (1984), table 3, p. 502. Converted from lb.

Table 4.4. *Reeling mills in the Bursa and Lebanon regions, 1840–1913*

	Bursa			Lebanon
date	mills in city/region +	basins in city/region	city % basins	
basin/mills				
1840				/1
1845	1	60		
1846*	/2	/120		
1847*	/3	/240		
1847	3/	90/		
1848*	/4	/320		
1848	5/			
1849*	/8	/600		
1850*	/11	/780		
1850	5 active	/650		
1851*	/15	/910		
1851	8/, 4 w/steam			
1852*	/21	/1,230		
1853*	/25	/1,345		
1855*	/29	/1,610		
1855	15/29	/2,000		
1856*	/53	/2,200		
1856	37/85	/3,000		
1857*	/64	/2,788		
1858*	/82	/3,712		
1859				91
1860	/83	2,100/3,752	56%	
1861*	/88	/4,185		
1862*	/90	/4,345		
1862	/91	/4,500		
1863	62/92	2,662/4,622	58%	
1869	/70	/3,400		
c.1869	56/90 operational	/5,400		
1870				67/3,000
1873				85/4,000
1883				95/6,500
1900	/88	/4,767		145/
1901	47/103	2,350/5,406	43%	
1906@	44/103	2,364/5,591	44%	
1906#	38/131	2,370/7,685	31%	
1909	38/152	2,083/9,519	22%	
1913				195

+ region, defined as Bursa province and İzmit district, includes the city of Bursa.

Sources: *FO (1873), J. Maling at Brussa, 10/5/1872; @ Bursa VS 1325/1907, pp. 258–260; # Delbeuf (1906), p. 131; FO and A&P, Sandison at Bursa; Warsberg (1869); RCL 12/31/1899; RCL 11/30/1909. Owen (1987).

disease-induced gap in Europe's supply, the number of mills leapfrogged, rising from 29 to 83 between 1855 and 1860. In just five years, productive capacity, as measured by the number of reels, rose 375 percent. During the 1860s, the number of factories climbed again, to some 90, containing 5,400 reels.

Productive capacity at Bursa reached record levels just as silkworm diseases from Europe began attacking the Ottoman silk industry. On the one hand, the number of basins reeling silk in the Bursa area rose significantly between 1857 and 1863. But, on the other hand, silk production fell almost 50 percent (tables 4.3 and 4.4). During the initial onslaught, entrepreneurs built mills to take advantage of the higher prices obtaining for ever-scarcer raw materials. By 1863, however, there were too many factories for the shrinking supplies and they began closing their doors.[66] That is, the buildings hardly had been erected to meet the boom when the bubble burst. For the next several decades, silk reeling was in sharp decline. Many mill operators went bankrupt or suspended operations. In the early 1870s, the surviving "factories [routinely] are working short time or not more than 200 days in the year."[67]

Similar patterns of boom, collapse and factory closings occurred in the other production centers. At İzmir, the value of the silk trade had risen ten-fold between 1857 and 1860 but diseases reached the region in 1859. During the 1860s, all the İzmir-area mills closed and, despite the various attempted remedies, remained so through at least the 1880s.[68] Similarly, the silk mills at Amasya went bankrupt and re-opened as flour mills for several decades.[69] At Edirne, the mills managed to hang on and annually spun 7,000 kg. into the 1870s.[70] At Salonica, the silk mills had increased to 34 in 1860, 19 in the town and the rest in surrounding villages. Many survived but were in serious decline during the late 1870s.[71]

Bursa entrepreneurs tried a number of remedies, including importing disease-free silkworm eggs. Local producers began to import eggs from Japan in 1864 to offset disease-induced shortages[72] and, in the 1880 season, for example, Japanese yellow cocoons accounted for 70 percent of all fresh cocoons sold on the Bursa market.[73] This measure helped but total raw silk output continued to slide because the strategy had serious drawbacks. Japanese silkworms were relatively small and twice as many were needed to produce the same amount of silk. Also, it was discovered, the silk was inferior in quality and commanded commensurately lower prices. The reputation of Bursa silk suffered, reducing European demand. During the early 1880s, production at Bursa sometimes had slumped to as little as one-fifth that of the boom years during the middle 1850s.[74]

A method to end the disease-borne crisis appeared after 1870, thanks to five years of research by Louis Pasteur. The great French scientist found a relatively simple technique to control and essentially eliminate these silkworm diseases. The method involved using microscopes to identify healthy eggs and cocoons and so build a disease-free population.[75] Some Bursa merchants and mill

Table 4.5. *Global raw silk production, 1871–1913 (in 000 kg.)*

	West Europe	East Europe, Near and Middle East	Far East	total
1871–5	3,700	700	5,200	9,600
1891–5	5,500	1,100	8,700	15,300
1901–5	5,200	2,400	11,500	19,100
1908	5,450	2,800	15,800	24,050
1913	4,100	2,460	20,760	27,320

Source: Gueneau (1923), p. 46.

operators studied in France, returning to implement the Pasteur method and raise the so-called Baghdad white cocoon, of higher quality than the Japanese variety.

Widespread adoption of the Pasteur remedies, however, was slow because of continuous declines in international silk prices that followed the massive entry of East Asian silk into Europe. After 1869, the newly-opened Suez Canal promoted the flow of huge quantities of raw silk from China and Japan. During the early 1870s, Oriental raw silk exports already were seven times greater than from the entire Middle East (see table 4.5). In the presence of vast new supplies, global raw silk prices fell steadily until 1892, when they levelled off, at one-half to three-quarter the rates prevailing in 1868. (see table 4.6).[76]

Global demand for raw silk caught up with East Asian production after 1892, when an equilibrium developed between world-wide production and consumption. The United States emerged as the greatest global consumer of silk, quadrupling its imports between 1870 and 1914. France, the major market for Middle East raw silk, provided a similarly favorable market, importing six-sevenths of the raw silk needed by its weavers.[77] In this context, the Ottoman Public Debt Administration, seeking to increase silk tax revenues under its control, enacted an effective program to boost production. Encouraged by these measures and by international demand that provided an assured market, Ottoman raw silk producers responded.[78]

Many new mills therefore opened, especially at Bursa but also in Edirne and the Lebanon, towards the end of the period. In the Lebanon, between the 1890s and 1909, raw silk output rose ten percent while the number of factories increased by one-third (table 4.4). At Edirne, the number of functioning mills remained steady, at three, from the 1870s until 1907, when two mills were added in successive years. At Souffli, three new mills opened between 1903 and 1909.[79] The number of mills around Bursa rose by 50 percent as regional annual raw silk production rose from *c.* 154 tons to 677 tons in the two decades after 1890. Aggregate Near and Middle Eastern raw silk production (statistically including Russia and the Balkan states) rose from 1,100 to 2,800 (see tables 4.4 and 4.6).

Table 4.6. *Annual average prices of Bursa and Syrian raw silk, 1850–1911 (francs/kg.)*

	Bursa raw silk on Lyon market	Syrian "thread"
1850	120	
c.1852	35	
1880–84	56	
1885–89	48	
1890–94	46	46
1895	39	39
1896	36	36
1899	55	51
1900		42
1901		40
1902		44
1903		49
1904		41
1905		43
1906		49
1907		59
1908		51
1909		53
1910		51
1911		50

Sources: for Bursa: 1850–2, RCL 11/30/1899, p. 1016; 1880–96: AE CC Turquie, Brousse, 3/31/1897. For Syrian "thread": Owen (1987), table on p. 274.

These impressive production increases, however, took place in a setting unfavorable to the founders of the mills, the investors who had backed them, and the workers they employed. Overall, after 1892, international (nominal) raw silk prices did rise slightly. Thus, the international atmosphere was more favorable than between 1868 and 1892, when prices fell steadily. But each time prices climbed somewhat, there was a very sharp fall, followed by a gradual rise and another price collapse. Consequently, in 1910, the price of raw silk was only about 10 percent higher than it had been in 1892. This modest rise, moreover, occurred in the context of substantial increases in general commodity prices, that took place after the end of the world depression in 1896. Thus, raw silk prices comparatively did poorly and relatively declined in the final prewar years. Overall, the price trend for raw silk through 1914 was unfavorable for producers.[80]

To hold down production costs, silk mill operators used a mix of policies, among them the adoption of new technologies to increase efficiency. These innovations were several and included the Pasteur practices. Also, new machinery killed cocoons more quickly, in a way that increased raw silk yield; other equipment spun more threads per reel than previously.[81] Other technical innovations to cut costs included efficiencies of scale. In the Bursa area, the mills grew larger in size, by an average of approximately 80 percent. But this does not seem to have been true elsewhere. Although the number of mills in the Lebanon increased by a full one-third between the 1890s and 1909, their raw silk output, as seen, rose by only ten percent (Table 4.4). At Edirne, the new mills were smaller on the average than those built in earlier decades.[82] Thus, technical changes helped the mills to remain competitive. But many cost reduction strategies involved the control of labor, the creation and maintenance of a skilled, cheap, and disciplined work force.

Working conditions in the silk mills

Beginning in mid-1840s, the workforce of the silk factories became a visible presence in several Ottoman towns. In every area – Salonica, Edirne, İzmir, Bursa and the Lebanon – all the reelers were female, usually young girls, and the remainder of the workforce – e.g., cocoon sorters – overwhelmingly so. Except during the earliest days of factory formation, they worked for exceptionally low wages, and in an erratically boom-bust industry. Work hours fluctuated with the season of the year while employment itself was tied to the seasonal nature of the cocoon production that supplied the factories. Very many reelers were from cultivator families and most of the rest from the poorer strata of Ottoman urban society.

In the city of Salonica during the mid-1840s, when it held an estimated population of 70,000 persons, the silk mills employed just under 2,000 workers. Most were "poor children" (certainly girls), working about 14 hours per day. Here, and in the other areas, mill workers' wages were seen as supplemental, to be added to the gross family income pool. At Salonica, six months' wages for two working children reportedly then supported their entire family for a whole year.[83]

At Bursa, in 1850,

hundreds of raya [non Muslim] women and children have a further recent resource for employment at the silk filatures ...[84]

In 1863, the mills in the city of Bursa, with a population of under 70,000 persons, employed 3,300 individuals. Mills in immediately adjacent villages employed 400 persons and factories elsewhere in the region employed 2,500 persons. Thus, there were 6,200 workers, and only the 400 directors and engineers were males. Reelers and reeler supervisors formed the largest single group, of 4,600 persons; 400 plaiters twisted the skeins, 600 persons sorted the cocoons and another 200 reeled coarse silk.[85]

The emerging nexus of silk spinning factories required a concentrated industrial work force, no easy task since this entailed unfamiliar work disciplines and

the employ of female labor outside the home. To run the new mills, entrepreneurs at Bursa during the 1840s (as well as in other locations at different
times) imported Italian and French directors to manage the factories. They also
summoned French reelers, experienced and skilled women. These women were
hired with a two-fold purpose. As skilled workers, they would instruct local
residents in the new technology. As women, their presence within the factory
would make it easier for local women to take the revolutionary step of accepting
work outside the home. Marie Blache, for example, was a 32-year-old widow
with a child from Loriol/Drome in France, hired by the entrepreneur Falkeisen
as an instructor and forewoman at Bursa.[86] (Blache later married M. Brotte, also
French, who operated a silk mill, and their descendants remained important in
the local industry.)[87] At the outset, the foreigners at Bursa trained only Ottoman
Greek women. Because recruitment was slow at first, the reelers originally
received wages that were "remarkably high" when compared with the cost of
living. Some of the new Greek reelers who had been doing laundry at the homes
of resident foreigners quit those jobs, leaving them to Ottoman Turkish
women.[88]

To reduce wages and obtain a more abundant work force, employers in the
town of Bursa adopted several strategies during the early 1850s. First of all, they
built many of the factories in or next to the residential quarters of the Greek and
Armenian communities, the first targeted sources for labor recruitment. In this
way, workers walked to the factory and more easily integrated their out-of-the-
home jobs with existing divisions of labor within the household. The employers
also reached an agreement among themselves and implemented a passbook
system to prevent workers from quitting work at one factory to gain higher
wages at another. In common with similar systems in Europe and the United
States, Bursa workers had to present their new employer with a passbook
containing their employment record and the written release of former
employers.[89]

As the number of mills increased, the available workforce became insufficient
and increasingly expensive. So, some mills operators built dormitories next to
the factories and inaugurated recruitment campaigns to bring workers from
outlying villages.[90] At the beginning of the reeling season, caravans of workers
arrived in town and were housed in the dormitories. Some were married women
but unmarried girls formed the vast majority.[91] Apprenticeships began around
10–12 years of age and during this period the girls received about one-half the
regular spinners' wages. In the dormitories, they lived frugally, despite one
foreigner's accusation, in 1860, that "the silk factory girls lay out too much of
their earnings in dress." In fact, the girls returned home at the end of the reeling
season with almost all their wages, mainly, it seems, to help support the family.[92]
The workday in the mills varied by season and, in the 1860s, it ranged from 13.5
hours in the summer (including 1.5 hours for meals and breaks) to 7.5 in

winter.[93] At Edirne, similarly, 300 female reelers during the early 1870s labored 13 hours daily in the summer and 10 during the rest of the year.[94] In the early twentieth century, the Bursa workday reportedly reached 14–16 hours. According to one source, breaks had become briefer,[95] perhaps to reduce costs or to meet the booming demand in France.

During the first factory years, mill owners at Bursa diversified the labor pool, breaking the Greek monopoly of the workforce. By 1854, the 2,200 "young women" or "young girls" who worked now included Armenians as well as Greeks. To facilitate the entry of Christian Armenian workers, so the story goes, the Pope issued a special decree affirming the morality of such labor and giving permission to enter these Ottoman satanic mills. In the Lebanon, similarly, the *ulema* were summoned to persuade Muslim workers during the 1850s while, *c.* 1869, local archbishops approved the employment of Christian women.[96] But, as the number of mills at Bursa continued to multiply and labor became relatively scarcer, Armenian workers demanded higher wages. And so, in mid-1855, Turkish women began entering the mills "for the first time." Jewish workers reportedly were kept out by their Christian and Muslim rivals, forming, in 1900, for example, under 3 percent of all silk reelers in the Bursa area.[97] The total number of Turkish and Jewish workers was not large and Ottoman Greeks remained the dominant single element. But these additions to the labor pool allowed mill operators to increase production without causing critical labor shortages or pushing wages to unacceptable levels. Labor supplies, now drawn from a more diverse ethnic and geographic pool, became abundant and wages fell accordingly. During 1861, admittedly a particularly difficult year, Bursa reelers received a daily wage only one-half that paid in 1857. Thus, the multiple mechanisms that employers used to attract workers did succeed.

Workers and their families became accustomed to, and then, probably, dependent on the new work and the cash incomes. The reeling girls and their families spun and wove less for home use, buying dress fabrics and other luxuries, such as sugar and coffee. The luxuries soon became necessities and the reeling girls and their families, as well as the cocoon-raising households, became reliant on cash wages. Thus, they became vulnerable to the fluctuations in this volatile industry. As disease began attacking Ottoman silkworks, factories in the Bursa area closed their doors, as early as 1860. "Few keep at the work the full year."[98] In early 1861, most mills were closed. But the few operators who remained open had "the advantage of work being much cheaper, paying ... to the girls employed ... but half their former wages."[99] The diseases continued to spread and, towards the end of the 1862 cocoon harvest season, worker resentment exploded, taking the form of inter-communal violence.

The ostensible issue was violation of an ancient Muslim cemetery. An Armenian mill operator had purchased land, covered with mulberry trees, from its owner, a "Turkish woman." After obtaining the necessary permissions, he built and opened a new mill, adding to the growing over-capacity of the crisis-bound industry. After it was completed, some "Turks," alleging that the building rested on an abandoned and no-longer visible Muslim cemetery, demanded its demolition by the authorities. And, they warned of another Damascus if they were ignored, referring to the recent worker riots in that city. On July 24,

a numerous mob ... met in the Grand Mosque, excited by some fanatics among the ulema, softas or sheikhs, and after some pourparlers with the authorities who requested them to disperse

marched to the mill, pulled it down and "next set fire to the mass of leveled ruins." Throughout this episode, the British consul who reported the event kept referring to Muslim fanaticism as the root cause. But, in his closing remarks, he gave away the game. *All* (my stress) the silk mills of Bursa, he commented, would be in peril unless the authorities took decisive measures. Thus, his remark reveals, it was not the presence of a cemetery but of low wages and unemployment that impelled the riot.[100]

This account also sheds some light on the rioters' perceptions of themselves – were they workers or Muslims? Contemporaries often observed that French-operated mills employed Greek and Muslim women while Armenian- and Greek-owned mills used only co-religionists.[101] If this is true, by destroying a mill that was Armenian-owned, the Turkish workers eliminated a source of employment for rival workers. Thus, the riot had the form of internal-communal violence but the content of worker protest to save jobs. In response, the factory share of raw silk being produced at Bursa dropped to 65 percent, down from 85 percent during the preceding year of 1862 (table 4.3). In the short run, this workers' action was successful.

Employment in the Ottoman silk mills generally fell during the later 1860s and remained at comparatively low levels until the revival of the late 1880s. During these several decades, the workforce at Bursa may have shrunk to as few as 2,000 persons, less than one-third the number in previous years.[102] Reeling then revived and by the 1890s employed 4,500 workers at Bursa. In 1900, there were 7,000 workers. The workforce continued to grow, spurting to new heights beginning in *c.* 1906. By the end of the decade, some 19,000 workers were employed in the reeling mills of the Bursa region, a record for the twentieth century.[103] These formed nearly one-half of the estimated 40,000 persons who then worked in Ottoman reeling mills. In the Lebanon mills, perhaps 14,000 persons were working while the scattered mills around Edirne, Salonica and elsewhere held the balance.[104]

During the early years of factory spinning, mills often (but not always) had been established in towns. In the Lebanon, small villages were the original and remained the characteristic setting for mills that were tiny in size and often manually operated. But in the Salonica area, during the 1850s, it will be recalled,

Table 4.7. *Workers and wages in the reeling mills (wages in piasters/day),*
1839–1913)

	Bursa		Edirne		Salonica		Lebanon	
date	wages	number	wages	number	wages	number	wages	number
1839						739		
1840						1,167		
1841						1,103		
1842						1,237		
1843						1,447		
1844						1,470		
1845						1,977		
1846–50	3–5							
1851	3–5					2,000		
1854		2,000						
1857	10							
1858–72	6–8							
1860	6–6.5	5,000						
1861	4–5							
1862	"wages declined"							
1863	6–8	6,200						
	summer							
1864	6–7							
1873			3–4.5	300				
1883								8,000
1900		7,000						
1903				4–500				
1909				600				
1911								14,000
1913	4	19,000						

Sources: Bursa: FO and A&P, Sandison at Bursa; FO (1873); Turkey (1970), pp. 21–23.
Edirne: FO (1873); RCC 1905, #412, Adrianople for 1903; RCC 1910, Adrianople for 1909
Salonica: FO Blunt at Salonica; US NA Abbott at Salonica, 5/19/1852. Wages are of reelers
only.

19 of the 34 mills were located in the city itself[105] while the town of Bursa had
been the original locus of the steam-powered mills in that region. Such comparatively westernized Ottoman towns were relatively comfortable bases for the
French and Italian merchants who possessed the new technology. In 1860,
Bursa town held 56 percent of the total productive capacity of regional silk
mills.[106] But, by 1909, the town's relative importance had fallen sharply and
held only 22 percent of regional productive capacity (table 4.4). Small villages
such as Ortaköy held thirteen mills with 616 basins while the village of Küplü
had ten mills with 730 basins. These new rural mills possessed several advantages over urban-area factories. Mill workers who lived and labored in Bursa had
acquired a half century of experience in factory work and were on the path of

developing class consciousness (see below). The workforce in the country mills, by contrast, not only was less expensive but also was probably more docile as well.

Overall, Ottoman silk mill workers had been, and continued to be, poorly paid. Nominal wages more or less had doubled between the first decade of factory reeling and the proliferation of silk mills in the later 1850s. Gaining control over wage scales, the employers stabilized wages, helped by sagging demand for workers. During the 1860s generally, wages were down 20–40 percent from their 1857 peak.[107] Thereafter, wage data are extremely scarce, available only at the very end of the period, in 1913. At that time, reelers' wages at Bursa were the lowest in Ottoman industry. The average Ottoman factory worker, typically male, then received a daily wage of 12 to 15 piasters. Textile workers daily averaged 6.1 piasters, silk weavers in factories earned 6.0 piasters but reelers, characteristically female, daily received only 4.0 piasters.[108]

A comparison of these wages with Ottoman prices demonstrates that the relative position of the reelers deteriorated over time. As seen (table 4.7), nominal silkreeling wages in the 1860s were 6–8 piasters and only 4 piasters in 1913. But, at the same time, Ottoman commodity prices went in quite the opposite direction. Overall, these increased slightly between the 1860s and 1870s and then stabilized until 1908 (falling until 1896 and then increasing). Prices thereafter rose sharply and in 1913 were much above those of the 1860s. The real wages of Ottoman silk workers clearly had declined significantly after the 1860s (see table 4.7).

Conclusion

Both the mill operators and their workers suffered from the nature of the industry as silk reeling became the largest single manufacturing employer in the Bursa and Lebanon regions and the second ranking Ottoman export industry, after carpetmaking. The mill operators competed in a business that inherently was seasonal in nature, depending on a single annual harvest of cocoons. During this brief harvest season, entrepreneurs required relatively vast amounts of capital to buy the creatures for reeling. According to one estimate, each Bursa operator needed 30,000–40,000 kg. of fresh cocoons, then valued at 0.5 million piasters, to keep the mill supplied for eight months' work.[109] During the cocoon harvest (which at Bursa occurred between June 20 and July 20), huge quantities of the raw material poured onto the local market, producing frenzied competition among mill operators.

The few bales of raw silk that already have appeared on the market have been snatched up by speculators at higher prices than at Lyon.[110]

Chronically short of cash, the operators frantically sought to be the first to ship bales of silk to Europe so they could obtain gold or credit from Lyon and Milan to continue cocoon purchases and thus keep their mills running for the season.[111]

Inadequate supplies of cocoons continuously plagued the industry, in times of healthy and diseased silkworms and in periods of boom as well as of bust. During the crisis of the later 1860s, existing factories had the capacity to reel 318,000 kg. of silk but received supplies of only 178,000 kg. Thirty years later, disease was under control, demand was very steady and production was booming. Output climbed sharply but, in the early twentieth century, continued cocoon shortages kept the mills operating at only 50 percent of capacity.[112] Even then, because of East Asian production, raw silk price trends were not favorable and there was very severe pressure to minimize costs. Under market conditions that were very strong at the turn of the century, considerable uncertainty remained in the work place. During the comparative prosperity of the later 1890s and subsequent years, operators routinely were encountering supply difficulties while cash shortages remained common, as they had been earlier. The combination meant that many mills continued to operate only part time. In extreme cases *c.* 1900, factories reportedly stood idle for up to six and seven months per year.[113] Ottoman silk reeling remained an industry of exceptional volatility, a risky investment for capitalists and a low-paying, irregular and undependable job for workers.

5 Carpet making

Introduction: patterns and trends in production

The making of so-called "Oriental rugs" is easily the most famous industrial activity of the late Ottoman Empire.[1] This is not because of the workers' behavior or the important place of rugmaking in the late Ottoman economy. Rather, the fame derives from the special place of these carpets in Western aesthetic sensibilities. In the romantic ideal, each Oriental rug is imagined as an art object, uniquely fashioned by its creator. The reality of the rugs, however, is quite different. Since at least the later nineteenth century, thousands of oriental rugs have been mass-produced in virtual sweatshop conditions – ofttimes by children. These conditions scarcely intrude on the admiring art aficionados who support an impressive array of publications in order to understand these hand-knotted products of Ottoman artisans. Luxurious art books continue pouring out to satisfy an apparently insatiable demand while the presence of journals such as *Halı* and *Oriental Rug Review* attests to the continuing Western fascination with rugs in the present day.

Ottoman rug making centered in Anatolia, where its introduction often is associated with the arrival, during medieval times, of nomadic Turkish tribes. Among these were the Kaçar, who settled down and made rugs in the west Anatolian town of Uşak. At first, very few rugs were sold, in a morning market where the rugs were spread on the "dokuzsele" bridge for prospective buyers. Süleyman the Magnificent, legend says, imported experts from the area of Azerbaijan and they began making a new style peculiar to the town of Uşak. Agents from İstanbul bought rugs to furnish imperial mosques, palaces and tombs in the Ottoman capital. At this time, Ottoman subjects likely obtained most of the rugs being produced although some already were finding their way to many parts of Europe.[2]

The relationship between Ottoman carpet producers and Western consumers reaches back at least to the sixteenth century, when English and then Dutch merchants and diplomats began buying Uşak rugs for personal use and for sale. Rugs began to be sent abroad, at first to the palaces and churches of Europe, satisfying the luxury trade and being recorded in the paintings of Lotto, Holbein

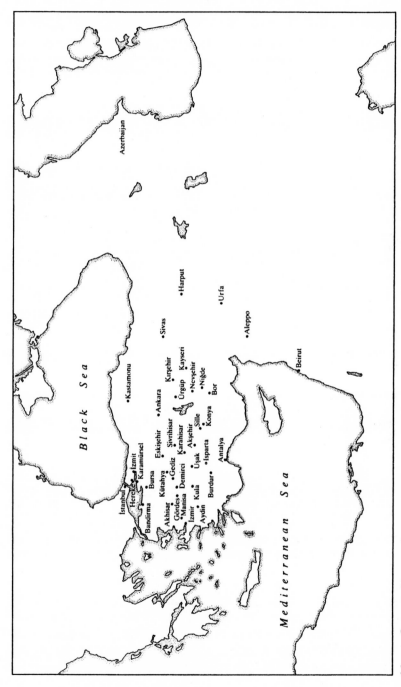

Map 5. Carpetmaking, c. 1820–1914.

Table 5.1. *Rug exports from İzmir and the Ottoman Empire, 1857–1913 (value in millions of piasters)*

	Ottoman Empire	İzmir	
	value	*qty.*	*value*
1857		1,096 b.	5.7
1866			2.9
1867			2.9
1867			3.9
1872			0.8
late 1870s	17.4	2,600 b.	13.5
early 1880s	15.8	3.100 b.	14.5
late 1880s	21.9	3.200 b.	21.5
mid-1890s	32.2		
1896		0.6 mil. kgs.	
1897		1.0 "	
1898		1.3 "	
1899		1.1 "	
1898		350,000 sq. m.	30.5
1899			32.6
1899		420,000 sq. m.	35.8
late 1890s		5,500 b.	33.4
1900		400,000 sq. m.	33.0
1900–1909		7,200 b.	35.2
1910–1913		8,800 b.	

b. = bale; sq. m. = square meter.

Sources: Farley (1862), p. 94; USNA T 238, Smyrna, 8/18/1866 and 1/4/1868; Salaheddin (1867), p. 46; Buhi, 9, III, 1/17/1902; RCC, Smyrne for 1899, Reel no. 33; Luckerts (1906), p. 2. JCCC, 7/26/1902 and GB A&P Smyrna, 1874–1914; derived from Quataert (1986), table, p. 475.

and others. But, already in the sixteenth century, "cartloads, camel-loads and horseloads" of these rugs went to Europe, suggesting a certain volume to the trade. Purchased mainly by the upper classes, these medium to coarse-grade rugs were produced in comparatively large quantities specifically for export. The foreign market developed further during the early eighteenth century, as sales accelerated in England and Holland, and, to a lesser extent, in the German and Italian lands. A sizeable and well-organized export industry in carpets existed in western Anatolia by the later eighteenth century.[3]

Commercial rug making continued to expand during the first half of the nineteenth century, when it reached semi-mass market proportions. By 1825, carpet buying had become common among less wealthy European families, prompting an output boom.[4] From at least the early 1840s, for example, the United States received shipments of rugs from İzmir.[5] Rug making in Uşak had become the major occupation in the town and their sale was "a considerable ...

Table 5.2. *Role of Uşak in the Anatolian rug industry, 1873–1910*

date	percentage	comment
1873	77	of exports from İzmir (value)
1881	75	of production in west Anatolia (value)
1890	66	of exports from west Anatolia (value)
1896	73	of production in west Anatolia (volume)
1899	56	of exports from İzmir (value)
1900	57	of exports from İzmir (value)
c. 1901	35	of production in west Anatolia (volume and value)
1902	57	of exports from İzmir (value)
1906	55	of exports from İzmir (value)
1907	52	of production in Anatolia (volume)
1910	23	of exports from İzmir (value)

Sources: see sources cited in Quataert (1986), table on p. 482; also k und k, x, 4, 1901, Brussa; Buhi, III, 9, 1/17/1902 and 7/2/1902; Buhi, 9, 1906, p. 719. *Ikdam*, IV 2 1325.

branch of merchandize at Smyrna ..."[6] During the 1840s and 1850s, the Ottoman government actively promoted rug production at Uşak and in the neighboring center of Gördes. It sought to improve quality and promote sales inside the Empire but "especially in Europe."[7] By the mid-1850s, total carpet exports from İzmir had reached an impressive 1,096 bales, worth 5.7 million piasters[8] (table 5.1 and 5.3)

Thereafter, until World War I, Ottoman rug making, almost always located in Anatolia, witnessed a growth spurt that authentically can be called extraordinary. Rug exports from İzmir, that remained the leading exit point, scored impressive gains. In the two decades after 1857, the volume of rug exports from İzmir more than doubled; it then doubled again by the late 1890s and, incredibly, doubled once more between the late 1890s and World War I. By 1913, the volume of İzmir rug exports had risen eight-fold since the 1850s (table 5.1)! The town of Uşak long had dominated the industry and, in the 1870s, for example, accounted for some three-quarters of total rug output in Anatolia. At Uşak, production doubled in volume between the 1880s and the mid-1890s, and then increased by another one-third before reaching its peak in *c.* 1900 (tables 5.2 and 5.4). Rug making also increased at other established centers of production, for example at Gördes, where it more than doubled in volume between 1885 and 1902 (table 5.5). In addition, commercial rug making developed in hundreds of new locations. In the city of Sivas, for example, some 2,000 looms initiated commercial production in the late nineteenth century (table 5.6 and 5.7). Similarly, at Isparta, 800 looms were working in 1906, virtually all of them introduced not earlier than 1900 (table 5.7). According to one enumeration, there were at least 15,000 looms in commercial operation in Anatolia *c.* 1906 (table 5.7), as compared to perhaps 2,000 in the early 1880s.[9]

Table 5.3. *Uşak carpet prices, wages, working conditions and Anatolian wool
production, 1834–1914*

(piaster/pik) date rug price	(kg., million) wool prod.	(piasters) wages	(hours) workday knots/day
1834 10		12/wk[1]	
1852 23[2]			
1854 31[3]			
1867		1.5[4]	
1867	2.3		
1868	4.1		
1869	4.6[5]		
1873	3.9[6]		
1876 49[7]			
1881	0.8[8]		
1882 35–50[9]			
1883		18–21/wk[10]	
1890		1.5[11]	
1890		2.0[12]	
1892		2–3	10[13]
1896			5,500[14]
1900 70 "fine"			
1900 40–62 "normal"[15]		2–5	14+[16]
1900 50–55 *tek ilme*			
1900 37–45 *çift ilme*[17]			
1902		8	14[18]
1906		7–9[19]	
		3[20]	
1906 51–58 *tek ilme*			6,000
1906 40–46 *çift ilme*[21]			
1908		4–6[22]	
1914		11 max.	
		5.5 ave.[23]	
In the period of the early Turkish republic:			
at Isparta		9–12	6–8,000[24]
at Uşak			2.8–4,000[25]
generally		5–7	5–8,000[26]

1. Texier (1862), pp. 425–6; 10 piasters = 2 fr 70 c per sq. pik of 63 cm. of plush, that is, first
   quality.
2. CRUS for year ending 9/30/1872; price in 1872 per pik is nearly double the 1852 figure.
3. USNA T 238, 6/23/1854, "Turkey" carpet prices at İzmir 1/7/1853 to 6/30/1854.
4. Salaheddin (1867), p. 46.
5. USNA Film T238, 12/11/1869, Smyrna.
6. Scherzer (1873), p. 171.
7. A&P 1876, Smyrna, export price at İzmir.
8. İzmir annual wool export to Istanbul, 68,000 kg. BCF 1881, Smyrne 9/30/1881.
9. Titall in Scala (1882).
10. Dutemple (1883), p. 222.
11. Cuinet (1890–94), IV, p. 407.
12. US Special Consular Reports, I, 1890, p. 308.
13. Rougon (1892), p. 249; also see Stoeckel (1892), p. IV.
14. HHStA, Januar 1896; 550 knots per hour for ten hours a day.

15. Buhi 1904. "Normal" and "fine" Uşak qualities most probably are the same as the *tek ilme* and *çift ilme* grades.
16. k und k 1901, x, 4, Brussa.
17. k und k 1901, x, 4, Brussa; 121 piasters/Ottoman pound; *çift ilme* is the quality usually exported.
18. CRUS LXX 266, November 1902, p. 414.
19. US Monthly, September 1906, #12, pp. 129–30.
20. k und k 1906, x, 2, Smyrna.
21. Buhi 9, 1906, pp. 712–13. In 1907, Konya province provided Uşak with 100 tons of raw wool. GB AS 1907, #4009.
22. US Monthly Reports #339, December 1908, pp 126–27.
23. *Board of Trade Journal*, 5/28/1914, pp. 510–11.
24. Dirik (1938), p. 47.
25. Banaz (n.d.), p. 14.
26. Atalay (*c.* 1952), p. 54.

Table 5.4. *Carpet production at Uşak, 1873–1910*

	production		
date	piks	looms	loom workers
1873	150,000		3,000
1883	c. 170,000	600	3,500
1885		800–900	
1889	300,000		
1892	300,000	1,000	2,500
1896	446,000	950	8,500
1900	490,000	1,200	6,.000
1902		1,200	6,000
1906		2,000	4,250
1910	200,000	1,175	

Sources: see table in Quataert (1986), p. 477, from which this largely is derived. Also see *İkdam*, IV 2 1325.

This growth partially built on trends established in the preceding period and derived from a number of causes. On the supply side, the need for remittances to pay for imported European goods certainly played an important role in increasing rug production.[10] The merchants seeking to sell imports to cash-short Ottoman peasants found the means to do business in commercial carpet making. This reorientation, as seen below, was not merely an extension of the previous practice of occasionally knotting a rug for the market. The means of making carpets were modified drastically to meet foreign needs just as raw silk reeling had been brought from homes and workshops into factories (see chapter 4).[11] The importance of carpet making in facilitating the flow of imported goods certainly heightened during the 1860s–80s collapse of Ottoman silk production, when the cash income from silk suddenly was reduced. As disease struck and reelers and silk merchants lost their jobs and markets, carpet making awaited, offering new opportunities. There probably is a connection between the fall of

Table 5.5. *Carpet production at Gördes and Kula, 1885–1906*

	workers		looms		production (piks)	
	Gördes	*Kula*	*Gördes*	*Kula*	*Gördes*	*Kula*
1885					34,000	20,000
1890					33,000	3.8 mil. ptrs.
1892	2,000	1,500–2,000	600	500–600		
1902					73,000	20,000
1904	2,000	2,000	1,100	900		
1906	2,000	2,000	600	600		
1907					160,000	15,000

ptrs. = piasters

Sources: Georgiades (1885), p. 64; Cuinet (1890–94), III, p. 408; Rougon (1892), pp. 253–54; Buhi, III, 9, 1/17/1902; Buhi 1904, p. 291; Buhi, 9, 1906, p. 734. *Ikdam* IV 2 1325.

Table 5.6. *Sivas rug production, early twentieth century (millions of piasters)*

1900	2.0	(1.1 exports)
1900	2.6	
1900	3.6	plus 7.5 mil. in kilims
1901	2.9	plus 6.2 mil. in kilims
1902	2.7	
1906	2.9	

Sources: A&P 1901, 85, 6450, Anderson at Sivas; RCL 1900, Lettre de Sivas, p. 205; RCC, Sivas for 1901, Reel no. 34; Luckerts (1906), p. 32.

Ottoman silk reeling and the rise of carpet making during the third quarter of the nineteenth century. Other factors promoting rug making included the development of railroads, that accelerated the flow of materials (and merchants) in traditional centers such as Uşak and new ones that emerged late, for example, Konya. But, railroads never reached some carpet-making centers that boomed late in the period, such as Sivas, and so the impact of railroads on carpet production should not be overstressed.

Turning to demand, the domestic market probably was not the crucial element in the vast nineteenth-century expansion of the industry. During the 1860s and 1870s, Ottomans were using perhaps 10 percent of all rugs (and furniture fabrics) being produced in Anatolia.[12] Thereafter, the Ottoman population increased but there are no statistics regarding domestic rug consumption. In the mid-1890s, the emerging production center at Isparta began making one style primarily for sale within the empire, suggesting a domestic market of some

Table 5.7. *Profile of the Anatolian rug industry, c.* 1906

location	production (mil. ptrs.)	(piks)	no. of workers	no. of looms
Uşak	18.3	490,000	6,000	2,000
Gördes	6.2	80,000*	2,000	600
Kula	5.0		2,000	600
Demirci	2.5	45,000	1,000	400
Kütahya		80,000	150	30
Karahisar			200	40
Eskişehir			150	30
Sivas province	2.7			10,000
Ankara province	12.5			
Konya province	5.0	70,000		
Sille			600	150
Akşehir			150	30
Permata			250	55
Isparta			3,000	800
Burdur			100	20
Niğde			150	26
Bor			200	35
Ürgüp			100	18
Nevşehir			120	24
Konya city			100	18
Hereke	1.6		180	800

Source: Buhi, 9, 1906, table on p. 734. For another, less complete survey, see Buhi 1904, p. 291.

significance.[13] But, given the ongoing westernization of Ottoman tastes, an increase in per capita Ottoman rug consumption seems unlikely.

Far more significant on the demand side was the maturing industrialization in the West that brought in its train comparatively greater incomes and a rising consumerism. With more money to spend, Europeans and Americans adopted increasingly lavish tastes in furniture and home decoration, including a more extensive use of rugs. The growing gap between per-capita incomes in the Middle East and in the West generally rendered Ottoman manufactures more competitive and made rugs affordable to more Westerners than ever before. The rise in consumerism, for its part, was marked and spurred by the phenomenon of expositions and exhibitions, where the proliferating goods were seen, admired and, later, bought. The Crystal Palace Exhibition at London in 1851 displayed Ottoman rugs as well as wool yarn, flatweaves and silks. Rugs similarly appeared in the Paris Exposition of 1855, and later exhibitions such as those at London in 1862, İstanbul in 1863 and Vienna in 1891. The rugs of Anatolia also played a part in the American Centennial Exhibition of 1876. These and other expositions helped teach the European and American middle and then working classes to want "Oriental" rugs. As the nineteenth century wore on, these rugs became a familiar part of everyday life in the United States and Western Europe. Foreign demand seemed insatiable and merchants and producers in the Ottoman Empire (as well as in Qajar Iran) scrambled to meet the need.

The particular nature of the rugs shaped the industry in a singular way. The appeal lay in their quality as hand-made goods, in the Westerners' perception that each rug was a singular object, unlike any other, no matter how many there might be in the marketplace. The rugs were an escape from the mounting tedium of western industrial life, with its growing standardization and endless array of identical mass-produced goods.

In the course of the century, therefore, nearly everything about rug production changed except for the knotting stage itself. Designs shifted back and forth according to the tastes of buyers in Hamburg, London or Buffalo. The wool yarn finally became machine-spun to relieve labor shortages although merchants remained unhappy with the result. Artificial and synthetic dyestuffs were adopted, rejected and re-adopted while merchants sought to centralize the dyeing process. The knotting of rugs increasingly moved from the household to the workshop. But through all these changes there was one constant – the loom. There seems to have been only one change in the final production phase, that occurred near the end of the period, in the era of greatest demand. A trident-like device was invented that permitted warp threads to be made in multiples of three to five, substantially raising productivity.[14] Descriptions of the loom otherwise are remarkably similar between 1800 and 1914. The Ottoman rug remained hand-made, but barely so.

Changing rug designs

As is well known, each of the various traditional centers – Uşak, Gördes, Kula – originally produced its own distinctive style of rugs, at least so goes the theory in art history.[15] A decisive stylistic change occurred towards the end of the first quarter of the nineteenth century. Until then, a wider variety of colors was used, including reds, blues, greens, brown, buff, yellow, black, bright orange-red and cream. Thereafter, the range of colors in the standard thick pile rug was reduced "rarely embracing more than two tones of red, two of blue, and one tone of green."[16] One may look to the designs as an index of the industry in responding to its foreign customers' needs. Made-to-order rugs of *any* design, however bizarre or weird, were commonplace, made with the help of patterns, the so-called "cartoons" that could be either photographs or drawings, schematic and otherwise. Art historians know this to be the case for the famous Hereke factory, where carpet making was taken up late in the nineteenth century. The factory never developed or possessed its own style of rugs. Instead, it made rugs only on specific order, sometimes following pictures torn from European magazines, or one of the photographs kept in an album containing pictures of several dozen rugs, many of them Persian, including the famed Ardebil rugs.[17] Made-to-order rugs also were commonplace at Uşak and many other Anatolian locations. Perhaps it is best to begin with an example from the late 1860s, when Uşak knotters made a rug "for a gentleman of Smyrna, the centre of which represented the arms of Italy."[18] In an early twentieth-century rug book, there is an illustration of a silk rug produced in Kayseri. Entitled a "Bird's eye view of Paris," the scene depicts the City of Light complete with the winding Seine and the Eiffel tower.[19] Knotted copies of European oil paintings were relatively common, including motifs from the Louis XV epoch. The French painter Watteau seems to have been a particularly popular subject, for we find copies of his works being knotted in both Anatolia and Iran during the early twentieth century.[20]

Uşak made great quantities of rugs from patterns supplied by European or American dealers. A participant's eyewitness account describes how the "cartoon" system worked at Uşak in the early twentieth century. The agent in Europe would send a design or photograph, sometimes requesting that up to three identical rugs be woven from the "cartoon." The İzmir agent receiving the order either gave the picture to his own artists or sent it to a merchant in Uşak. Once in Uşak, the picture was distributed to the knotters. Artist copying was seen as a very profitable business in Uşak, at least by the author of this account, who drew when he was 18–19 years old.[21] By c. 1900, artists usually prepared the patterns in Europe according to old Turkish designs and merchants gave them to the producers.[22] At Isparta, knotters made high-quality rugs from "scale paper patterns," but the end result was a product "much like European or American machine-made goods."[23]

Knotters mainly worked from memory, sometimes aided by referring to Turkish designs or Persian imitations that families passed down for generations.[24] Pictures and patterns commonly were used to introduce knotters to new designs or styles. In such cases, an expert worker received the pattern from which she made a model for distribution to the other women who made the rug. These women used the reverse side of the model to mark the pattern that they followed when knotting.[25] At Uşak, distortions often resulted. The pictures frequently were not to scale and the knotter made the adjustments as she worked. This practice was replaced in the early twentieth century by the Oriental Carpet Manufacturers, a trust that came to dominate the industry. The firm deskilled the craft by providing proportionately drawn patterns for knotters.[26] As production mounted and brought in new workers, it became very difficult to recapture the old schemes; and so the better carpets were made using drawn patterns.[27]

It does seem that pictures and patterns became more common as new and less-skilled workers were brought in to knot rugs. But the use of patterns and pictures was hardly a late nineteenth-century innovation, as the earlier-mentioned arms of Italy example makes clear. Also, in 1852, a government inspector had visited Uşak and made a series of recommendations to develop the carpet industry, among them the abandonment of old designs in favor of new ones. Knotters working for the Uşak merchants, he said, should be given printed pictures of new patterns. The inspector himself distributed instructions and pictures to various workshops in Uşak, an action that greatly improved designs, he said.[28]

Over the century, the industry waxed hot and cold over whether traditional or modern designs should prevail. While the inspector favored new ones, the industry generally remained divided. Trends variously shifted in favor of, then against, modern or traditional styles. In the 1860s, for example, the merchant house of Schiffmann at Uşak successfully introduced "modern" designs (of an undisclosed nature) to local makers. But his competitor and one of the major merchants in the town, Hacı Ali Efendi, focused on making antique designs that were more popular with the crowds who saw them at the İstanbul Exhibition of 1863.[29] At about this time, a new Uşak pattern came into existence, created specifically for the American market. Called Zarif Ali, these rugs had very deep colors such as bordeaux red and blue.[30] During the 1870s, new designs and garish colors were replacing tested Turkish patterns, to the supposed endangerment of the industry.[31] Simultaneously, other merchants actively promoted the making of antique Persian designs at Uşak.[32] During the 1890s, similarly, modern designs using so-called "Oriental" motifs, but with brighter and more striking colors, appeared. An 1896 source tells of the abandonment of efforts to imitate European floral patterns and other models.[33]

Extension of production into new villages, towns and cities meant the blurring of regional distinctions in design, a trend already advanced by the 1870s. So-called "Uşak" rugs in fact were being produced at many different locations outside of the Uşak region.[34] "Persian" rugs were made in Uşak and elsewhere in Anatolia. A 1904 rug book speaks of Turkish Kirmans, fine Uşak rugs of Persian design, a practice already at least three decades old in the town. At Sivas in the early twentieth century, the Aliotti merchant house, working with the Spartali firm, directed the making of large, high-quality Persian-style rugs.[35] Konya producers were then imitating Uşak rugs; Akhisar knotters made rugs similar to the Gördes rug; and Kırşehir workers produced a mix of Arabian and Persian forms.[36] In the Niğde region, where knotting flourished under the direction of the Greek and Armenian churches, a variety of patterns coexisted. Some were "frighteningly ugly," based on outdated and "terrible" European tastes. To counter-act this tendency, a government official at Nevşehir took old carpets from the mosques and distributed them among the knotters so they could imitate the old designs.[37]

Dyestuffs

Towards mid-century, professional dyers monopolized the work at Uşak (but not all Anatolian locations). There were independent dyers, who reportedly produced fugitive colors, but rug merchants owned most dyehouses where the workers were considered to be exceptionally skilled. These dye masters had surprising skills that they had learned on the job and could make colors exactly matching those already in a rug. There were separate recipes (*tarifname*) for each color and the formula was written under a yarn sample attached to a somewhat large notebook.[38]

Changing rug designs had an important impact on dyestuff usage and both dramatically were affected by the revolutions in the European chemical industry. As seen, local Ottoman sources had supplied most dyestuffs from nature while indigo came from abroad, at first from India and then the New World. Cochineal from the Western Hemisphere first entered Anatolia as a competitor of the madder root in 1840, to the dismay of some rug merchants who found its purplish-red color too harsh.[39] Then came the synthetic and coal tar dyes, that rug makers almost immediately adopted. The availability and cheapness of these artificial and substitute dyestuffs added to the confusion caused by rising production during the earlier part of the nineteenth century. The quality of dyeing at Uşak c. 1850 already was being questioned. Whether this was due to falling standards or demands for different fashion colors is not clear. The government inspector charged to increase production found the colors (and designs) to be old-fashioned. Most local dyes, he asserted in 1852, were not fast and he recommended adoption of inexpensive chemical dyes. Turning to mechanization, he weighed the several sides of the issue. Factories could meet any increased demand, he said. Coal was not locally available; thus steam engines were out of the question although water power could be used. But since mechanized factories would create widespread unemployment among local rugmakers, he advised against their foundation. He insisted, however, on the need for chemical dyes.

If fast and bright dyes are used to dye the yarn, and if care is taken so that the designs used are continuously changed, it [a rug] will be cheap to make and demand will increase.[40]

Problems of mechanization and dyeing appear again in an 1868 report that discussed rising production in response to foreign demand.

[I]t is to be regretted, however, that the introduction of European machinery and the use of inferior dyes in their manufacture has greatly tended to deteriorate their quality.[41]

The new synthetic and artificial dyes had serious disadvantages for rug makers. Peasant dyers could not read the labels and sometimes used the dyes without mordants, producing a quickly fading color. The colors could be very poor and unstable, especially in the case of the anilines, if handled incorrectly. But, nonetheless, there were numerous advantages to using chemical dyes. Many in the rug trade believed that only these dyes could meet European and American fashion demands. The colors required variously were described as sparkling, or deeply rich and contrasting (as opposed to light and pale) and livelier.[42] In addition to serving fashion needs, the new dyes avoided the labor-intensive preparation of natural dyestuffs, a problem that became increasingly critical as rug production boomed in labor-scarce Anatolia. Artificial dyes avoided many other problems associated with the natural materials. For example, although quality red dyes required the use of six-year-old madder roots, many mixed in plants that were only one–three years old, producing inferior dye.[43] Also, these new dyes, particularly anilines, were far cheaper than natural dyestuffs. And, finally, since the aniline dyes were much easier to use, they offered a way to circumvent professional dyers, reduce labor costs, and rapidly expand production.

The German manufacturers either visit the district personally or send their agents, who penetrate into the chief centres of the interior where carpets are manufactured, show their dyes to our men and teach them how to employ them.[44]

And so, makers quickly and widely adopted both synthetics and anilines. For a while, aniline usage proliferated willy-nilly and seemed to be totally displacing natural dyes.[45] A see-saw struggle developed as some merchants promoted while others opposed anilines. Some certainly changed their minds as the negative consequences became more apparent. The struggle among natural, aniline and synthetic dyestuffs never was resolved conclusively in the rug industry as a whole or even in a particular location. The situation was very confused: as producers in one region were adopting the anilines, others were discarding them.

In the early 1870s, some makers used the new dyes to create popular designs and "sparkling colors."[46] Overall, these dyes seem to have been adopted most enthusiastically during the third decade of the century.[47] Uşak makers, according to one source, employed natural dyes until the 1890s when they finally succumbed and adopted anilines on a widespread basis. By *c.* 1900, according to one long-time Uşak resident and worker in the rug industry, Uşak workshops were dyeing with aniline.[48] But another eyewitness, a European, who visited the town in 1891, places aniline adoption at a somewhat earlier date. There were eight large and continuously busy dyeworks in the town, he said. "The coal-tar colours are therefore now largely used and are imported from Germany and France." First, he said, they were used to supplement the vegetable dyes but they quickly became the only dyes employed. The advantages, he said, were their simplicity of use and ability to provide modern colors. People "demand elaborate designs, rich assortment of colours, and brilliant shades, which can readily be got," he stated, with the anilines.[49] While the Uşak dyers thus appear to have switched over to anilines and synthetics by the early 1890s, they prevented outsiders from taking over their business. An İzmir rug merchant with a big American trade had founded a steam dyeing establishment to corner the trade, intending to use chemical dyes to color all the wools for the industry. But, before 1900, he gave up the effort.[50] At Kula, by *c.* 1900, the secret dye recipes

have not been merely superseded by the introduction of European aniline dyes, but are even said to have already completely passed out of knowledge.

This was not entirely true since some Kula producers maintained use of vegetable dyes; but generally they were abandoned.[51] In other areas, in the early twentieth century, some İzmir merchants placed their orders with knotters, supplying both patterns and aniline-dyed wool. Konya producers, in 1903, reportedly had abandoned anilines and returned to vegetable dyes but, four years later, they chiefly used chemical colors.[52] Several other accounts add that makers also obtained fashion colors in the 1890s by mixing natural dyes with one another. Some used only vegetable dyes for the finer rugs while others used the various synthetics as well; and aniline dyes were used for lower-quality rugs.[53] Makers still employed cochineal, for example, in the İzmir area during the mid-1890s, but red aniline, that faded, was found in the most common rugs.[54]

As their use expanded, knowledge of the shortcomings of anilines – their fugitive colors – became more apparent and well-known. Warnings and efforts to resume the employ of natural dyestuffs mounted. Already in 1878, for example, a London-based rug firm successfully reintroduced

the old colours ... to local dyers [who] had lost the art of extracting the various colouring matters from the native dye-stuffs.[55]

In 1888, the governor of Aydın province prohibited the use of anilines but the decree was rescinded after pressure by British merchants in İzmir.[56] The newly developing carpet industry in Sivas suffered terribly, one local observer complained, because it relied completely on anilines that produced a shockingly poor product.[57] Anilines helped merchants to obtain very cheap carpets for the low end of the market, especially during the early twentieth century.

This marked increase [in British imports of carpets] is accounted for by the greater cheapness of oriental carpets, which no longer confines their use to the rich...[58]

This trend continued until the outbreak of World War I. "It is noteworthy that the increase is greatest in the cheaper grades of carpets."[59]

By the turn of the century, many Ottoman and European merchants, dyers and officials were mounting a sustained campaign to improve production standards and focused primarily on the dyes. Aniline usage continued to mount but natural dyestuffs and the better quality synthetics made a comeback. There are indications that sales of Anatolian rugs faltered briefly c. 1900 in favor of Persian rugs. Some were too shoddily made and drove away customers.[60] The İzmir carpet firms established their own dye centers using madder root and cochineal for reds, indigo for blue, yellow berry and saffron for yellows. One large İzmir carpet house (Aliotti in cooperation with Spartali) opened a knotting factory in Sivas and sought to imitate old plant dyes and their pale tones, hiring a dye expert from Italy for the purpose.[61] The İzmir merchants generally hired European dyers to employ French and German alizarin at Uşak, Gördes, Kula and Demirci. In the early twentieth century, a number of İzmir export firms formed a close ring that fined any member who brought in aniline dyes.[62] In part, the merchants were warring against their own past practices and sometimes against the policies of their agents in the interior. These agents earned much, probably most, of their income by compelling loom owners to use their dye-houses, where cheap and inferior chemical dyes had come to prevail.[63] Joining the chorus, the organizers of the 1909 Industrial and Agricultural Exhibition at Bursa warned that most rugs were being made very quickly, with the cheapest kinds of aniline dyes that faded in a year. To solve the problem, they called for the use of synthetic alizarin rather than aniline.[64]

The formation of the Oriental Carpet Manufacturers in 1907, by a number of İzmir merchant houses, was a part of this general effort during the early twentieth century to control production standards. Founding members included both the big rug merchants and a number of wool dyers.[65] To improve dyeing quality, the company operated a model dyehouse in İzmir, directed by European chemists. It seems clear that high quality synthetics were employed[66] although only vegetable dyes reportedly were used.[67] The company generally is credited with raising dyeing standards.[68]

Wool yarn

The carpet industry relied mainly on Ottoman-made wool yarn but also used other materials such as cotton yarn, hemp and silk. Thus, in the new workshops at Sivas, they employed cotton in both the warp and the weft and linen in the weft. The Kula industry was using hemp for the warp in 1906. The substitution of cotton for wool mounted in the early twentieth century, when demand pressures were sharply increasing raw wool prices. Thus, we find cotton in the weft of rugs from the city of Kayseri in 1906, and in the warp of some from Gördes, Demirci and sometimes Isparta.[69]

Throughout the period *c.* 1830–1914, the Anatolian rug industry received its supplies of wool exclusively from domestic sources, notably the Kastamonu area on the Black Sea and the interior regions of Konya and Ankara.[70] Some rug-making families obtained the wool from their own sheep and personally carried out all the necessary steps – washing, drying, separating, cleaning, carding, sorting – prior to the actual spinning. This remained true for commercial carpetmakers at Sivas and Ankara into the twentieth century. There, the knotters sold their rugs to travelling Armenian buyers or to merchants in nearby towns, often, it was said, for the market price of the prepared wool alone.[71] At other locations, notably Uşak, a more elaborate system was employed, with connections to the nomadic animal raisers of the high plateau. Nomads sheared the wool and sold it to merchants who had extended them credit and who often travelled to the great market center of Sivrihisar, located in the middle of the high plateau.[72] Buying of the wool occurred in the early spring at Sivrihisar and was over after the second shearing, at the end of March or early April. The merchants arranged for delivery to villagers around Uşak who cleaned and washed and spun the wool for a fee, probably on a piece-work basis. At Uşak, agents of İzmir buyers and exporters rather than loom operators usually purchased the prepared yarn.[73] During the 1880s, Uşak-area spinners annually used 600,000 kg. of raw wool, that yielded about one-half that amount of spun wool.[74] In 1906, the town annually required up to 2.9 million kg. of raw wool while the industry altogether used *c*. 5.1 million kg.[75] In good years, the carpet industry overall required up to 80 percent of Anatolian wool production.[76] Wool exports thus fell sharply because of expanded rug output and wool prices rose accordingly, from 3.2 to 8.3 piasters/kg.[77] At the end of the period, the carpet industry was said to be faltering because of high prices for wool and the low quality of the rugs.[78]

Over the century, mounting demand for carpets had produced considerable pressure to mechanize the labor-intensive yet unremunerative task of spinning wool yarn. In the middle 1840s, several merchants, Hacı Mehmet Ağa and Gördesli Ahmet Ağa, with the help of the Uşak judge (*kadı*), Acemoğlu Ali Ağa, acted to promote Uşak and Gördes carpet production. They sought government loans to import (unspecified kinds of) machinery from Europe.[79] Mechanized wool spinning offered a way to circumvent the problem of a limited labor force and increasing demand. Machine production of wool yarn for carpet making however, was problematic.

The advantage of a hand-twisted yarn is that the tufts of the carpet blend together in the process of wear, forming a grand harmonious whole.[80]

In addition, machine-spun wool yarn of the period often was too stiff for the knotters to handle and simply could not be used. For much of the century, available technology was unable to produce wool yarn suitable for hand knotting. Thus, spinning machinery adopted at Uşak *c*. 1880 was abandoned because "the result was eminently unsatisfactory."[81] In addition, Uşak-area hand spinners mobilized in defense of their jobs. A few years after this failed effort to mechanize, two capitalists sought to build a spinning factory for carpet yarn but were prevented by the government after protests of the "inhabitants."[82] In the late nineteenth century, however, the technology became available to machine-make a spun wool more suitable to hand knotting. Factories quickly proliferated and, by 1905, machine spinning essentially had replaced hand-spun wool. At

Uşak, three consortia of Muslim rug merchants established the wool spinning factories, as early as 1895, followed by two others in the first years of the new century.[83] One of the entrepreneurs was Tiritoğlu Mehmet. Born of a poor family, he made his fortune from carpets, dyes and the factory and came to rival the town elites.[84] At nearly the same time, in 1902, an Englishman (Sykes) cooperated with several Bosnians to build the largest of the factories, at the port town of Bandırma. This mill came to play the leading role in supplying Ottoman knotters, except for those at Uşak. In 1907, it provided 84 percent of all the yarn used in fourteen rug making centers in west and central Anatolia. At Uşak, however, the factory furnished just 2 percent of the yarn consumed.[85] Other mechanized mills included two at İzmir, one founded by an independent competitor of the Oriental Carpet Manufacturers. This was the Blackler Spinning Company, founded in 1910, that employed 100 workers and daily produced 700 kg. of wool yarn.[86] Hacı Halilağazadeler established the other mill at İzmir while Çolakzadeler founded one at Kula.[87] A small spinning mill opened in Eskişehir at this time, re-spinning carpet remains into thread, apparently for use in making textiles, not rugs. The opening of this factory, using the wastes of the rug industry, suggests how significant an activity carpet making had become.[88]

Despite these successes, machine spinning remained plagued by technological and social problems. Much of the factory-made yarn in 1909 was too dirty since it had not been properly cleansed before combing. Also, combing on cylinders crushed and broke the fibers. The resulting yarn was short, weak and oily and the dyes could not penetrate it as needed. The Oriental Carpet Manufacturers allegedly was at fault since its agents made contracts to knot with the factory-made yarn and dye with fugitive mineral dyes.[89] The social problem involved Uşak-area hand spinners who, since the 1880s, had mobilized to block factory formation. During several days in mid-March 1908, crowds sacked the three factories, destroying the engine rooms and carrying off the wool. They had begun by listening to the Friday sermon in the mosque and then, in a well-organized fashion, marched on the factories. Egged on by competitors of the consortia that had built the mills (they were especially concerned about the rise of Tiritoğlu Mehmet), and by members of the Young Turk revolutionary underground, the hand spinners were protesting the loss of jobs that factories caused.[90] The rioters included the nearby villagers who hand-made the yarn and nomads (*yürüks*) who made the warp, and also residents of the small town of Gediz (some 40 km. away) who spun the weft.[91]

Diffusion of rug making

In the early nineteenth century, commercial rug making on any scale was confined to western Anatolia, mainly to the towns of Uşak, Kula and Gördes. In these and a few other locations, such as the small village of Saruhan near İzmir, the industry already had turned towards market production. At Uşak in the 1860s, for example, a single merchant house reportedly controlled 300 looms, some exceptionally large, up to seven meters in width![92] From these few centers, carpet making spread to hundreds of other locations – villages, towns and cities – in western, central and, finally, eastern Anatolia.

The initiators of this diffusion were many and the process varied considerably. Sometimes government officials played the critical role. But, without question, the major agents were the merchant houses, primarily those of İzmir and also of İstanbul. Turkish Muslim firms independent of these houses, notably at Uşak, also played an important role. Most of the recorded activities are of foreigners while one of the few Ottoman houses for which we have information entered the rug trade at Uşak in 1772. By 1900, some 90 percent of the İzmir rug trade had concentrated in six merchant houses. In rank order, the most important were the firms of Spartali and Co.; P. de Andria and Co.; and Sydney LaFontaine. Next came the house of W. Griffith and that of Partridge, followed by that of Habib and Polako.[93] Three firms – de Andria, Habib and Polako, and Spartali – had been operating in İzmir since the late 1830s. The American Blackler family, involved in the Partridge firm, also had been in the İzmir carpet trade since the 1830s.[94] The İstanbul houses, by contrast, largely had remained aloof, focusing instead on the trade in carpets from Iran. At the very end of the century, however, some İstanbul houses entered the Anatolian industry, with momentous consequences that will be seen below.

A unique type of diffusion took place *c.* 1880, when a fire devastated the town of Demirci, until then "unknown in the rug trade." The majority of this community of 20,000 were left homeless and desperate. Some hundreds of them went to Gördes, which possessed a well-established carpet industry. They learned the trade, returned home, and taught their fellow townsmen. Skilled dyers were attracted to Demirci, found water of "a good solvent quality" and opened shops.[95]

Kütahya knotters, for their part, learned their craft from Uşak artisans *c.* 1889–94 and reportedly surpassed their teachers in quality. The source of this initiative probably was the İzmir-based English merchant Sykes, whose factory later supplied the town with wool yarn.[96] In several locations, missionaries set up rug-making operations. At Urfa, a German charitable organization formed a carpet "factory" while, at Harput, American capital set up the rug industry, directed by an Ottoman subject (certainly Armenian) who had trained in U.S. carpet factories. Using cheap or free labor from the American orphanages in the area, the industry not surprisingly focused on the U.S. market. A missionary-sponsored rug workshop, employing 600–700 girls and women, seems to have operated at Aleppo.[97]

The memoirs of an Ottoman official-cum-entrepreneur from Isparta vibrantly illustrates the pitfalls and difficulties of the diffusion process. The official tells how, in 1888, he travelled to the ancient rug making village of Ladik, near Konya, to examine *seccade* carpets, with coats of arms, that he had commissioned. Inspired, he sought to develop the industry in the village of Subran, near his home town of Isparta. Enduring local ridicule, he hired a woman from the rug center of Kırşehir, allegedly after overcoming his fear that she was too old. He then applied for the services of a master (dyer probably) from the Feshane factory in İstanbul. Failing that, he sent an agent to Uşak but the entrepreneur Tiritoğlu Mehmet Pasha prevented the man from learning any craft secrets. The storyteller, in 1891, then set up a small joint stock company with another local official. They opened workshops, spun wool by hand, used chemical and natural dyes and sent their *seccade* rugs to İzmir. They sought to bypass the İzmir merchant houses and deal directly with London but their marketing connections, and probably their capital, were inadequate. The venture collapsed and the company was dissolved. Some local Greeks at Isparta then tried their hand, but also failed. The town finally became a production center in *c.* 1908, when an Isparta Armenian living in İzmir opened a branch of the Oriental Carpet Manufacturers.[98]

The changing carpet industry in the Sivas region derived from a combination of state and merchant effort. Until *c.* 1890, rugs were made solely in the countryside around the town of Sivas. The governor then introduced Khurasanian and Persian designs and established 300 looms, dispersed in the town of Sivas itself. These rugs were different in color and design and were far finer, with twice as many knots per square unit (pik), than the country rugs.[99] Three Armenians in 1900 formed a company to mass produce rugs and they set up a 20-loom workshop in the town with 80 workers. The young Armenian who managed the operation had worked in the carpet business in the United States.[100] At the same time, an agent of an İzmir merchant house (perhaps the Aliotti firm) arrived to buy rugs for export but found Sivas designs and colors unacceptable. Therefore, he sought to bring the scattered rug makers of the town together and furnish them with designs and colors provided by a master dyer. In exchange for this, for advances and for a guaranteed market, he required "a reasonable and necessary lowering" of the workers' wages.[101] Just two years later, there were as many as 2,000 looms working in the city. The İzmir house of Aliotti, in cooperation with the Spartali firm, now was doing business in the area and was credited for the vast increase in the number of looms. They had installed some "grand workshops" in Sivas with nearly 1,000 female workers, making rugs that rivalled the better Persian grades. In 1911, rug factories in this town employed "many thousand little [Armenian] girls;" in addition, there were a large number of home looms.[102] Outside the city, 350 villages in the Sivas region reportedly held 10,000 looms (table 5.7).[103] The Sivas rug industry was seen to be prosperous and expanding, now under the control of the Oriental Carpet Manufacturers.[104]

In the city of Konya, as in Sivas, state officials and merchants both worked to develop the industry. But while İzmir merchants played the key role in Sivas, İstanbul merchants made the initial efforts at Konya. A European named Keun played an early and important role. He had resided in Konya since 1887, first as representative of the Ottoman Bank. By 1897, when he was British vice-consul, Keun had developed the local rug industry; to some extent it was located in the city of Konya but mainly it centered in the village of Sille, one hour away, where he had established a workshop (*fabrique*).[105] As agent of the Giustiniani firm located in İstanbul, Keun developed an extensive network making good quality rugs. In 1900, looms under his control produced 20,000 meters, worth 2.2 million piasters.[106] To provide high-quality models to an already-growing industry, the local governor held a forty-day rug exhibition in the provincial capital in 1900, displaying old carpets of earlier centuries next to modern Anatolian ones. A few years later, the government established a school of arts and crafts at Konya in order to increase the number of carpet looms. Local authorities at Kırşehir, that in centuries past had been an important center, aggressively promoted the industry. In 1900, they were planning an exposition of the best modern rugs and, in 1902, instituted a quality control system, requiring each locally made carpet to have a city trademark, in the form of a lead seal, attesting to a certain standard of design, workmanship and color.[107] By 1906, Konya province held some 1,200 looms with 5,000 knotters (table 5.7) an industry that was growing rapidly, thanks to the efforts of the Giustiniani house and other firms based in İstanbul.[108]

Here, it seems, is a key for understanding the emergence of the Oriental Carpet Manufacturers. The Keun/Giustiniani program in the Konya region was part of a larger effort mounted by İstanbul merchant houses. Beginning in 1897, these houses quickly succeeded in forming a vast home industry network in the interior, aimed at the export market.[109] The İstanbul merchants' actions in turn were part of a larger challenge to the ambitions of the İzmir-based firms. The three consortia of Uşak Muslim rug merchants who founded the wool spinning mills in that town similarly threatened the position of the İzmir houses. The situation was critical for the İzmir merchants. The international market was huge and booming and the demand for rugs seemed insatiable as prices continued to drop. The struggle was among the İzmir, İstanbul and Uşak merchants over who would control and benefit from the boom. To consolidate and enhance their hold over this expanding market, most of the important İzmir rug merchants banded together to found the Oriental Carpet Manufacturers. The Uşak merchant/manufacturers survived this onslaught and remained prominent in the industry well into the period of the Turkish republic. But the İstanbul firms succumbed completely to the Oriental Carpet Manufacturers. In its first year of operations, the trust triumphed in Konya.

The carpets go to Smyrna, where the trade is in the hands of a newly formed syndicate of carpet manufacturers, all opposition to them having broken down.[110]

By 1912, the province of Konya held some 4,000 looms with 15,000–20,000 working girls, more than three times the number just a few years earlier. The great part belonged to the Oriental Carpet Manufacturers as the İstanbul presence vanished.[111]

The famed factory at Hereke entered the rug industry as a part of the general diffusion of rugmaking in the late nineteenth century. It seems likely that there were several false starts, as early as the 1840s and again in 1862.[112] These were followed by several more successful efforts. In 1891, artisans from several locations were summoned to introduce new designs. The weavers variously are said to have come from Manisa and Sivas as well as Gördes, Demirci and Kirman (in Persia). Since Manisa and Sivas were not yet important in the industry, this attribution probably is incorrect.[113] Other accounts, likely accurate, attribute Hereke rug production to the migration, in *c.* 1888, of a family of Uşak weavers. By 1900, rugmaking had taken hold and Hereke knotters were receiving their yarn from a Karamürsel factory. A German-trained dyer, working in a factory setting, colored the yarn using alizarin but not aniline dyes.[114]

Working conditions, the workforce and the division of labor

Rug output increases in the nineteenth century sparked sweeping changes in the nature of work as well as in the structure and composition of the workforce. At Uşak, the industry reached out to neighboring communities, profoundly affecting the pattern of their lives. Some villagers in Banaz sub-district (*nahiye*), for example, abandoned agriculture in favor of a more reliable income from hauling wood off Murat Mountain to the dyehouses of Uşak. Other villagers on the Banaz plain made the looms, some of them very large. Their pace of life and work must have changed radically when the number of looms in the town doubled in two decades. The changes at Uşak, with a late-nineteenth-century population of *c.* 13,000, seem to have been extraordinary, particularly in the decades after 1870. When the river running through the town proved inadequate for the washing and dyeing needs of the booming industry, Uşak merchants raised 200,000 piasters and diverted part of the Banaz stream, some 2.5 hours away.[115] During this era of intense change, men joined women in spinning yarn, the number of knotters tripled, yarn factories were founded and the women even began knotting at night, with kerosene lamps like miners' lights. A railroad came to town while an industrial work force of several thousands went to work in the new mills.[116]

As it adapted at Uşak, Kula and Gördes, the industry radiated outwards into new regions. There, a workforce of another religion and ethnicity was more poorly paid and labored under conditions strikingly different than in the traditional centers. In part, the new centers emerged because Uşak's limited population could not satisfy the demand for carpets. But the diffusion mainly occurred because the Uşak community resisted merchant pressures to lower wages and more fully regiment and control the production processes. And so, merchants developed the industry in other regions of Anatolia, finding and molding a more pliable and poorly paid labor force.

Because rugs were very profitable, the Oriental Carpet Company that was established sought to establish carpet making in locations [outside Uşak] where the workers would work for less money.[117]

As a result of these actions, the relative importance of Uşak fell. In the 1870s and 1880s, the town provided some three-quarters of all rugs exported from İzmir. Thanks to the efforts of the İstanbul merchants and then the Oriental Carpet Manufacturers, Uşak knotters, *c* . 1910, accounted for as little as one-quarter of total Anatolian rug output (table 5.2).

The trend in wages for knotters and prices for completed rugs suggests that both workers and merchants fared best during the early part of the period. In "recent years," said an 1870s source, rug prices had risen some 40 percent. Certain lower-quality Uşak rugs increased some 50 percent in price while, in the 1860s alone, some of the higher grades rose one-fifth in price (table 5.3).[118] Overall, between the 1830s and 1880s, prices for some grades of Uşak rugs increased three- to five-fold while knotters' nominal wages doubled. Thereafter, the picture became less rosy. Between 1882 and *c*. 1900, carpet prices perhaps climbed slightly; thereafter, they remained steady through the first decade of the new century. Knotters' wages at Uşak remained unchanged after 1882 while, in new production areas, lower wage scales prevailed and remained stable. Several conclusions emerge from this brief survey of prices and wages. First, the importance of the value of the labor input decreased over time as carpet prices improved relative to knotting wages. Second, knotters' real wages fell during the general price rise after 1896 and perhaps were declining as early as the 1880s. Third, merchants suffered from stagnating prices in the post-1896 period of general price inflation, when most commodity prices were rising. Similar to their sisters in silk reeling, carpet knotters were mired in a low-wage industry with declining real wages at the end of the period. As in the case of the silk-mill operators, the rug merchants competed by freezing or reducing wages. And, just as silk mills proliferated outside the town of Bursa late in the century, rug merchants found more vulnerable and cheaper labor sources outside of Uşak.

As the industry expanded, the ethnic and religious makeup of the work force became substantially more mixed although the relative proportions remain uncertain. Workers at the Hereke mill included both Greek and Turkish girls, each group with its own dormitory. But, since this was a state-run operation, we should not generalize from the composition of this particular workforce.[119] According to one post-war report, a full 85 percent of the enumerated Ottoman rug-making workforce had been Muslim. This count, however, included only 24,000 workers and we know that there were at least twice that many in the industry as a whole.[120] Nor can we draw any conclusions from the post-World War I emergence of Greece and Egypt as more important rug producers than republican Turkey, thanks to the arrival of Greek and Armenian refugees from Anatolia. It is not simply that the post-war industry in Anatolia collapsed because Christians had been the majority of the labor force and they had disappeared. The wartime devastation of Anatolia between 1914 and 1923 played an important role, crippling the industry for a time. Furthermore, since rug making there did recover,[121] a body of skilled workers must have been locally available. Overall, Ottoman Muslim Turks tended to dominate the workforce in older production centers. At the established centers of Uşak, Kula and Gördes – that all had strong Muslim majorities – the rug workers overwhelmingly had been Muslim Turks.[122] And, the Turkish Muslim majority persisted in the industries of these towns as they expanded. But, the ethnic-religious pattern elsewhere differed significantly. In the newer centers, the rug merchants and agents – who largely were either foreigners, Ottoman Greeks or Armenians – recruited from the local Christian population. For example, the three Armenians who set up the knotters' network in Sivas *c.* 1900 (probably) found their workers within the local Armenian community and may well have been aided by Church authorities.[123] Christian Armenians and Greeks were more important, likely the majority of the workforce, in the newer centers.

Several general statements seem applicable to the workforce and the nature of labor. First, girls and women were and remained the vast majority of the weavers. Second, the division of labor became more pronounced as commercial production advanced over the century. And, third, the household diminished in relative importance as the site of carpet making as merchants imposed more control over production. Workshops became more important in knotting while factory increasingly replaced both workshop and household labor in the spinning and dyeing phases of production. Behind these statements about change, however, lie rich and complex realities about continuity. In many areas, notably at Uşak, households remained the usual setting for the manufacture of carpets. And, when change was the norm, there were many different kinds of adaptations as well as multiple exceptions to the generalizations.

The organization of production varied considerably from place to place and over time. Among nomads and in countless villages offering the occasional rug for sale, the family together or a single person, usually the mother/wife, performed all tasks associated with rugmaking. In villages around Sivas *c.* 1900, for example, the woman washed, carded, spun and dyed the wool, after either buying the dyes from a peddler or making the dye herself, and then knotted the rug.[124]

In commercial production, the division of labor varied considerably and became increasingly refined in many locations. For most of the century, men at Uşak had washed and dried the wool and turned it over to women for combing and spinning. They mainly spun by hand, during virtually every moment of their "spare" time. Villagers around Uşak, as we have seen, provided much of the yarn, spinning with wheels as well as by hand.[125] Much yarn likely was contracted by agents of the merchants. But, through the mid-1880s at least, a local market also existed for the yarn to which buyers and sellers flocked every Thursday.[126] Some gender switching of tasks occurred during the mid-1890s when men at Uşak briefly took over at least some of the yarn spinning to free women for knotting tasks. The male assumption of traditionally female jobs was only temporary, and was abandoned as mechanized spinning mills were built in the town to relieve the labor shortage in knotting.[127] As the twentieth century opened, centralized production of spun yarn, in the new factories at Uşak, Bandırma and elsewhere, became commonplace although hand spinning remained important.

Earlier in the century, women at Uşak also had dyed the yarn but this became a male task as rug production increased. Similarly, Sivas women had dyed yarn but abandoned the work as local production expanded and was commercialized late in the century; in 1900, only a few old women there remembered the formulas for using natural dyestuffs.[128] By *c.* 1850, there were centralized dyehouses in the town of Uşak, both merchant-owned and independent. All of them dyed in every shade and were not restricted to a particular color.[129] At Kula, by contrast, dyeing remained a decentralized and female craft until at least the 1880s. There, every woman had her own dye pot just outside the door while the single centralized dyehouse made only indigo blue.[130]

In the Anatolian rug industry overall, the household fell in importance because merchants usually set up workshops in the new production centers. But, at Uşak, despite all the changes that had taken place and the increasingly refined division of labor, knotting remained a home industry. The looms at Uşak were without exception in private homes, either in the courtyard or the large public room.[131] The mistress of the home organized production, finding the workers as well as the materials, and often employed one–three knotters. At Uşak and Gördes, but not at Kula, which was another established center, different persons carried out the spinning, dyeing and knotting functions.

Uşak women loom owners functioned in a variety of relationships with agents and merchants.[132] Some received cash advances, pledging to produce for the agent but otherwise remaining independent. Others received advances and promised to use only the agents' dyeworks while a third kind of operator at Uşak exclusively used the dyed yarn that the agent brought to the house. All three forms of loom owner-agent/merchant relationship – that reflect the operator in quite different stages of dependency – were present in the town during the nineteenth and early twentieth centuries. Thus, loom operators, all women, variously obtained the dyed yarn from the dyehouses of the agents and of the independents. They assigned a few women to regulate the warp and to apportion the design; both tasks received higher wages than knotting.[133] Girls as young as six years learned knotting from their mothers and, after two years' apprenticeship, began to receive wages. Knotters were placed about two feet apart at the loom and, depending on the size of the carpet, there were up to ten workers.[134] They passed the time singing folk songs; some of them, apparently, were ribald and scandalized passersby.[135] The knotters received piece rates and every evening the mistress of the house measured the work against the warp threads. Piece work remained standard throughout the industry in Anatolia.[136] While only girls and women knotted at Uşak, men performed this task at a number of locations, including the long-established centers at Kula and Gördes as well as at more recently founded weaving centers such as Sivas.[137]

Knotting in households prevailed in the Anatolian industry until a relatively late date. By 1906, a few workshops for carpet knotting had emerged. Sometimes called factories (*fabrique/fabrik/fabrika*), these simply were rooms or structures that had been rented or built. Women and girls walked from their homes and assembled in the factory to knot at looms provided by the operator/owner. In 1906, centralized knotting shops existed at Kütahya, Sivas and Eskişehir, some belonging to İzmir merchants who were among the founding members of the Oriental Carpet Manufacturers.[138] In addition to establishing workshops, merchants persuaded many households to begin rug making, providing them with the looms, buying the rugs on completion, and paying piece work rates.

The Oriental Carpet Manufacturers confirmed and accelerated trends already present in the Anatolian carpet industry – notably the ongoing centralization of spinning, dyeing and knotting. These trends had been set earlier by future members of the firm as well as by their Ottoman and European competitors in İstanbul, İzmir and Uşak. The company spun the yarn in the Bandırma factory of a founding member and dyed it in a new central dyehouse at İzmir. It shipped this colored yarn to women and girls knotting on company-owned looms in workshops located away from home. These centralized worksites proliferated under the company's auspices but they were not its creation. The firm formed seventeen of these workshops in west and central Anatolia and appointed women directors who in turn hired the other women and girls, to work under her direction, on company looms. In many locations, carpet workshops probably were the first worksites outside the household that assembled comparatively large numbers of women, with important social implications. At other locations, usually where rug making had been common, (including Uşak, Gördes and Kula), it placed agents who ordered rugs from autonomous knotters; these, however, used only company-dyed yarn.[139] By 1910, the firm employed 50,000 knotters in Anatolia.[140]

The workshop model favored by the Oriental Carpet Manufacturers and some of its rivals offered the merchants many advantages. It had been relatively more difficult to supervise knotting in the household, where domestic demands constantly interrupted the workplace. Workshops allowed for more effective quality control since supervisors were physically present and could intervene at any time. Output would rise since the women could be more effectively disciplined to knot rather than care for the children, the house or the fields. Techniques such as drumming out the knotting count maintained or increased the pace. In sum, workshops certainly facilitated increases in productivity although caution must be used in determining how much. A number of factors, including rug design and quality, affected productivity; per capita output varied considerably. The best household knotters at Uşak, according to a well-informed source, made as many as 12,000 knots per day and apprentices produced 5,000–8,000 knots.[141] The private 1892 diary of a rug merchant, however, remarks that 3,000 knots per day was average and 7,000 was exceptional.[142] Rates of 5,000–6,000 knots per day for a skilled worker seem to have been usual at Uşak, and these are comparable to output elsewhere. At Sivas, *c.* 1900, workers at home produced 4,500–5,000 knots per ten-hour day while at Konya, in 1907, they averaged 6,000 knots.[143] Workshops of the Oriental Carpet Manufacturers, however, maintained a substantially greater workplace. At Isparta, knotters in 1914 were averaging 9,600 knots for an eight-hour day, while skilled workers produced as much as 14,000 knots.[144] Thus, knotters of the firm in shops were working two to four times faster than those in households.

It is also clear that knotters in areas of new commercial production received wages far lower than workers in the Uşak industry. This was true both for workers in homes as well as in workshops. Household knotters working for the three Armenian entrepreneurs at Sivas in 1900, for example, received an extraordinarily low wage, of 0.5–1.0 piasters per workday. This was as little as one-eighth the rates then being paid at Uşak for an equivalent number of knots. Several years later, when the Aliotti house opened its workshops at Sivas, pay improved somewhat but still was as low as one-quarter the Uşak wages.[145] The workshops of the Oriental Carpet Manufacturers paid similarly low wages, again by comparison with the Uşak industry. In 1914, for example, the company paid Isparta workshop knotters wages that nominally were one-half or less than the piece rates that had prevailed at Uşak eight years earlier.[146]

If the workshops offered merchants the opportunity to lower wages and increase productivity, there were disadvantages. Workers who gathered together at a central spot – for knotting, dyeing or spinning – were more likely to organize than those scattered about in homes. And they did. In 1908, workers of the Oriental Carpet Manufacturers joined in the great wave of strikes sweeping the

Ottoman Empire. In August, some 50 men and 250 women working at the dyeing and knotting facilities of the firm in İzmir struck for a full week, demanding higher wages. They seized the plants and, in the struggle, one woman striker killed a soldier.[147]

In these workshops and, to a lesser extent, in the industry overall, the working environment had changed and rug making had become a radically deskilled craft. Factory-spun and dyed yarns were supplied to knotters who sat before geometrically drawn patterns that required no adjustments and no decisions, only imitative copying without deviation. For many, the art of rug making had become a series of mechanical tasks, carried out by individuals engaged in specialized functions, not seeing the product through from conception to completion, with no room for the individual's creative input.

Conclusion

The decline of decline

Historians' discovery of significant rural and non-factory manufacturing in Europe, when large-scale mechanized production supposedly dominated, inspired this search for manufacturing in the nineteenth-century Middle East. We did not find an Ottoman world overwhelmed by European manufacturing. Instead, widespread and vigorous industrial activities revealed themselves, largely based on non-mechanized forms of organization, located in urban areas and the countryside. Homes and workshops remained the locale of most Ottoman manufacturing, as they had for centuries. Men, women and children continued to card, spin, dye and weave. Important quantities of yarn still were handspun while handweaving actually increased over the period. Natural dyestuffs regained popularity late in the century, at least in the carpet industry and some other activities. Continuity thus is a major theme of Ottoman textile history.

But continuities camouflage change. If the largely rural framework of the Ottoman world remained intact, within it were changes, adaptations and transformations in the processes of industrial production as well as input mixes. The relations of production were far different than before, not only in the new factories but also in the many homes that increasingly engaged in market production. That is, the shell remained but inside was a significantly restructured manufacturing sector. Some manufacturing activities for the market were in new locations, where they had not existed before, ranging from Arapkir to villagers' homes on the Bosphorus. Textile producers' reliance on hand-spun yarn, hand-woven cloth and naturally derived dyestuffs had given way, by 1900, to the massive use of machine-made threads and cloths and laboratory-based dyes. To this list of the major technological changes in Ottoman textile production we need add: the sewing machines in their tens of thousands, the jacquard looms in their several hundreds, and the several dozens of mechanized factories.

Ottoman textile manufacturing clearly had changed in the nineteenth century. But had it declined? Was there a deindustrialization of the Ottoman economy? The absence of even crude guesses concerning changes in Ottoman gross national product and the agricultural, manufacturing and service contributions enormously complicate resolution of the problem. There certainly was significant expansion in agricultural and industrial production as well as in the service sector during the nineteenth century. The answer to the deindustrialization question certainly depends on your viewpoint and your definitions.

From an international comparative perspective, Ottoman industry surely did decline. It was further behind Western manufacturing in terms of output, technology and contribution to the national income in 1914 than it had been in 1800. The gap, already present at the beginning, had widened geometrically over the century. If, for example, a graph were drawn representing the numbers of Ottoman and West European (or American) mechanized cotton spindles in *c.* 1914, the Ottoman figure would not have been visible on the graph since it equalled only 0.02 percent of its British counterpart.[1] Western industry grew at nearly unbelievable rates and overshadowed manufacturing everywhere else in the world (except Japan). The point about the phenomenal growth in Western industry need not be belabored here.

Why were so many Ottomans unable to continue competing with European and American manufacturers, often even for the home market? The objective of this question is not to explain why an Ottoman industrial revolution never occurred. Such an inquiry would lead to the sterile conclusion that the Middle East did not follow a Western path of development. This approach does not seem fruitful since no country outside the West did during the nineteenth century, except for Japan. Here is not the place to reiterate the long list of factors impeding Ottoman big factory mechanization.

Successfully competing was not necessarily a matter of making a comparable product for a cheaper price. British cotton cloth in the 1830s did cost considerably less but it was not made as well as the Ottoman. Middle Eastern producers often made goods that were quite high in quality and sold for commensurate prices. To drop their prices sufficiently to meet foreign competition, particularly in the earlier part of the period, meant lowering standards. Some Ottoman manufacturers failed to grasp this essential point and went under. Many did not recognize the rapid fashion shifts to Western styles, that disadvantaged local producers most gravely during the initial moments of the encounter between European and Ottoman manufacturers. They certainly were not helped by a standing policy of the British government (lifted in 1841) to restrict the export of textile technology. This policy, some historians argue, also explains the failure of nineteenth-century Spain to compete. Similar restrictions, however, did not prevent the diffusion of technology in Europe and the industrial rise of France and the various German principalities.[2]

Nor would some Ottoman manufacturers adopt the new technologies, including machine-spun yarn and cloth and, later on, laboratory dyestuffs. Social choices were made that precluded the adoption of cost-cutting technologies. Existing relationships prevented some artisans from making needed changes, for example, those of guild weavers with guild dyers. In this case, adoption of factory-made dyes would have snapped the social relations between the two groups. Similarly, the presence of putting-out networks retarded innovation in many textile centers. The prevalence of home industry meant price–wage structures that made investment in mechanized factories risky. That is, dense exchange networks emerged using factory-made yarns, cloths and dyes and their presence acted to retard further industrial development via mechanization.

The Indian and Japanese experiences may have some relevance in explaining the pattern of nineteenth-century Ottoman industrial evolution, In Japan, a homogenous merchant *gono* class of rural entrepreneurs tightly controlled the market, both vertically and horizontally. Their capital had originated in the supply of food to Japanese cities and they used the surplus to finance large-scale industrial production. But in the Ottoman Empire and in India, foreign and local merchants in India split the market, both horizontally and vertically. The economy, consequently, was decentralized and unintegrated, a character that prevented any group of merchants from accumulating capital that might have led to greater industrialization. In the Ottoman case, at least, ethnic division that existed among Turks, Greeks and Armenians probably served to fragment the market, and capital accumulation, still further. In the Ottoman world, the small landholding patterns that prevailed in most areas exacerbated the capital shortfalls prompted by the accumulation difficulties of the merchants. The merchants' sharing of a split market plus small landholdings meant very little capital became available for investment in Ottoman industry.[3]

Many manufacturers failed not because of social choices but for reasons literally out of their control. Even the most enterprising spinner or weaver was hardpressed to work without raw materials. Many, as seen, failed early in the century for the want of dyestuffs, siphoned away by higher international prices. Later on, during the cotton crises of the American Civil War and the early twentieth century, hand spinners and weavers suffered as Ottoman and foreign merchants re-routed raw cotton supplies away from them in favor of direct exports.

Some important industries suffered or failed for political reasons. Diyarbakır weavers at one point lost (and later regained) their Baghdadi customers because Mohammed Ali Pasha had occupied the lands in between. Kayseri merchants and their Black Sea spinners and weavers suffered severely from the Ottoman government's failure to maintain the imperial boundaries during the 1828–29 war. The consequent decision of Trabzon merchants to switch from exporting Ottoman manufactures to Abaza to importing European goods via İstanbul was a rational choice compelled by political, diplomatic and military events. But it was disastrous for Ottoman manufacturers. Manchester was a terrible foe but so were closed Russian borders sealing out Ottoman products. The lost wars of 1877–78 and 1897–98 also cost Ottoman manufacturers traditional markets and customers, in times that already were difficult.

When industries failed, where did the workers go? Some certainly spent more hours in agricultural tasks than they had before. This would have been an especially attractive possibility during comparative boom periods in agriculture, in the decades surrounding the Crimean War, when Ottoman agricultural exports rose at record levels, and after 1896. Workers abandoned cotton spinning for silk reeling and, later on, switched from silk reeling to work in the carpet industry. Many who gave up handspinning of cotton more profitably and productively spent those hours weaving cloth, using imported yarn. Here was a powerful engine of positive change in Ottoman manufacturing. Some silk and cotton hand spinners and weavers and their jobs, however, died together. It is probable that they accepted steadily decreasing wages and were not replaced upon death. The vast expansion of the Ottoman civil bureaucracy and military drained away many young men from manufacturing. In *c.* 1900, there were approximately 500,000 civil service jobs that had not existed a century before. Similarly, the Ottoman military forces had increased over the century. At the beginning of the period, Sultan Mahmud II's army employed 120,000 men while, during the Balkan Wars of the early twentieth century, over one-quarter million Ottoman men fought.

But let us return to the question of the fate of Ottoman manufacturing and the issue of deindustrialization. We already have agreed that, compared to developments in the West, Ottoman manufacturing relatively had fallen by the wayside and therefore had declined in international relative terms. To continue further: by decline and deindustrialization, do we mean a fall in the nominal output of Ottoman industry over time? That is, did aggregate Ottoman industrial production absolutely rise or fall over time? Adopting this unit of analysis gives a different answer than the international comparison. Overall, it is my impression that the volume of Ottoman textile production was greater in *c.* 1914 than it ever had been during the nineteenth century.[4] To proceed further, however, did *per capita* manufacturing output rise or fall in these Ottoman lands between *c.* 1800 and 1914? According to one estimate, the population of the lands that were still Ottoman in *c.* 1911 doubled during the period, thanks largely to immigration. Thus, a *per capita* increase in manufacturing would have required at least a doubling of output. Did this occur?

Between 1800 and 1914, the absolute numbers of persons working in textile manufacturing certainly increased, if the yarn spinners are excluded. The decline in the numbers of yarn spinners was not as much as once believed and the number of dyers might have risen thanks to demand for natural dyes in the carpet industry and despite the vast increases in imports of artificial and synthetic materials. Overall, the aggregate number of textile manufacturing workers rose but the overall Ottoman population probably increased at a proportionately greater rate. Does this mean Ottoman deindustrialization? Not necessarily. The answer partly depends on productivity trends in Ottoman agriculture and manufacturing. Production increases in agriculture derived largely from an extension of the area under cultivation; an impressive number of steel plows came into use but otherwise there were few technological changes and productivity improvements.[5] Productivity increases in textile manufacturing likely surpassed those in agriculture during the period. There are a number of factors that substantially increased industrial productivity and argue in favor of *per capita* increases *if* the above assertion, that aggregate output rose between 1800 and 1914, is true. First, we should consider the massive adoption of imported machine-made yarn. Most hand spinners stopped spinning altogether, or nearly so. The purchasers of the foreign yarn found the capital in some combination of industrial and agricultural activities. Some spent more time in textile production – weaving, printing, sewing, reeling silk or knotting carpets – or in some other industrial activity. Others devoted more hours to agriculture. All those who stayed in textile making and used machine-made yarn worked at higher levels of *per capita* productivity than before. Second, consider the addition to *per capita* output deriving from the Ottoman spinning mills that ultimately furnished one-quarter of domestic yarn needs. Third, the several tens of thousands of workers in the few scores of mechanized cloth factories were vastly more productive than if they had been hand weavers instead. Also, consider the productivity increases rendered by the adoption of sewing machines. In the early twentieth century, more than 10,000 machines annually were being sold in the empire as a whole, at least 6,000 in the Anatolian provinces alone. Each machine represented a vast increase in the productivity of the household or workshop sewer. In sum, even though aggregate data are lacking, the argument in favor of *per capita* increases in manufacturing output cannot be dismissed out of hand. Thus, *per capita* manufacturing decline or deindustrialization might not have occurred.

As seen, the inability to compare output trends over time has greatly impaired our understanding of nineteenth-century manufacturing production and of the deindustrialization issue. More specifically, I believe that the actual importance of the international markets that were lost during the eighteenth century has been greatly over-inflated. Several issues seem relevant here. These industries were of interest and importance to European observers in a way that the domestically oriented industries of the next century were not. They received an exaggerated amount of attention from contemporary European observers and later historians using their works. The issue centers on the size of the export markets that were lost and the volume of the domestic Ottoman market during the nineteenth century. Take, for example, the famed mohair cloth industry at

Ankara, a paradigmatic case of Ottoman manufacturing decline. At their peak, the Ankara weavers exported *c.* 20,000 pieces. By eighteenth-century standards, this was a vast quantity but its volume seems less impressive when compared to output levels during the next century. Compare this figure, for example, with the 60,000 pieces of cotton cloth that weavers at Van, a minor center, were selling in nearby markets during the 1880s. (The mohair pieces certainly were of finer quality and represented more labor input and value added.) The Ankara-Van comparison suggests that the Ankara output stands out mainly because Europeans were buying the goods and because eighteenth-century world trade functioned at levels substantially below those of the subsequent century. Haven't we actually over-estimated the economic importance of these lost export industries?

Comparison of the eighteenth-century export industries with those of nineteenth-century production, both for international and domestic use, is important in quite a different way. There can be no doubt that the overall quality of the goods being made fell over time. This decline likely undermined and reduced the master or independent weavers. Many were compelled to turn to the production of coarser goods, inflating the labor supply in this sector, a trend that drove down wages and prompted the emergence of industries in which part-time work became more common. One result, arguably, was increased female participation in the workforce (see below).

There was no overall decline of Ottoman industry but the performances of specific industries varied considerably. And we have seen that the decline of some of them was real. The output of the red-yarn makers of Ambelakia, the mohair weavers of Ankara, some of the cotton weavers of the Black Sea region and the silk weavers in İstanbul diminished over time. Output at the major center of Diyarbakır, in a worst case scenario, remained steady. But there is the chance that production there increased. At some locations, such as Aleppo, a closer look has shown that textile production certainly rose over time. Even the silk weaving at Bursa increased during the period, if we consider 1800 and not 1810 as the baseline of comparison. These two examples are particularly significant since the purported failures at Aleppo and Bursa were said to be emblematic of the general decline of Ottoman industry. The cases of restructuring and growth were found to be numerous. Many artisans continued to earn their livelihoods in textile making but used different material inputs. These include the head-covering decorators who adopted imported cloth and the cotton weavers in countless locations who abandoned homespuns and natural dyestuffs in favor of imported substitutes. It also (may) include the Diyarbakır cloth makers who took up British yarn and began raising their own silk to cut costs. It definitely counts those, such as the makers at Aintab and Aleppo, who vascillated between local and imported material inputs. And then there are the industries that were created or expanded vastly to meet emerging market opportunities, both foreign and domestic. These included the lacemakers of

İstanbul and the Anatolian carpet knotters, who produced a hand-made product that scarcely was such in 1914.

Beyond the decline paradigm

This book does more than challenge the paradigm of industrial decline and deindustrialization. It has placed the Ottoman domestic market at the very center of the manufacturing story and demonstrates that internal demand was the engine that drove Ottoman textile production. Thus, the book breaks from the Eurocentric view of the Ottoman economy, that placed prime importance on the connections between the Western and Middle Eastern economies and ignored the domestic market. It has tried to emphasize those forces working within the Ottoman economy. The effort, however, has been only partially successful because so many European sources were used in the absence of available Ottoman alternatives.

Changes in Europe and the global economy obviously influenced Ottoman manufacturing to an important degree. The ending of the Napoleonic wars unleashed the full competitive force of ongoing British industrialization upon cotton spinners and weavers in the Ottoman lands. The lives of thousands in Bursa and the Lebanon were changed irretrievably by clashes between militant workers and demanding industrialists at Lyon. Several decades later, they were dramatically altered by events in East Asia that flooded Europe with silk. Similarly, rising consumerism and the expansion of the Western middle classes profoundly altered the rhythms of existence at Uşak, Gördes and dozens of other rug-making towns in Anatolia. The significance of far-away events on the Ottoman economy is well known and widely accepted.

The role of internal dynamics within the Ottoman society and economy have been neglected in the Eurocentric view. Such neglect was dangerous since, as this book shows, the domestic market kept much of Ottoman manufacturing alive. The story of Ottoman textiles often can be told only from the perspective of the internal market.

When domestic Ottoman patterns are considered, a new periodization for textile manufacturing history emerges. The periodization is no longer centered on stagnation and decline, based on the end of the Napoleonic wars or the 1838 Anglo-Turkish Convention. Rather, we see the period dividing into two parts, with *c.* 1870 as the hinge, and with adaptation, adjustment and innovation as major themes. The Western impact was most devastating during the first period until approximately 1870, when the competitive threat was new and least clearly understood. The trough seems to have been reached between the 1830s and 1850s. But, even then, some existing industries increased output while new ones emerged serving the domestic market. At this time, we also see the rise of the first major new export industry, silk reeling. During the post-1870 era, there were substantial increases in many cloth industries and in mechanized yarn spinning for internal markets. And, there was the maturation of the second great export industry, carpet making.

Part of this industrial revival indeed was tied to changes in Europe. The shift of the mature industrial economies away from the production of consumer goods to capital equipment clearly offered new opportunities to Ottoman, as well as Indian, Italian and other entrepreneurs. An international division of labor was underway as the value of Japanese silk cloth exports skyrocketed while that of Indian cotton textiles and of Ottoman carpets more than tripled between 1880 and 1900.[6] Similarly, the onset of the 1873–96 global depression made Ottoman manufacturers more competitive. Also, better prices for Ottoman agricultural exports after 1896 spelled stronger sales to peasants who had always been important to textile producers. These international events partly explain the concurrent post-1900 booms in the output of various textiles at, i.a., Harput, Aleppo, Arapkir, Bursa and (perhaps) Diyarbakır.

But there are the internal factors as well. We need to recall, for example, that manufacturing increases in some areas began before the onset of the depression (and prior to import duty increases). They thus were responses to domestic impulses and not only echoes of far-away events. Also consider, for example, the continued preference of many Ottoman consumers for products of local manufacture, even though often more expensive than Western goods. While the price of a manufactured good was important, it was not always crucial and other considerations influenced the sale.[7] In many cases, Ottoman buyers would pay more, if able, for the local product of better quality. This taste preference is a form of resistance to European manufacturing and represents a choice among options made by Middle Eastern consumers.

Resistance to European goods and to industrialization bubbled up throughout the nineteenth century and is a recurring theme in the manufacturing story. In some instances, such as the redundant spinners, opposition may have been blunted by the rapid shift to new jobs, in this case, to weaving with imported yarns. The resistance varied from burning factories to insisting on "traditional" clothing. Ottoman shopkeepers, for example, beat up fellow subjects and foreigners seeking to sell competitive European products. Local leaders campaigned against adoption of Western clothing, warning of the disastrous consequences for Ottoman textile producers.[8] Resistance to Western goods was not unusual and over the century evolved, taking a final form in the post-1908 boycotts against Austro-Hungarian and Greek goods.

Ottoman workers, entrepreneurs and the population at large, moreover, passively and actively resisted the formation of factories. This opposition was important and, according to some analysts of Indian manufacturing, could outweigh the lack of capital in explaining the industrialization path not taken. When the adoption of new technology required reduced labor costs, entrepreneurs' fear of resistance by workers could block innovations.[9] Resistance sometimes took the guise of concern about the air and water pollution that a factory might bring. These objections were repeatedly raised in the Balkan, Arab and Anatolian provinces alike, by officials and the general population. Such objections have a face value but they also camouflaged the fear of economic competition.[10] Or, take the example of the entrepreneurs who, in 1875, sought to found a water-powered yarn factory in the town of Niausta. The local government stated that the mill could not interfere with the existing livelihoods of town dwellers. Therefore, since women had been producing wool yarn in town workshops, the factory could spin only cotton, not wool. Nor could the mill diminish the water supplies needed for the gardens, orchards and fields.[11] Similarly, when a British subject opened a factory at İzmir for printing muslins, local Armenian manufacturers, whose factory offered a similar product, protested. İstanbul consequently ordered a halt to the operations.[12] Also recall the efforts to erect wool spinning mills at Uşak, that foundered on the hand spinners' protests. Wool yarn factories later were built at Uşak anyway, only to be sacked and burned by angry hand spinners in March 1908.[13] At Adana, a knitting factory "was burnt down and never started again."[14] Resistance and factory burning also accompanied the emergence of the steam reeling factories at Bursa during the 1850s. Sometimes the evidence of resistance is unclear. For example, a fez factory, constructed in Salonica in 1908–9, burned down almost immediately and was not rebuilt.[15] At Trabzon, a British firm imported the machinery for a cotton and woolen weaving plant "but while in store a fire damaged them greatly so that most of the parts will have to be renewed."[16] The presence of such attitudes and behavior in Ottoman society clearly indicates the importance of internal factors in the evolution of Ottoman manufacturing.

The contents of this book deviate from a historiographical tradition that had focused on a nineteenth-century elite world full of elite actors – the Westernizing bureaucrats, intellectuals and policy-makers. This tradition had rendered the Ottoman manufacturing sector invisible, a domain of common artisans and manufacturers that could be of only passing interest. Thus, while the present assault on the decline paradigm is important, perhaps the greater contribution of this book is its view from below. The role of the state is de-emphasized and more attention has been paid to actors and events in Ottoman industry than to governmental goals regarding manufacturing. Comprehensive data regarding labor still are lacking but a preliminary picture has begun to form. There is little information on the workplace in many important centers such as Buldan, Kadıköy or Rize; but working conditions in Uşak, Trabzon and a few other locations suggest situations that may have prevailed more widely. In these locations, when workshops were the norm, the owners usually worked alongside the hired (or family) labor. Work hours usually were dictated by the sun, contracting in winter and stretching out in summer. In cases of household production, the hours given to manufacturing surely fluctuated according to season and family needs. When market demand was very strong, new gender divisions of labor sometimes occurred. In other instances, exceptional measures were taken, such as the Uşak carpet knotters who put on miners' helmets to work into the night. Thus, this book has helped to people Ottoman history, however imperfectly. It also depicts *activity*. Industrial centers teemed with workers at places such as Buldan and Kadıköy in the west and Rize, Gürün, Diyarbakır and Aleppo in the east. Once-unknown villages such as Bor and remote, faraway cities such as Bitlis and Van were shown to be alive with manufacturing workers. This nineteenth-century empire was jammed with (at present nearly invisible) networks linking Ottoman manufacturer and consumer. If traced on a map, these thick networks would resemble a diagram of telephone and electric lines in a great city of today, such as London or New York.

A certain division of labor among the four regions of industrial activity has become sufficiently clear for us to begin to understand the different regional economies that were present in the late Ottoman period. The Ottoman West at Salonica and in Macedonia worked mainly in wool, from local raw materials, while the north Anatolian towns (except Rize) usually wove cotton cloth, employing yarns brought from outside. The Ottoman East mainly worked in silk and silk-cotton mixes, employing a combination of local and imported materials. Western Anatolia was the most diverse manufacturing region, making comparatively important quantities of various cotton, silk and wool textile products. This area relied on local sources for the latter two textiles and a mix of imports and indigenous materials for its cotton fabrics. In two areas, the Ottoman Balkans and northern Syria, cotton cloth production was mounting very late in the period. The increase may have been a response to new supply opportunities as cotton weavers in western and central Anatolia turned to rug making, or simply a result of rising peasant consumerism in the face of improving agricultural prices. Natural advantage could be important, for example, in the operation of the mechanized yarn factories near the cotton fields of Adana and İzmir or the wool cloth industry in Macedonia that supported large sheep herds. Similarly, the carpet-making districts had easy access to the flocks of the Anatolian high plateau.

To a large extent, these regional concentrations were legacies of the past and the precise combination of factors prompting their original rise remains unclear. Aleppo, Diyarbakır, Buldan and Rize continued to possess important textile sectors. It certainly is true that, as in Europe, regional specialization in several of the regions took place when commercialization transformed locally idiomatic forms of peasant production into market activities. Quite likely this is the origin of the woolen industries and of cotton textile production in west Anatolia, that drew on locally abundant raw materials. The Aleppo and Bursa silk industries, however, owed their emergence to competition with the Iranian silk industry and efforts to take advantage of its weaknesses. The rise of Aintab as an important cotton cloth maker, for its part, closely parallels the European pattern of regional specialties emerging in response to competition for wider markets, a struggle that we have seen was taking place in late-nineteenth-century north Syria.[17]

Merchants originally were more important in areas where the basic materials were not available than in regions possessing supplies of cotton, wool, silk or flax. During the nineteenth century, as both foreign and domestic machine-spun yarns played larger and larger roles, merchants' significance surely increased. Industries such as cotton and wool weaving at Arapkir and Gürün respectively and carpet making at scores of locations all derived from the organizational efforts of the merchants, either foreign or Ottoman.

Distance from the coasts in itself did not protect manufacturers from foreign goods. It could play a role, not on its own but in combination with factors such as taste preference. Thus, nineteenth-century industries expanded in distant eastern mountainous regions far from the sea but they also did so in western coastal regions and even in the capital itself.

Population densities certainly played a role in determining the location of industry. In most manufacturing communities, the densities seem comparatively high, considering the very low levels in the Ottoman Empire overall. During the nineteenth century, the population of many manufacturing centers had become too large to be supported solely from agriculture. The soils often were marginal by absolute standards but, as in parts of the Sivas region where carpet making became important, they were of moderate fertility in comparison with other Ottoman areas.

All of the textile manufacturing areas for which we have information were relatively well-watered. The general lack of water in the Middle East was important and surely reduced the possibilities for its manufacturers. It should be recalled that steam did not replace water power in Europe and the United States until late in the nineteenth century. This option of water power for early industrial development was not available in most of the Ottoman world. On the other hand, no factories emerged among the rich coal fields of northern Anatolia, where patterns of migratory labor to İstanbul were deeply rooted.

The markets of the four textile manufacturing zones varied considerably and several were expanding late in the period. These extensions, moreover, were a net increase in the Ottoman market, not rising sales in one region at the expense of manufacturers in another. Sometimes, producers sold their manufactured cloth outside the region for further work and sale to the final consumer. The local market was present but seems to have been secondary for the Macedonian wool weavers who sold in virtually every corner of the empire. The intra-regional market had greater significance for west Anatolian weavers although they also did ship outside the region, to the eastern Black Sea coast and to

İstanbul. In the Black Sea hinterland region, most cotton cloth production and the slight silk fabric output focused on local and regional consumers, including those in nearby Russia. But Tokat cottons and the wool and cotton cloths of Gürün sold more widely, in the Persian borderlands and Mediterranean coastal areas, and in Egypt. The linens of Rize went everywhere in the empire, and to Egypt and Persia. Manufacturers in the north Syrian region sold very widely, finding customers throughout Anatolia, the Iraqi provinces, İstanbul and Egypt.

The Ottoman case thus seems partially to support Franklin Mendels' "proto-industrialization" arguments that linked rural manufacturing for extra-regional trade to high population densities and poor soils.[18] Thus, the rich soils of Aydın province nourished a flourishing home and workshop manufacturing sector that focused largely on local needs. There does appear to be a close correlation between the infertility of the lands around Diyarbakır, Aleppo and Uşak, and the prevalence of manufacturing for the long-distance market. But there seem to be many exceptions to the rule. The comparatively rich Black Sea hinterland, for example, supported manufacturers who sold their goods in Russia.

It also seems important to note that domestic rivals eroded the dominance of several traditionally significant textile production centers, in quite different ways. The near-hegemony of Uşak in carpet making faded with the century, because of Ottoman and foreign merchants' activities elsewhere in Anatolia. Similarly, Aleppo textile makers lost sales to Aintab producers. In both cases, manufacturing activities became more diffuse while output at the old centers in particular and of the respective industries in general reached record levels.

The variety of organizational forms in Ottoman manufacturing was tremendous: there were independent peasant and urban household producers, putting out networks in both town and country, urban workshops and mechanized factories. Overall, the changing comparative importance of these various forms is not clear. The size and number of factories is comparatively well known and measurable; these were only a very modest beginning, played a small role in overall output and paled in comparison with even the least industrialized European state, such as Spain. We can be similarly certain about craft guilds, many of which continued to exist in a formal fashion while declining quite sharply in significance. Craft guilds' economic importance essentially had vanished by 1850. Most of the guilds that subsequently retained economic vigor were connected to service functions, notably the porters and boatmen.[19] Beyond the factories and craft guilds, little is certain. Did urban, workshop-based manufacturing for sale diminish or rise in relative importance? Here we need to consider production in Aleppo, Diyarbakır, Mosul and elsewhere and the many (new and old) activities that bustled in İstanbul. And what is its relationship to the considerable rural textile manufacturing taking place? The relative shares of manufacturing contained in urban and rural areas in general cannot be estimated. More specifically, did it take place mainly in workshops or in homes? The organizational form of many manufacturing activities remains unclear. For example, were the wool and cotton weavers of Gürün, Arapkir and Maraş working in homes or workshops?

Handspinning of wool and cotton yarn remained a household task, as it always had been. But silk reeling after *c.* the 1860s essentially ceased to be a household activity in most areas.[20] Lacemaking was home-based, with the exception of the missionary workshops. In the carpet industry, the rising production at Uşak occurred in homes. In the other regions, workshops were the site for knotting in many of the new carpet-making centers, such as the city of Sivas. A great deal of cotton, linen, silk and wool weaving – organized in whatever fashion – certainly occurred within households but the small workshops of Aleppo suggest alternative forms of organization.

In the manufacturing sector as a whole, the household probably increased in importance during the nineteenth century, a function of efforts to reduce production costs. There were considerable differences among the industries. In some, the significance of households as a unit of production rose while it declined in others. Even within a particular industry, the significance of households varied just as it might change over time.

Equally difficult is the question of the organization of production within the household; was it of the putting-out variety or were these independent producers? A key to the answer may lie in the nature of their output. Coarser, well-made, cotton textiles of one type or another, as seen, were the major product in many areas. Frequently there was a tendency to cheapen the product, e.g., the century-long transformation of Aleppo *alaca* cloth from a silk-cotton to a cotton product. These cheaper goods were a way of coping with shrinking profit margins; but they offered merchants very low net returns. In some areas of the world, such as nineteenth-century China, merchants responded to such small profits by extending equally minuscule efforts and money on the organization and management of a putting-out system. In China, consequently, there was an expanding market but without the emergence of putting-out systems.[21] If this happened in the Ottoman lands, then independent producers would have prevailed among the household workers for the market.[22]

The household was a bridge connecting Ottoman industry and agriculture, as its members move back and forth, from the one to the other, depending on natural and market conditions. Weavers tilled and farmers spun. The continuing predominance of agriculture and of small landholding tenure patterns in the Ottoman economy played a key role in shaping the nature of its industry. The prevalence of small peasant holdings, for example, helps explain the significant levels of yarn that were being hand spun late in the period. Their production of food, for subsistence and sale, allowed many peasant textile producers to continue competing for domestic and international markets. The marginal value of the labor at home was always more than zero and so household textile production continued. This was true for many town dwellers as well as for peasants. We have a few glimpses of nineteenth-century urban geography in manufacturing towns such as Rize, where linen weavers' homes seem to have been scattered among gardens and orchards. Such examples suggest the mixed occupational character of Ottoman textile makers in many towns and cities.

Girls and women were more important in textile manufacturing at the end of the century than they had been in *c.* 1800. Females' labor always has been present in Ottoman manufacturing for the marketplace but this scarcely had been remarked upon. One of the fascinating parts of the research presented here has been the discovery of women's work in so very many areas of manufacturing life. When the sources became sufficiently specific in describing a manufacturing activity, it turned out that female labor usually was present.[23] Sometimes, the sources themselves sought to deny this and referred to the workers as males or in gender neutral terms when, without question, they were females. Female labor was an integral part of nineteenth-century Ottoman manufacturing. It was not a remarkable or unusual phenomenon, but rather a central, everyday, recurring presence.

The growing participation of girls and women is most visible in the export industries that grew so dramatically – raw silk, carpets and lace. They formed a very strong majority of the knotters and probably all of the reelers and lace-makers. They also clearly dominated (although men also spun) the various spinning industries, of cotton, linen and wool; females also had formed an important part of the Ankara mohair spinning industry. This is hardly unique to the Ottoman world and shares much with the gender division of labor in many countries. In nineteenth-century Ireland, to give but one example, it was women's work to spin and to weave linen cloth for home use while the men commercially wove.[24] In the various Ottoman textile weaving industries, the gender division remains unclear but, overall, there were many more women and girls present than I originally had suspected.

There was no single gender division of labor in textile making. Again, this finding shares much in common with patterns in many regions of the world where men and/or women might weave, dye and print. Rather, it varied by region, by industry and date, and changed depending on circumstances. Women, we know, commercially wove various kinds of cotton cloths in many villages of İzmir, Sivas and Trabzon provinces and wove linen for sale in towns of the Kars district. In the city of Trabzon, they wove silk cloth and printed head gear. Aleppo master weavers were male, but many of their workers were females and children. Moreover, many Aleppine Armenian families worked as weaving units, with women and men sharing the task. Given this geographically, chronologically and occupationally diverse list of known female participation, it seems reasonable to assume that they worked in a wide variety of other manufacturing activities as well. Men seem to have dominated weaving in the town of Diyarbakır but there is no information on the gender identity of cloth workers in many locations, such as Gürün, Arapkir, Rize, or in Macedonia. Also, there is no evidence of girls and women joining craft guilds although they frequently supplied them with spun yarns. The guilds seem to have worked to assure men's position in urban production.

Thus, very many women and girls engaged in household spinning, weaving, knotting, embroidering and lacemaking. In addition, female and child manufacturing work outside the home was commonplace, irrespective of location or ethnicity. It is not true that non-guild workshops and factories employed only men. This is a false assumption about Middle East privacy norms and must be abandoned. Child and female workers predominated in all of the mechanized cotton spinning and silk reeling mills. They were an important, likely the major, part of the workforce in the Uşak wool yarn factories. Women also worked in the wool cloth factories at Niausta in the Balkans and Eyüp in the capital and in the umbrella workshops of İstanbul. (In addition, they were important elements of the workforce in İstanbul shoemaking, see below, and in the tobacco factories at İstanbul, Salonica and Samsun.)

The vital role of girls and women in Ottoman textile production, as well as in shoemaking and tobacco processing, derived from the low wages that they received. Whatever comparisons are possible, their wages everywhere and always were small fractions of those obtained by men for the same or equivalent work. The combination of very low-wage households and female labor best explains the continuing ability of Ottoman industry to compete for the domestic market and to sell products abroad.

In the end, it is unlikely that the manufacturing growth measured in these pages would have led to the emergence of the Ottoman Empire as a major industrial power. The answer will never be known for certain since the results of World War I totally shattered the Ottoman world, its boundaries and its economy. Most of the major manufacturing centers were deprived of all or some of their former markets. The north Syrian region became part of two separate nations. Aleppo lost its Anatolian buyers while the customers of Maraş and Rize and Gürün vanished behind the tariff walls of the new mandate states of Syria and Lebanon. And, the Ottoman economy lost all of the comparatively large industrial infrastructure in Salonica and Macedonia even earlier. Elsewhere, for example, around Adana, the skills acquired by the founding entrepreneurs of mills became scarce as many fled or died during the war. Similarly, at least part of the trained workforce that had emerged in the various areas and industries was killed or deported. That is, the clusters of factors that had nourished and sustained the regional concentrations of textile manufacturing had been thoroughly broken apart. We cannot trace the outcome of prewar industrial trajectories by using subsequent manufacturing trends. Great Power policies of de-industrialization of the Arab Middle East during the post-war period and the failure of the republican Turkish private sector to industrialize tell us little about Middle East manufacturing in 1914.

Thus, World War I was a decisive watershed in the manufacturing history of the region. Even so, the character of the industrial activities before the war does suggest that the significant capital accumulation needed for massive infra-structural investment was not occurring. On the macro-economic level, factors discussed earlier, such as the division of markets between foreign and Ottoman merchants, surely played a role. In Salonica, where industrial concentration was perhaps the most dense, factory owners were placing much of their profits in non-industrial enterprises. The long manufacturing experiences of Bursa (and the Lebanon) similarly led nowhere in terms of enhancing the Ottoman indus-trial base. The capital being amassed was spent in other endeavors. Capital-intensive, high-wage industries were hardly present in the late Ottoman landscape.

Ottoman textile manufacturing remained a low-wage, often labor-intensive, low-capital endeavor. Capital inputs rarely rose above the level of a sewing machine except, of course, for the silk mills, and a few other mechanized factories and jacquard looms in workshops. Whenever wage data are given, they reveal very low labor costs. Conditions of high labor exploitation prevailed and many sweatshop industries emerged late in the century. In the provinces, these certainly included the missionary lacemaking workshops and the vast rug work-shops opened by İstanbul and İzmir merchants and the Oriental Carpet Manu-facturers trust. Conditions seem to have been particularly bad in the city of Sivas. At İstanbul and several other of the largest cities, such as Salonica and İzmir, sweat-shop industries had become common at the end of the century and ranked among the most successful enterprises – for example, ready-made clothing and umbrella making. In part, as suggested earlier, the low-wage structure derived from the emphasis on the production of coarse goods, at the expense of finer textiles. Such coarser goods include not only the wool *aba* and various cotton textiles, but also the cheap, mass-produced rugs that poured out of Anatolia late in the period. But very low wages prevailed in other industries as well.

Among these was the shoemaking industry of İstanbul, with an evolutionary pattern quite similar to many textile-making activities. At first caught off guard by the popularity of Western-style shoes, the industry appeared to be disappear-ing *c.* 1850. But, by 1900, the industry had been restructured; it not only regained its İstanbul market but also exported very large quantities of shoes to the provinces and to Egypt. Shoemaking became a decentralized, non-guild craft dominated by small manufacturers. Workshops were located in different quarters of the city; in one quarter, therefore, the workers were Armenian while in another they were Greek. Each quarter apparently specialized in different kinds of shoes. Merchants placed orders with the workshops and provided the masters with the materials. Employing from five to as many as fifty male and female workers, the master worked in and supervised a minute division of labor. Some workers cut, while others sewed or punched holes or made heels or soles. The work was of high quality and wages were extremely low.[25]

This example, when considered with those presented in textiles, underscores the low-capital, labor-intensive nature of late Ottoman manufacturing. Low wages were an essential component, without which Ottoman industries could not survive. Still worse, there is evidence that, for most of the time, textile workers suffered from declining real wages (as did the İstanbul shoemakers). This certainly was the case in the export-based industries of silk reeling and carpet making, for which the documentation allowed a detailed comparison of prices and wages since *c*. the 1880s. Real wage declines also were taking place in the industries producing for the domestic Ottoman market, such as Rize linen weaving where, between 1896 and 1910, prices for top-quality linen fell steadily. Similarly, the piece rates paid in the important Diyarbakır textile industry declined after *c*. 1860. Real wages in other domestically oriented textile manufacturing sectors likely had declined during the first decades of the British textile influx, *c*. 1820–60s. They may have stabilized during the depression of 1873–96 but certainly fell thereafter.

Some industries could not survive except with the very cheapest of labor. At Salonica, tobacco processing became lucrative because of skyrocketing American demand after 1900. Local wages increased accordingly and, in response, the local silk mills simply closed down. But the Aleppo textile industry had a different experience. The wage strikes by Aleppo textile workers in 1903 and 1904 anticipate by one-half decade the explosion of labor strikes for higher wages that occurred after the 1908 revolution. They thus preview the massive unrest triggered by the real wage declines that had been accumulating in the Ottoman manufacturing (and transportation) sectors. But, in addition, they suggest a certain improvement in the profit margins of some Ottoman industries in the early twentieth century. The textile workers' wage demands at Aleppo won success because profit margins were sufficiently large to afford the new rates. The wage hikes in 1908 similarly reflect surpluses on which many Ottoman industrial entrepreneurs could draw, however reluctantly, to keep the workers weaving, printing and sewing.[26] The strikers' successes meant at least some relief; but it did not halt the decline of real wages for most textile workers.

Thus, industries survived, grew or were born in the various areas for many different reasons but always because labor was skilled, cheap and worked hard. Low wages, paid to women, children and men working most often in households, workshops and sweatshops enabled Ottoman textile industries to compete for domestic and international markets. "Small was sometimes beautiful, but more often it was dependent, oppressive and exploitative."[27]

Notes

Introduction

1 Eldem (1970), pp. 302ff.

2 Jean Quataert (1988) is a good summary of the debates and issues.

3 It is not much more helpful to repeat the enumeration of workers engaged in manufacturing, in the early twentieth century, when the empire possessed perhaps 26 million inhabitants. At this time, there allegedly were 303,000 industrial workers in İstanbul, Anatolia and the Syrian provinces and an additional 105,000 in Lebanon, Jerusalem and Iraq. Eldem (1970), p. 287.

4 See my chapter on agriculture in the forthcoming *The Ottoman Empire: Its Economy and Society*, Cambridge University Press, for a summary.

5 Eldem (1970), p. 286. The political role of these workers would make a fascinating study.

6 Pallis (1951), p. 75 and, for example, BBA HH 54918, 1204/1789–90.

7 BBA Cev İkt 1393, VIII 1267/1851.

8 This may be a reference to shipments to Egypt that paid this 12 percent duty. See FO 195/700, Skene, Aleppo, 6/8/1861. But did the duty apply to shipments to Anatolia as well, as FO 195/741, Aleppo, 6/5/1862 clearly states?

9 BBA Cev İkt 1024, two petitions, dated X 11 1262/October 1846. Appeals to poverty should be judged carefully; this was part of the language that guilds customarily used in their appeals to the state.

10 FO 195/741, Aleppo, 6/5/1862.

11 BBA I MV 25281, V 22 1283/October 1866.

12 A&P 1875, 77, 3837, North Syria for 1874, Aleppo, 5/26/1875.

13 BBA I MM 2276, III 28 1292/May 1875.

14 AS 1890, 745, Aleppo for 1889.

15 For a summary of the arguments, see Tomlinson (1985).

16 For more details, see my contributions in the forthcoming *The Ottoman Empire: Its Economy and Society*.

17 Genç, for example, (1975).

18 BBA Cev İkt 579, IX 19 1260/1844.

19 See, for example, BBA MV 24162, 1282/1865 and MV 403, 1257/1841.

20 For example, BBA I, MV 636, 1258/1842.

21 BBA Cev İkt, 347, X 1220/1805–1806; ŞD 2196, XI 3 1295/1878; ŞD 2236, XII 16 1295/1878; ŞD 2580, VIII Şaban 1296/1879.

22 Genç (1975); Petmezas (1989); Quataert (1990). During the eighteenth century, guilds had declined in Europe and in other regions. See Perlin (1983); Pollard (1981); Jean Quataert (1988).

23 See, for example, the works by Issawi (e.g. 1966); Sarç (1940); Ubicini (1856).

24 Keyder (1989), p. 15.

25 Records of the new taxes levied on non-guild manufacturing have not yet become available but this situation is changing with ongoing classification of archival documents in İstanbul.

26 For example, BBA Cev İkt 1165, I 8 1225/1810; Cev Mal 16795, IX 2 1257/1841.

27 Abou el-Haj (1991).

28 Quataert (1990).

29 Ergin (1330–1338); Cevdet (1309); Lüfti (1292–1328).

30 BBAI MV 8615, VII 7 1268/1852.

31 See, for example, the 1860s commission report cited in Sarç selection in Issawi (1966) and discussed in Quataert (forthcoming).

32 Salahhedin Bey (1867).

33 Turkey (1970); also see Quataert (1984), p. 296.

34 Cevdet (1309); Lütfi (1292–1328); also see the Turkish Historical Society's official history of the Ottoman Empire, *Osmanlı Tarihi*, in eight volumes, variously authored by İ. H. Uzunçarşılı and E. Z. Karal.

35 Sarç (1940); Önsoy (1988).

36 This is equally true of Ottoman history produced in Europe and the United States and includes the present author.

37 Landes (1966) and (1969).

38 Issawi (1966); Hershlag (1964); also Cook (1970).

39 Issawi (1966), pp. 227 and 274 ff.

40 Owen (1981); also Owen (1984).

41 Issawi (1982), pp. 150 and 154; quote from p. 152.

42 Pamuk (1987); the chapter is entitled "The decline and resistance of Ottoman cotton textiles, 1820–1913," pp. 108–29.

43 Pamuk (1987), p. 128.

44 Pamuk (1987), p. 115.

45 Jean Quataert (1988) is a good summary.

46 See Pollard (1981) and Jean Quataert (1988) for the works of Franklin Mendels and Hans Medick. Mendels too, like W. W. Rustow and Landes, believed in the stage theory; he held that protoindustrialization was the first stage on the road to mechanized factory production. Medick later argued that protoindustrialization did not necessarily have to lead to development.

47 Berg (1985), p. 17.

48 Berg (1985), p. 38.

49 Greenberg (1982), pp. 1246–47.

50 Berg (1985), p. 24.

51 Hopkins (1982), p. 56.

52 Berg (1985), p. 40.

53 Berg (1985), p. 42 and Greenberg (1982), p. 1246.

54 This is admittedly an impressionist statement based on comparing the volume and value of eighteenth- and nineteenth-century exports that are specified throughout the text.

55 Issawi (1982), p. 24.

56 Mendels (1972).

57 Park and Anderson (1991), p. 536. Hanson (1980), p. 148.

58 Harrison (1978).

59 Tomlinson (1985).

60 Bronfenbrenner (1982).

61 Simmons (1985).

62 Chandavarkar (1985).

63 Simmons (1985); Chandavarkar (1985) essentially is expressing grave uncertainty about the reasons for the transition to big factory industrialization.

General introduction

1 Twomey (1983), p. 45.

2 Pamuk (1987), p. 115.

3 İnalcık (1979–80) and Veinstein (1989).

4 See, for example, FO 195/113, Sandison at Bursa, 2/15/1840; FO 195/208. Sandison at Bursa, 3/10/1844, report on Bursa trade for 1843; FO 78/750, report on Bursa trade for 1847. FO 195/393, Sandison at Bursa, 1/28/1861 shows the prolonged duration of the fashion changes.

5 Owen (1981) and Sami (1983).

6 Owen (1981).

7 See Owen (1981) and the various works by Issawi.

1 Raw cotton, dyestuffs and yarn production

1 A&P 1873, 67, 3655, Wilkinson at Salonica, 8/12/1872; Bowring (1840). Volumes originally given as 90,000 and 60,000 cwt. and 250–500 tons.

2 USNA, Film T194, Constantinople Dispatches, Reel 3, –/18/1858; CRUS for year ending 9/30/1859; except for Asia Minor, originally given in okes. BCF 1879, Smyrne, 4/2/1879; originally stated as 29,000 bales of 180 kg./bale.

3 RCC Reel 35, İzmir for 1902; Buhi 18, 1913, 9/24/1912; Buhi 1904. Stich (1929), p. 88. Ottoman cotton exports, 1878–1913, averaged 10,400 tons/year: Dağlaroğlu (1941), pp. 16–17.

4 Quataert (1973), tables on pp. 289–90; Eldem (1970), pp. 77ff; Tillmann (1916–1917), p. 4, asserts that increasing Ottoman yarn production was causing exports of raw cotton to decline, from 7,712 tons in 1906 to 6,861 tons in 1908.

5 Issawi (1982), pp. 30–31, originally stated as 0.5 and 7.48 million qantars.

6 Bowring (1840); Cunningham (1983), p. 47; Leake (1824) but the journey was in 1800, p. 97; MacGregor (1844), p. 121.

7 RCL 5/31/1904 is a special issue on yarns that has considerable information on the comparative importance of imported and domestic, dyed and undyed, yarns. Compare Scherzer (1873) with AS 5247, Smyrna for 1912–1913. Both state that the 90/10 bleached/dyed proportions in yarn imports remained the same at İzmir for the next

however, asserts that the consumption of dyed yarn had been declining, especially the cheaper qualities once from Belgium.

8 Georgiades (1885), p. 48; Stich (1929), p. 79; USNA T238, Reel 6, 9/26/1863.

9 AS 1887, #197, Constantinople for 1886, Fawcett, 6/9/1887.

10 Warburg (1918); Atalay (c. 1952); RCC Reel 33, Nr. 84, Mersin and Adana for 1900, p. 11.

11 MacGregor (1844), p. 121; RCC Reel 33, No. 49, Sivas in 1899. Buhi, 9, 1906. The booming carpet industry of the post-1850 period helped keep alive natural dyeing techniques.

12 Buhi, X, Heft 9, 8/20/1907; RCL 5/31/1904, Lettre de Marache; Buhi Heft 13, 2/14/1902.

13 RCC Reel 34, Nr. 150, Trebizonde for 1901. Buhi, IV, 13, 11/20/1902.

14 A&P 1896, 89, Richards, Ankara for 1895, 5/8/1896.

15 RCC Reel 32, #271, Commerce of Smyrne for 1893; this probably was used in rug manufacturing.

16 AS 3931, Smyrna for 1906; it was British-owned but with German machinery and German technicians.

17 k und k 1912, Smyrna; also Junge (1916). US D of C and Labor, Bur of F DC, Special Agent Series, March 1912. AS 5247, Smyrna for 1912–13, notes that İzmir did not dye blue or red, importing the blue yarns from Britain and the reds from Austria-Hungary and Germany.

18 RCC Reel 32, No. 7, Aleppo for 1899.

19 Buhi III, Heft 10, 1/22/1902, Aleppo; k und k, 1907, VIII, 1, Aleppo.

20 Buhi, III, Heft 10, 1/22/1902 Aleppo; Buhi x, Heft 9;, Buhi, Heft 13, 2/14/1902. k und k, 1907, VIII, 1, Aleppo.

21 Scherzer (1873).

22 AS 5247, Smyrna for 1912–1913; RCL 5/31/1904.

23 RCL 5/31/1904, Lettre du Comité de Brousse, 4/30/1904. RCC, 1910, #838, Edirne for 1908. USCR LXIX No. 260, May 1902; RCL 5/31/1904, Lettre de Harpout, 4/1/1904.

24 RCL 5/31/1904; see also AS 2950, Constantinople for 1902.

25 AS 2950, Constantinople for 1902; AS 3140, Constantinople for 1903. AS 3170, Smyrna for 1901–3; Buhi, Januar 1902, III, Heft 9; RCL 5/31/1904.

26 US D of C and Labor, Bur of F & DC Special Agent Series, March 1912, Izmir. UPA vol. 16, 1908, British Trade in Mesopotamia. k und k 1907, VIII, 1, Aleppo. Pamuk (1987), p. 192.

27 BBA Cev Harc 2133 VI 1207 and 2677 VI 1207/1793; Cev İkt 1114, 25 VIII 1228/1813. İnalcık (1979–80) and Veinstein (1989).

28 BBA Cev İkt 1114, VIII 25 1228/1813.

29 BBA Cev Maliye 442, VIII 15 1238/1822. At least these are the sources that the state mentioned in its records, perhaps indicating only areas supplying state yarn needs rather than the most important yarn production center.

30 Svoronos (1956), pp. 243–7. A&P 1873, 67, 3655, Wilkinson at Salonica, 8/12/1872.

31 BBA Cev Maliye 652, VIII 4 1245/1829.

32 BBA HH 51599, 51599a-b, 1250/1834–5; MV 13393, VIII 3 1271/1855; Cev İkt 1415, 1229/1814.

33 İnalcık (1979–80); Olivier (1801); Cunningham (1983), p. 44.

34 Eton (1799), p. 234.

35 Urquhart (1833).
36 Urquhart (1833), pp. 47–51 and Stavrianos, (1953), pp. 298–99.
37 Stich (1929), p. 78.
38 Olivier (1801), p. 44.
39 Petmezas (1987), who also tells of an 1817 effort by Ambelakia merchants to adapt to the British competition. They imported a German spinning machine (and a German mechanic) but the experiment foundered and was abandoned on the death of the mechanic. Also, Urquhart (1833), pp. 47–51.
40 İnalcık (1979–80) and Cunningham (1983), p. 77.
41 Pamuk (1987).
42 See Pamuk (1987), chapter 6.
43 BBA MV 2441, 22 XI 1263/1847.
44 BBA Cev Maliye 361, VIII 13 1251/1835 and Cev İkt 1487, VIII 16 1255/1839.
45 BBA MV 505, X 8 1257/1841.
46 BBA MV 6181, III 25 1267/1851 and MV 22267, III 30 1280, when wages were raised.
47 BBA MV 1183, XII 26 1260/1845.
48 BBA MV 1460, III 21 1262/1846 and Dah 5253, VI 14 1261/1845.
49 BBA MV 14224, VIII 27 1271/1855.
50 Urquhart (1833), p. 148.
51 US T 238, reel 2, 12/31/1843, D. Offley; at this time, the city shipped 22.9 million piasters worth of raw cotton.
52 FO 78/289, 10/11/1836 and 5/11/1836, Brant at Trebizond.
53 FO 195/113, Sandison at Bursa, 3/10/1844 and 6/2/1844.
54 FO 78/750, Bursa trade for 1847 and FO 195/113, Sandison at Bursa, 2/15/1840.
55 FO/289, Abbott at Erzeroom, 10/11/1835; FO 195/112, Stevens at Erzeroom, 2/15/1840.
56 FO 195/253, 12/31/1845, Carpenter at Tarsus; FO 195/205, Suter at Kayseri, 2/26/1852.
57 FO 78/289, 11/8/1836, Brant at Trebizond.
58 FO 78/289, 11/8/1836, Brant at Trebizond.
59 FO 195/459, Holmes at Diarbekir, 3/31/1857.
60 FO 195/112, Brant at Erzeroom, 7/16/1839.
61 FO 195/112, Brant at Erzeroom, 7/16/1839; FO 195/253, Suter at Kayseri, June 1844.
62 Bowring (1840), p. 37.
63 "Genç kızlar, anneler muhtaç kadınlar herbiri bir saikin tesirile pamuk alırlar." Hayri (1922/1338).
64 Nuri (1922/1338).
65 US T681, Jewett at Sivas, 5/26/1887 and 5/26/1893.
66 RCC, Reel 34, Nr. 149, Sivas in 1901; Buhi, X, Heft 9, 8/10/1907.
67 A&P 1859, 30, Skene on 1857 Aleppo trade; Buhi, I, Heft 9, 8/20/1907.
68 FO 195/278, Dalyell, 2/22/1862; FO 195/939, Taylor at Erzeroom, 3/18/1869; A&P 1873, 67, Taylor at Erzeroom, 11/14/1872.
69 Diyarbakır VS 1302/1884–5 and 1321/1903.
70 Buhi, X, Heft 9, 8/20/1907, noting the use of 10,000 packets of regional yarn. Usual packet weight was 4.5 kg.. In addition, the weavers purchased yarn from the Adana mills.

71 Buhi, X, Heft 9, 8/20/1907. The total cotton harvest equalled 950,000 kg.. RCL 5/31/1904, Lettre de Harpout, 4/1/1904. Cotton yarn "chiefly is made by villagers who avail themselves of their distaffs in traversing the wheel."

72 Shields (1986), pp. 73–74 and 174, quoting from French consular sources.

73 A&P 1859, Skene for 1858, 2/14/1859; RCL 5/31/1904, Lettre de Harpout, 4/1/1904. Local yarns were *c.* 14 percent of all yarns used at Maraş.

74 RCL 5/31/1904, Lettre de Marache, 3/30/1904.

75 RCL 5/31/1904, Lettre de Marache, 3/30/1904. The hand spun cost 9–12 piasters per oke.

76 *Ibid.* Nr. 10 Adana yarn sold for 18.28 piasters per oke while Nr. 20 English yarn sold for 19.71 piasters. Hand-spun Maraş yarn cost 9–12 piasters while the lowest-number European yarn, Nr. 16, cost 18.57 piasters and Nr. 4 Adana yarn cost 10.85 piasters.

77 Pamuk (1987), p. 219, using the 1911 borders of the empire as the unit of comparison.

78 Specifically, the government had prohibited the export of more than one example of each piece of machinery. FO 78/298, 6/22/1836, Treasury to Nouri Efendi.

79 A&P 1899, 103, 6241, Sarell on the trade of Constantinople, 1893–97.

80 Luckerts (1906). The Harput factory supplied the weft yarns for Tokat goods in 1896. A&P 1896, 89, Richards at Ankara for 1895, 5/18/1896.

81 The concessionaires were Şura-yı Devlet members İbrahim Niyazi and Cavid Bey and the Ottoman *chargé d'affaires* in London, M. J. Eestenklen. Turkey *Düstur* (1937–43), 7, pp. 275–83.

82 Clark (1969), p. 97. At Aleppo, there were four cotton gins (*filanden, pamuk fabrikası*) but no spinning mills at the end of the century. Halep VS 1317/1899, pp. 191–92 and 1321/1903, p. 218; k und k 1901, Aleppo.

83 Later, a weaving factory was added. This might be the concession granted in Turkey, *Düstur* (1937–43), 6, pp. 143–51, to Ahmet Refik Reşid and Refik.

84 A&P 1892, 84, Fawcett at Constantinople, 4/16/1892; Junge (1916), p. 437.

85 Clark (1969), p. 97.

86 Buhi, 1904.

87 RCC Reel 32, #271, Commerce of Smyrne for 1893; AS 3170, Smyrna for 1901–1903; RCC Reel #33, Nr. 130, Smyrne in 1900; RCL 5/31/1904.

88 Stich (1929), p. 89; AS 4242, Smyrna for 1907; Buhi Januar 1902, III, Heft 9.

89 In 1912, the mill used *c.* 6,500 bales of cotton, when total cotton exports from İzmir were 29,000 bales. k und k 1912, Smyrna; Stich (1929). In 1901, the government awarded Azapzade Saadetlu Hikmet Bey a 25-year concession to build a sack, yarn and sail-cloth factory in İzmir district (*sancak*). There were the usual tax exemptions and requirements that employees be Ottoman. Turkey, *Düstur* (1937–43), 7, pp. 643–45.

90 Stich (1929); similar figures in A&P 1913, 73, 7781, Waugh.

91 Buhi x, 9, 8/20/1907.

92 RCL 10/31/1910 but A&P 1913, 73, 7781, Waugh, says there were 690 gins in 21 ginning mills and RCL, Septembre 1912, Lettre de Mersin gives a figure of *c.* 1,200 gins. AS 4235 for 1908 offers a figure of 550 gins.

93 RCC 33, Nr. 84, Mersine and Adana in 1900. In 1889, the state had granted a 20-year concession to an Ottoman merchant, Hazar Nisan Efendi, to build a cotton and wool yarn and textile factory in Adana province. The concession provided the factory with a monopoly in the province, but with two caveats. It was not proper to close any textile

factory or workshop that already existed, nor was it proper to halt imports from Europe or elsewhere. The concession included the usual provisions for duty-free imports of machinery and Ottoman wool and cotton. Turkey, *Düstur* (1937–43), 6, pp. 466–67.

94 RCL 1904, Adana and Mersina for 1903.

95 Luckerts (1906); it contained 5,200 spindles in 1914, Eldem (1970), p. 131.

96 Clark (1969), p. 99; Eldem (1970), p. 131.

97 Eldem (1970) shows three mills with both spinning and weaving but British consular sources note only two.

98 US B of F and DC, D of C, Commerce Reports, 7/30/1915.

99 Clark (1969), p. 99; RCL Septembre 1912, Lettre de Mersine.

100 A&P 1909, 98, 7360, Doughty-Wylie, Adana.

101 RCL Septembre 1912, Lettre de Mersine.

102 Buhi III, Heft 10, 1/22/1902, Aleppo; Buhi, I, Heft 9, 8/20/1907.

103 USCR LXIX, Nr. 260, May 1902, Harput; A&P 1898, 94, 6125, Graves at Erzeroum for 1897; RCL 5/31/1904, Lettre de Harpout, 1 Avril 1904; Buhi X, Heft 9, 8/20/1907.

104 Clark (1969), pp. 95–96; A&P 1908, 116, 7252, Wylie, Konya.

105 BCF Salonique, 7/25/1883; A&P 1893–94, 97, 5581, Blunt, 9/30/1893; FO AS 1887, 75, Salonica for 1885; 1889, 623, Salonica for 1888.

106 A&P 1893–94, 97 5581, Salonica, for 1891–92, Blunt, 9/30/1893; RCC 1905, #515, Salonique in 1904; AS 4579, Chafy at Salonica for 1909.

107 k und k 1900, II, 7, Salonich; A&P 1893–94, 97, 5581, Salonica for 1891–92, Blunt, 9/30/1893.

108 AS 1886, 67, Smyrna 1881–2 to 1885.

109 RCC 5/31/1904, Lettre du Comité de Brousse, 4/30/1904.

110 RCC 1905, #412, Edirne province for 1903 and 1910, #838, Edirne for 1908.

111 Dağlaroğlu (1941), p. 83; RCC Reel 33, Salonica for 1900, Nr. 76; Reel 35, Salonique in 1902; A&P 1908, 17, 7253, Salonica for 1907 and 1910, 103, 7472, Chafy.

112 k und k 1902, XVIII, 2, Salonich.

113 RCC 1905, #414, Smyrne for 1903. But others felt that the local mills, with lower transport costs, had the advantage of buying local cotton at prices that Europeans found very high and hence blocked raw cotton export to Europe. RCC 1905, #506, Smyrne for 1904.

114 A&P 1899, 103, 6241, report on trade of Constantinople, 1893–97, Sarell.

115 Owen (1981), pp. 236–38.

116 Pech (1911), pp. 272, 320.

117 k und k 1901, XIX, 1; *ibid.*, from 1902 and 1903; also see RCL 5/31/1904.

118 AS 1889, 571, Adana for 1888 and AS 1890, 745, Aleppo for 1889; RCC Nr. 109, Mersine for 1892.

119 Buhi, X, Heft 9, 8/20/1907, Adana. A 1913 report notes two factories at Tarsus, with 20,000 and 6,000 spindles but makes no mention of looms. *Board of Trade Journal*, 3/27/1913 and AS Constantinople for 1912 which is the source of the Board of Trade report.

120 BCF Salonique, 7/25/1883.

121 A&P 1893–94, 5581, Salonica, for 1891–92, Blunt, 9/30/1893.

122 He closed it when workers continued to prefer bringing their own food. Except where noted, this account relies on Buhi, XIX, Heft 6, 4/18/1913. Also see k und k 1905,

XX, 6 Salonich; k und k 1906, XXI, 3, Salonich; AS for 1909, Chafy at Salonica.

2 Trends in cloth production in the Ottoman lands from Salonica to Aleppo

1 BCF 1877, Adrianople, 5/10/1877; k und k 1902, XVIII, 4, Adrianopel; idem for 1903, II, 1; idem for 1905, XX, 2.
2 Todorov (1983), pp. 212–13 and, generally, pp. 218–91.
3 Lampe and Jackson (1982), pp. 141 and ff for prosperity of the industry through 1878.
4 Michoff (1971), pp. 397, 426.
5 FO 195/193, Blunt at Salonica for year ending 12/31/1849. Selanik VS 1307/1889, p. 229.
6 A&P 1873, 67, 3655, Wilkinson, Salonica, 8/12/1872 and A&P 1897, 94, 6016, Heathcote for 1895.
7 Selanik VS 1307/1889, p. 227.
8 FO 195/176, Blunt at Salonica, 1/8/1841 and FO 195/476, Charles Blunt at Salonica, 12/29/1855.
9 AS 1886, 24, Salonica for 1883–84 and AS 1887, 75, Salonica for 1885; AS 1888, 394, Salonica for 1887; AS 1889, 623, Salonica for 1888; A&P 1896, 89, Blunt, Salonica for 1893–94; k und k, 1906, XXI, 3 Salonich.
10 BCF 1877, Adrianople, 5/10/1877; k und k 1902, XVIII, 4, Adrianopel; idem for 1903, II, 1; idem for 1905, XX, 2; idem for 1911; AS #5015, Adrianople for 1911. A Serbian factory that had contracted to supply the Ottoman army with 8,000 meters of cloth then bought 150,000 kg. of wool from Edirne as well.
11 Selanik VS 1307/1889, pp. 227–28; 1315/1897, p. 576; 1322/1904, p. 523; FO AS 1886, 24, Salonica for 1883–84. The Samsun region, for example, annually imported *c.* 1.0 million piasters worth of wool cloth from the European provinces during the early twentieth century.
12 Shields (1986); Masters (1988) and Ariel Salzmann's work on Ankara are examples of research on regions outside of the capital city.
13 i.a., see Göyünç (1983) and Güran (1984–85).
14 This situation should rapidly change as Ottoman historians exploit new kinds of local sources, such as the court records (*şeriye sicilleri*).
15 See Jenny B. White's dissertation "Family industry in Istanbul: Labor as a Construction of Social Identity," University of Texas, Austin, 1991. The archives of the Istanbul *müftülük* have been exploited by Rhoads Murphey.
16 BBA I, MV 505, X 8 1257/November 1841 contains seven petitions and a number of government decisions. The petitions all are undated. The eleven guilds included those making *peştemal, bezzaz, kemha, sandal, dülbent, aba* and *astar* as well as *iplik* and the dyers's guild (*boyacı*).
17 See Cunningham (1983), p. 91 for discussion of another large stone khan that is not the one mentioned here.
18 BBA I, MV 505, X 8 1257/November 1841.
19 BBA I, MV 505, X 8 1257/November 1841; I MV 934, IV 2 1259/May 1843.
20 The tax burden of the Üsküdar guild remained unchanged during this 1840s' period of crisis, no doubt adding to its woes. During the early 1850s, however, the state did

forgive overdue back taxes and began paying the salaries of officials who once had been supported by guild taxes. BBA I MV 8392, II 6 1268/May 1852; I MV 15036, IV 23 1272/January 1856.

21 Compare BBA I MV 8392, II 6 1268/May 1852 and in BBA I, MV 505, X 8 1257/November 1841.

22 BBA I, MM 4031, VI 12 1304/March 1887.

23 BBA I MV 403, V 15 1257/August 1841.

24 BBA I MV 21191, I 9 1279/July 1862.

25 Dumont (1982), p. 220. Quataert (1988), pp. 174–75.

26 Buhi 1904 and BCF 1889, Trebizonde.

27 For details, see my *Technology Transfer and Manufacturing in the Ottoman Empire, 1800–1914* (İstanbul, 1992).

28 RCL, Mars 1904 special issue on sewing machines.

29 Junge (1916b), p. 441. The number of machines is an estimate, based on the total imports, worth 7.8 million piasters, divided by the stated average cost of 160 francs (*c.* 700 piasters) each.

30 Buhi 1904, pp. 322–323; Herlt (1918). Value originally stated as three million francs.

31 Value originally given as 7 million francs.

32 RCL, 10/31/1909, pp. 440–46; Herlt (1918). Buhi 2/14/1902, Heft 13, pp. 522–23, shows similar patterns of very cheap labor producing ready-made clothing in İzmir and Beirut.

33 RCL 10/31/1909, pp. 445–46.

34 In this case, the guild members were Jews, see Galante (1985), IV, pp. 66 and 97, for Jewish textile workers at Aydın, making braid, shirts, and men's trousers.

35 AS 3931, Smyrna for 1906.

36 AS 3170, Smyrna for 1902–3.

37 RCC Nr. 506, Smyrne for 1904. Thus, more than one-half of Ottoman sewing machine imports passed through the port of İzmir.

38 Cuinet (1890–94), III, pp. 409–10. Originally stated as three million francs. Buhi, III, 9, 1902, Januar 1902. Value originally given as 1.75 million marks.

39 Cuinet (1890–94), III, p. 410. Value originally given as 60,000 marks. Quantity of *mendil* given as 10,000 *arşın*.

40 Aydin VS 1307/1891, pp. 748–49.

41 Fitzner (1902); GB Naval Staff (1919), I, pp. 120–21; also Cuinet (1890–94), III, p. 622.

42 Aydin VS 1307/1891, pp. 748–49. Also, Junge (1916). Invariably, these cloths were of white cotton and yellow silk. Cuinet (1890–94), III, p. 409. Compare with Buhi III, 9, 1902, Smyrna. This latter source seems to state, mistakenly, that all these looms were devoted to turban cloth making. More likely, it was the total number of looms in the town.

43 Buhi, 1902, III, 9, Januar 1902.

44 Cuinet (1890–94), III, p. 574.

45 Buhi, III, 9 Januar 1902.

46 FO 195/113, Sandison at Bursa, 2/15/1840; k und k for 1905, X, 3, Brussa. In 1905, this represented *c.* 2 percent of estimated Ottoman yarn imports. Pamuk (1987), p. 115. Bursa then held about 0.03 percent of the Ottoman population.

47 RCL 5/31/1904, Lettre du Comité de Brousse, 4/30/1904. This calculation based on

the statistics of the Mudanya-Bursa railroad, that carried 300,000 kg. of imported yarn to Bursa in 1903, when the city exported about 93,000 kg. of woven cotton textiles. Issawi (1988), pp. 400–1.

48 FO 78/750, reports on Bursa trade for 1847; also FO 195/208, Sandison at Bursa, 3/10/1844; FO 78/868, Sandison for 1850, 3/31/1851.

49 A&P 1859, 1/20/1858, Sandison for 1857; A&P 1862, 58, Sandison for 1860.

50 FO 195/741, Sandison, 6/28/1862 and FO 195/744, Bursa for 1863, Sandison, 5/18/1864. FO 195/774, Bursa for 1863, Sandison, 5/28/1864.

51 Bursa VS 1324/1906, p. 179.

52 Ibid.

53 k u k, 1902, VIII, 5 Brussa; k und k for 1905, X, 3, Brussa; k und k, 1906, X, 1, Brussa.

54 k und k 1912, Brussa. Bursa VS 1324/1906, pp. 179–80.

55 Cuinet (1890–94), I, p. 839; FO 195/1934, Richards, Ankara, 10/24/1896, similarly ranks *alaca* production second to carpet making in the Konya region. Niğde had 9,387 households (*hane*) but contained only 350 cloth looms (*dokuma tezgahı*) and no workshops (*fabrika*). *Yurt Ansiklopedisi*, 8, p. 6167. Buhi, X, 9, 8/20/1907, p./624, states that Cor [*sic*] contained 35 carpet looms that employed 200 workers.

56 A&P 1908, 116, 7252, Wylie at Konya. In the early 1840s, two European merchants set up business in Konya. The bazaar was well stocked with "all kinds of unbleached and bleached calicoes, muslins, shawl, and other cotton goods of British manufacture," as well as Swiss nankeens and prints. The 1840s' report makes no mention of local textile production.

57 Buhi, I, 9, 8/20/1907. Value originally stated as one-half million marks.

58 FO 195/112, Stevens at Erzeroom, 2/15/1840.

59 FO 78/189, Abbott, Erzeroom, 10/11/1835.

60 RCC Reel 34, Nr. 149, Sivas in 1901 and Buhi 9, 8/20/1907. The province bought some 2,000 Singer sewing machines in 1910, at 75–150 francs each. RCC Reel 40, E. Dussay, 1911. Value originally given as 550,000 francs. Genç (1987), pp. 145–170.

61 US T 682, Jewett at Sivas, 5/26/1893. Buhi 9, 8/20/1907; this does not include the looms at Amasya which were not given in this enumeration nor does it count the *donluk* looms.

62 FO 78/289, 3/31/1836 and 11/11/1836. If the practices followed in the 1890s are any indication, the Tokat weavers used European yarn for the warp and relied on local yarn in the weft to give greater strength.

63 Mordtmann (1925), p. 162. The town paid 391,405 piasters in *emlak, temettü and iane-askeriye bedel* taxes in 1867. BBA I, MV 25922, V 20 1284/September 1867.

64 Buhi, IV, 13, 11/20/1902, Trapezunt.

65 A&P 1898, 94, 6125, Longworth, Trebizond. Buhi, 9, 8/20/1907. RCC Reel Nr. 40, 1911, E. Dussap, Sivas. In 1907, each piece sold for between 0.75 and 3.00 piasters, depending on size, the number of colors used, and the quality of the cloth.

66 Buhi, 9, 8/20/1907. Value originally given as 500,000 marks.

67 FO 78/289, Brant, 8/11/1836 and 3/11/1836.

68 Cuinet (1890–94), I, pp. 650, 693; Buhi, 1904, gives the number as 400, in Christian hands.

69 Sivas VS 1306/1888, p. 217; Sivas VS 1321/1903, p. 181; k und k 1903, Konstantinopel.

70 A&P 1908, 117, 7253, Shipley, Erzeroom for 1907; RCC Année 1911, Sivas vilayet, #953, Reel 40.

71 RCC, Reel #34, Nr. 149, Sivas in 1901; Buhi, 9, 8/20/1907.

72 Buhi, 9, 8/20/1907.

73 RCC Anne 1911, Sivas vilayet, #953, Reel 40. Value originally given as three million francs.

74 Buhi, X, 9, 8/20/1907; also see BCF 1889, Trebizonde.

75 Cuinet (1890–94), I, p. 119.

76 FO 78/367, A. G. Glascott, 10/11/1839.

77 AE CC Turquie 10, 4/15/1890, pp. 193–193r; RCC Reel 31, #209, Trebizonde for 1893. A&P 1892, 84, 1050, Erzeroum for 1891; A&P 1897, 94, 6016, Erzeroum for 1897.

78 FO 78/289, 5/11/1836; UPA FO, VI, January 1868, 103; k und k, XX, 10, for 1903, Konstantinopel; Buhi 1904, p. 297; *Yurt Ansiklopedisi*, 9, p. 6359 quoting Trabzon VS for 1872 and 1901.

79 From 8 l to 3 l. A&P 1910, 103, 7472, Longworth at Trebizond. RCC Année 1913, Trabzon province for 1910 and 1911.

80 FO 195/939, 1/6/1869. Similarly, Erzurum purchases for Mosul cloth fluctuated from 302 to 24 bales, for Van cloth from 163 to 56 bales and of Harput cloth from 22 to 78 bales.

81 Buhi, X, 9, 8/20/1907.

82 A&P 1902, 10, 6568, Erzeroom for 1901; A&P 1910, 103, 7472, McGregor at Erzeroom.

83 FO 195/112, Brant at Erzeroom, 6/16/1839.

84 FO 195/1584, 1887, Barnham, 4/2/1887; AS 1891, No. 930, Erzeroom for 1889–90, 6/16/1891.

85 FO 195/112, Brant at Erzeroom, 6/16/1839. A&P 1873, 67, Taylor at Erzeroom, 11/14/1872.

86 BBA I, ŞD 2196, XI 3 1295/1878; see also BBA I, ŞD 2580, VIII 2 1296/July 1879.

87 AS 1889, #527, Erzeroum for 1887–88, Chermside, 4/10/1889. AS 1891, No. 930, Erzeroum for 1889–90, 6/16/1891; US T 681, Sivas supplement 6/20/1893, has a table showing annual cotton yarn and cloth imports into Harput province, 1885–92. A&P 1899, 103, 6241, Erzeroum for 1898, Massy.

88 This assessment compares the shipments of 200 bales of cloth to Erzurum with the use of 2,500 bales of British yarn plus the locally spun yarn in the 1890s.

89 Buhi 9, 1907, 8/20/1907.

90 A&P 1908, 117, 7253, Shipley, Erzeroom for 1907; A&P 1910, 103, 7472, McGregor at Erzeroom; and A&P 1911, 96, 7579, McGregor.

91 FO 78/289, Brant at Trebizond, 11/8/1836; FO 195/459, Holmes on Pashalik of Diarbekir, 4/14/1857 and Holmes at Diarbekir, 3/31/1857; A&P 1865, 53, Taylor for 1863; FO 195/799, Taylor at Diarbekir, 1/11/1864 and 3/31/1864.

92 FO 195/799, Trade and Agriculture for Kurdistan for 1863, enclosed in Taylor, Istanbul, July 1864.

93 FO 195/304, Stevens at Samsun, 5/10/1845; Luckerts (1906), p. 23. FO 195/799, Trade and Agriculture of Kurdistan for 1863, Taylor at Istanbul, July 1864. Earlier in the century, Mardin weavers had been famed for the manufacture of beautiful white woolen cloaks worn in the summer but it is uncertain if this is the same activity reported on here.

94 A&P 1873, 67 Taylor, 11/14/1872.

95 A&P 1873, 67, Taylor at Erzeroom, 11/14/1872; FO 195/1584, 1887, Devey at Erzeroum 4/7/1887; ibid., Boyajian 5/9/1887; AS 1886, #30, Erzeroum for 1885; AS 1889, #527, Boyajian at Diarbekr, Report for 1888; AS 1891, #930, Erzeroom for 1889–90. These statements about increases in cotton and cotton-silk production are based on imprecise statistics. In 1864, 3.1 million piasters of the former and 3.9 million of the latter were exported from the region. During the late 1880s and early 1890s, mixed cloth exports averaged *c.* 1.3 million piasters. Given the price declines that had occurred, the volume was probably about one-third below that of the 1860s. In 1908, 3.5 million piasters of mixed cloth was produced and 2.0 millions were exported. Again, considering price trends, these exports in volume certainly exceeded those of 1864. Cotton cloth production, for its part, reportedly had become directed solely towards the local market and was valued at 3 million piasters. This was certainly at least twice the volume produced for export in 1864.

96 A&P 1892, 84, #1050, Erzeroum for 1891, 4/16/1892; A&P 1893–94, 97, #5581, Fitzmaurice, 5/20/1893.

97 Buhi, X, 9, 8/20/1907.

98 Buhi, 9, 8/20/1907 and FO 195/799, Taylor at Istanbul, Julliet 1864. Statistics regarding the numbers of looms at Diyarbakır are unhelpful. An early twentieth-century source bemoans the decline of manufacturing at Diyarbakır and Mardin by comparing the number of looms of earlier times with those of his own day. Then, the German consular official said, Diyarbakır and Mardin held 23,000 looms (respectively 3,000 and 20,000); now (1907), however, there were 3,500 (1,000 and 2,500 respectively). But the contemporary British report from the 1860s enumerates 3,920 looms in the two areas (1,720 and 1,200 respectively).

99 See sources cited in table 2.5 and BCF, 1889, Diyarbakır, 1 July 1888. It should be noted that the lower figures, 17.0 and 12.5 percent, are given by European sources while the 50 percent figure is derived from official Ottoman statistics. Thus, the differences in market shares may derive from a reporting problem.

100 This section summarizes the material found in Shields (1986), esp. pp. 69–78, that forms the best account of Mosul economic life in the period.

101 In 1845, indigo dyeing in the town provided the most important single source of taxes, some 190,000 piasters, obtained from the indigo dyeing *mukataa*. Its holder had the monopoly over the activity. In addition, indigo dyeing in the villages provided 6,500 piasters, a sum that surely reflects governmental tax-collecting inabilities rather than dyeing activities in these rural locations. By comparison, the stamp tax provided 130,000 piasters. FO 78/598, 6/21/1845, Stevens at Samsun.

102 A&P 1858, 30, Skene on 1857 Aleppo trade.

103 BBA Cev İkt 1024, two documents, each dated X 11 1262/October 1846; FO 78/289, Abbott at Erzeroom, 10/11/1835; FO 78/264, Werry at Aleppo, 6/10/1835; CRUS Aleppo for 1857, p. 348.

104 FO 195/741, Trade reports for 1861–62, Skene, Aleppo, 12/31/1861; idem., 6/5/1862; FO 195/761, Skene, Aleppo, 12/31/1862.

105 A&P 1872, LVII, 3565, Skene at Aleppo, 12/31/1871; A&P 1873, 64, Skene on North Syria for 1872.

106 Scherzer (1873), pp. 183, 189.

107 Buhi, III, 10, 1/22/1902, Aleppo; k und k 1904, X, 1, 3; k und k 1907, VIII, 1.

108 Bowring (1840).

109 Bowring (1840), p. 84

110 A&P 1856, LVII, 2330, Barker on Aleppo trade of 1855.

111 A&P 1872, LVII, 3565, Skene for Aleppo, 12/31/1871.

112 BBA I MM 2276, III 28 1292/May 1875.

113 Buhi III, 10, 1/22/1902, Aleppo.

114 Luckerts (1906).

115 A&P 1856, LVII, 2330, Bulwer on Aleppo trade of 1855; FO 195/741, Aleppo, 6/5/1862; Scherzer (1873), p. 189, refers to *alaca* robes of half silk.

116 Buhi III, 10, Aleppo, 1/22/1902. In 1866, *alaca* was still made with silk. See BBA I, MV 25281, VI 1283/October 1866.

117 Buhi 9, 8/20/1907.

118 FO 195/302, Werry at Aleppo, 2/2/1850 and 2/1/1851. The revolt resulted from imposition of the *ferde* and *vergi* taxes on the city. FO 195/416, Werry at Aleppo, 1/29/1853.

119 FO 195/700, Skene at Aleppo, 12/31/1860 and 6/8/1861.

120 FO 195/761, Skene at Aleppo, 12/31/1862; FO 195/800, Skene at Aleppo, 12/31/1863.

121 FO 195/802, Skene at Aleppo, 4/2/1868.

122 A&P 1873, 64, Skene for North Syria in 1872.

123 A&P 1876, 75, 3925, Skene, Aleppo, 12/31/1875.

124 A&P 1877, 83, 4024, Skene for 1876; AS 1889, 500, Jago at Aleppo, 3/6/1889.

125 AS 1888, 342, Trebizond for 1887.

126 AS 1890, 745, Aleppo for 1889; ibid. 1891, 896, Aleppo for 1890.

127 A&P 1897, 94, 6016, Catoni, Aleppo, 8/24/1896 and also Catoni report for 1895–96.

128 RCC Reel 32, Nr. 7, Aleppo for 1899.

129 Buhi III, 10, 1/22/1902, Aleppo.

130 k und k 1901, X, 3, Aleppo.

131 A&P 1899, 103, 6241, Aleppo.

132 A&P 1900, 96, 6353, Aleppo for 1899, Barnham.

133 A&P 1910, 103, 7472, Aleppo for 1909, Catoni. The figure is surely too high.

134 k und k, 1904, X, 1.

135 See sources cited in table 2.8. This seems to be the same person, Skene, who had filed the 1862 report and forgot his own earlier testimony! The exception is the 1856 report cited by Issawi that was near contemporary to the time being discussed.

136 Bowring (1840); Buhi, 13, 2/14/1902.

137 FO 195/902, Skene at Aleppo, 4/2/1868.

138 FO 195/902, Skene, Aleppo, 4/2/1868; Halep VS 1317/1899, pp. 191–92; k und k X, 3, 1901, Aleppo; k und k VIII, 1, 1907, Aleppo.

139 RCC Reel 32, Nr. 7, Aleppo for 1899. Similarly, the increasing indigo imports at Diyarbakır were attributed to rising poverty; "the poorer the country gets the more will this article be in demand." AS 1886, #30, Erzeroum for 1885.

140 CRUS Aleppo for Year Ending 9/30/1858, Aleppo for 1857, p. 348; A&P 1872, LVII, 3565, Skene at Aleppo, 12/31/1871. In 1871, Aleppo weavers used two million lb. of yarn to make 2,000,000 pieces of cotton cloth. In 1855, they had made 2,600,000 pieces of cloth while, in 1857, they had used 1.0 million kg. of cotton thread.

141 Buhi, Heft 13, 2/14/1902; see Issawi (1988), p. 144.

142 k und k, 1904, I, p. 1. Productivity certainly was rising at this time; between 1902 and
1911, some 50 jacquard looms went into operation in the city.

3   **Patterns of cloth production in the Ottoman lands from Salonica to Aleppo**

 1 FO 78/189, 5/11/1836. Galante (1985), IV, p. 46.
 2 Cuinet (1890–94), III, p. 410.
 3 FO 195/112, Brant, 7/16/1839.
 4 BBA Cev Mal 16795, IX 2 1257/1841. Armenians of unspecified gender also were
    weaving.
 5 ZStA,AA 8729, Trapezunt for 1902.
 6 Buhi, IV, 13, 11/20/1902, Trapezunt; k und k, 1906, X, 3, Trapezunt.
 7 Issawi (1988), p. 401. FO 195/459, Holmes on the Pashalik of Diabekir, 4/14/1857 and
    Holmes at Diarbekir, 3/31/1857.
 8 Fukasawa (1987). FO 78/420, Brant at Erzeroom, 6/18/1840.
 9 Buhi, IV, 13, 11/20/1902, Trapezunt; k und k, 1906, X, 3, Trapezunt. It is not known
    if the shopowners were organized into guilds.
10 Cuinet (1890–94), III, pp. 537–39.
11 Issawi (1982), p. 152.
12 FO 195/304, Stevens at Samsun, 5/10/1845; Luckerts (1906), p. 23. FO 195/799,
    Trade and Agriculture of Kurdistan for 1863, Taylor at Istanbul, July 1864.
13 FO 195/153, Carpenter at Tarsus, 12/31/1845 and A&P 1875, 77, 3837, Aleppo,
    5/26/1875.
14 FO 78/367, A. G. Glascott, 10/11/1839.
15 FO 195/741, Whitaker at Gallipoli, 2/12/1862; A&P 1868–9, Gallipoli for 1867,
    Odoni; A&P 1872, 58, 3566, Gallipoli for 1871, Odoni.
16 Todorov (1983), pp. 212–13 and, generally, pp. 218–91.
17 E.g., BCF 1877, Adrianople, 5/10/1877.
18 FO 78/289, Brant, 8/11/1836 and 3/11/1836.
19 FO 78/289, 5/11/1836 and 11/8/1836, Brant at Trebizonde; A&P 1899, 103, 6241,
    Massy at Erzeroum for 1898.
20 A&P 1897, 94, 6016, Massy report on Adana for 1895–96; A&P 1898, 94, 6195, Massy
    at Adana; A&P 1900, 96, 6353.
21 A&P 1905, 93, 6884, Aleppo, 3/31/1905.
22 A&P 1912–13, 100, 7685, Fontana at Aleppo; A&P 1914, 95, 7883, Fontana at Aleppo.
23 Shields (1986), pp. 69–78.
24 Buhi, III, 9, Januar 1902.
25 A&P 1908, 116, 7252, Wylie at Konya.
26 A&P 1902, 10, 6568, Erzeroom for 1901; FO 195/112, Brant at Erzeroom, 6/16/1839;
    FO 195/728, Dalyell, 12/29/1862.
27 FO 195/1584, 1887, Barnham, 4/2/1887.
28 Buhi, XIII, 9, 8/20/1907; BBA Cev İkt 1393, VIII 1267/1851; Scherzer (1873),
    pp. 178, 184.
29 A&P 1898, 94, 6125, Ankara, Shipley, 7/11/1898 and A&P 1913, 73, 7781, Monahan
    for 1912.
30 A&P 1862, 58, Stevens, Trebizonde.

31 Nuri (1922/1338); Buhi XIII, 9, 8/20/1907.
32 See sources cited in chapter 2, Arapkir section.
33 AE CC Turquie, 10, 4/15/1890; Buhi, X, 9, 8/20/1907.
34 Buhi, IV, 13, 11/20/1902.
35 Buhi, IV, 13, 11/20/1902, Trapezunt; k und k, 1906, X, 3, Trapezunt and 1912.
36 FO (1871), pp. 795–97.
37 FO 195/799, Trade and Agriculture for Kurdistan for 1863, enclosed in Taylor, Istanbul, July 1864.
38 Russell (1794), pp. 161–62.
39 Thieck (1985), pp. 141–42.
40 A&P 1858, 30, Skene on 1857 Aleppo trade.
41 Buhi, III, 10, 1/22/1902, Aleppo.
42 Buhi, III, 10, 1/22/1902, Aleppo.
43 A&P 1902, 110, 6568, Barnham, Aleppo for 1901; Buhi, 9, 8/20/1907; Buhi, III, 10, Januar 1902, Aleppo.
44 This is the view of Faruk Tabak, Binghamton University, who is completing his dissertation on Aleppo during the eighteenth century.
45 There is no enumeration of privately owned factories in Egypt until late in the period; see Owen (1981), pp. 149–51. See chapter 1 for a discussion of factors affecting the formation of factories.
46 RCC 1905, #412, Edirne province for 1903; Edirne VS 1309/1891, p. 182.
47 k und k 1906, XXI, 3, Salonich.
48 k und k 1907, XXI, 5, Salonich.
49 Buhi, XIX, Heft 6, 4/13/1913, pp. 444–46.
50 For more details, see my *Technology Transfer and Manufacturing in the Ottoman Empire, 1800–1914* (İstanbul, 1992). Clark (1969), pp. 7–33; DeKay (1833), p. 124.
51 k und k, 1901, XIX, 1, Konstantinopel and 1903, Konstantinopel; Buhi 1904, p. 298.
52 k und k, 1901, XIX, 1 and 1903, Konstantinopel. Turkey, *Düstur* (1937–43), 6, pp. 472–82; BBA I MM 3225, VII 7 1298/1881; Clark (1969), pp. 100–1. *Bursa sergisi*, 7 Ağustos 1325, aded 5, pp. 58–59.
53 k u k 1910, Smyrna. A&P 1912–13, 100, 7685, Waugh for Istanbul.
54 Buhi 18, 1913, 9/24/1912, Smyrne.
55 Buhi, 18, 1913, 9/24/1912.
56 FO 195/889, Taylor, 4/18/1867; RCL 5/31/1904, Lettre de Harpout; Buhi 1907, 9, 8/20/1907; USCR, LXVI, 249, June 1901.
57 Buhi III, 1902, Adana; Buhi 1904, 8, 1/14/1902.
58 A&P 1913, 73, 7781, Waugh at Istanbul; RCL, Lettre de Mersine, Septembre 1912. AS 4235 for 1908.
59 A&P 1909, 98, 7360, Doughty-Wylie, Adana; Buhi X, 9, 8/20/1907.
60 Corancez (1816), p. 403 says 2,000 looms but others, such as Yavuz (1984), p. 195, and US Monthly Reports, February 1909, p. 114, give lower figures, usually 1,000. The last source states the total number of loom workers as 10,000.
61 Ibid.
62 Based on 1840 report of one Captain Conolly to the Asiatic Society. My thanks to Ariel Salzmann for this material. She is preparing her doctoral dissertation on industry in the Ankara region.

63 FO 195/253, Suter at Kayseri, 3/16/1846; Ankara VS 1307/1889, p. 233; US Monthly Reports, February 1909, p. 113.

64 Ankara VS 1311/1893, p. 238.

65 k und k, 1903, Konstantinopel. Ankara VS 1311/1893, p. 238.

66 Fukasawa (1987), e.g. pp. 46–48.

67 Statistics concerning this decline presently are not available.

68 BBA Cev İkt 347, X 1220/Dec.-Jan. 1805–6. My thanks to the late Jean-Pierre Thieck for his help in understanding the intricacies of Ottoman cloth finishing.

69 Fukasawa (1987), pp. 51–53.

70 FO 78/289, 8/11/1836; FO 195/101, Brant, 4/11/1832 and Suter, 12/31/1835.

71 FO 78/289, Brant, Trebizond, 8/11/1836.

72 FO 78/289, 8/11/1836; FO 195/101, Brant, 4/11/1832, and Suter, 12/31/1835.

73 A&P 1905, 93, Izmir, Altintop for 1904, 7/11/1905.

74 FO 195/939, 1/6/1869 and FO 195/889, 4/18/1864.

75 FO 195/939, 1/6/1869, Erzeroom and FO 195/889, 4/18/1864.

76 AE CC Turquie 10, 4/15/1890, pp. 193-193r; RCC Reel 31, #209, Trebizonde for 1893. Erzurum residents at this time annually bought some 110,000 piasters of the linen; e.g., A&P 1892, 84, 1050, Erzeroum for 1891; A&P 1897, 94, 6016, Erzeroum, for 1897.

77 Issawi (1988), pp. 373–76.

78 RCC Reel 34, Nr. 149, Sivas in 1901 and Buhi, 9, 8/20/1907; Mordtmann (1925), p. 155; Sivas VS 1321/1903.

79 Turkey *Düstur* (1937–43), 5, pp. 93–94.

80 BBA Cev İkt 1793, I 1220/1805.

81 FO 195/293, Blunt at Salonica, for year ending 12/31/1849.

82 Selanik VS 1307/1889, p. 228.

83 Cuinet (1890–94), III, p. 410. Value originally given as 60,000 marks.

84 Fitzner (1902); GB Naval Staff (1919), I, pp. 120–21; also Cuinet (1890–94), III, p. 622.

85 Cuinet (1890–94), IIII, pp. 537–39.

86 BBA Cev İkt 1393, VIII 1267/1851. Inequitable taxation was blamed: domestically made goods paid 24 percent in customs duties while foreign goods paid only 3 percent.

87 Buhi 1904 and BCF 1889, Trebizonde.

88 Scherzer (1873), pp. 178, 184.

89 HHStA,AA, PA XII, Karton 272, k und k Smyrna, 1/4/1896. Also see Aydın VS 1313/1897, pp. 501–2; RCC Reel 33, No. 32, Izmir for 1899 and No. 130, Izmir for 1900. RCC Reel 35, Izmir for 1902. Buhi, III, 9, Januar 1902.

90 Calculations based on Scherzer (1873), p. 184. Depending on quality and width, the imported cloth cost 10–15 centimes/yard. A finished printed piece, weighing *c*. 1/2 kg, sold for between 10 centimes and 1.25 francs/yard. Value originally stated as 1.7 million francs.

91 UPA FO Vol. 7, Biliotti at Trebizond, 12/31/1878.

92 A&P 1872, LVII, 3565, Skene at Aleppo, 12/31/1871; A&P 1873, 64, Skene on North Syria for 1872.

93 A&P 1893, 97, 5581, Trabzon for 1892, Longworth, 3/13/1893.

94 RCC Reel 34, Nr. 149, Sivas in 1901 and Buhi 9, 8/20/1907. The province bought some 2,000 Singer sewing machines in 1910. RCC Reel 40, E. Dussay, 1911. Value originally given as 550,000 francs. Genç (1987), pp. 145–70.

95 A&P 1873, 67, Taylor, 11/14/1872. Compare the piece rates for *şeytan bezi* in FO 195/799, Trade and Agriculture of Kurdistan for 1863, Taylor at Istanbul, July 1864 with 1888 piece rate for cotton cloth production in the town of Diyarbakır in BCF 1880, Diarbakr. 7/1/1889. The import of synthetic dyestuffs also was important although its precise role in reducing costs at Diyarbakır is not known at this time.

96 Sivas VS 1306/1888, p. 217 and 1321/1903, p. 191.

97 FO 78/289, 5/11/1836 and 11/8/1836, Brant at Trebizond.

98 FO 195/939, 1/6/1869, Erzeroom and FO 195/889, Taylor, 4/18/1864.

99 Cuinet (1890–94), III, p. 360.

100 US T681, H. M. Jewett, 3/1/1888. Value originally given as 11,000 pounds sterling.

101 AS 1886, Erzeroum for 1885.

102 A&P 1892, 84, #1050, Erzeroum for 1891, 4/16/1892; A&P 1893–94, 97, #5581, Fitzmaurice, 5/20/1893.

103 ZStA,AA 8729, Trapezunt for 1902.

104 Buhi, IV, 13, 11/20/1902. This marketing practice confused observers who sometimes reported the bundles of five pieces as one piece.

105 Tillmann (1916–17), p. 8.

106 Also see Junge (1916), and Stich (1929) for accounts derived from the German and Austrian consular sources.

107 A&P 1878–79, Biliotti at Trebizond for 1877–78.

108 AS 1887, No. 135, Trebizond province for 1886.

109 FO AS 342, 1888, Trebizond for 1887; AS 549, 1889, Trebizond for 1888.

110 FO AS 689, 1890, Trebizond, 1889. AE CC Turquie, 10, 4/15/1890.,

111 A&P 1892, 84, 1059, Trebizond for 1891.

112 A&P 1893–4, 97, 5581, Trebizond for 1892 and A&P 1895, 100, 5801, Trebizond, 3/15/1895. See also A&P 1894, 88, 5690, Trebizond for 1893.

113 This account is uncertain because different units of measure were employed by the various sources. In 1889, production was 40,000 *pics*, 6.8 m × 48–50 cm, while in 1910, *manusa* cloth production was a stated 60,000 pieces. AE CC Turquie, 10, 4/15/1890 and compare with A&P 1910, 103, 7472, Longworth and with the sources cited in the Trabzon section.

114 Buhi, IV, 13, 11/20/1902, Trapezunt; k und k, 1906, X, 3, Trapezunt; k und k, 1909, Trapezunt; and k und k, 1912, Trapezunt.

115 Buhi, IV, 13, 11/20/1902, Trapezunt; k und k, 1906, X, 3, Trapezunt; k und k, 1909, Trapezunt; and k und k, 1912, Trapezunt.

116 This was also the case in Aleppo and Aintab.

117 Burnus and handkerchief looms numbered two in 1902, three in 1909 and reportedly ten in the preceding year.

118 For example, see the output figures in Issawi (1988), p. 376.

119 Fukasawa (1987), pp. 47, 51–52.

120 A&P 1859, Skene at Marash, 2/14/1859.

121 RCL 5/31/1904, Lettre de Marache, 3/30/1904; table 2.8.

122 A&P 1859, 30, 2544, Sandwich at Aintab, 4/4/1858.

123 A&P 1859, 30, 2544, Sandwich at Aintab.

124 A&P 1859, 30, 2544, Sandwich at Aintab, 4/4/1858; FO 195/1202, Henderson at Aleppo, 12/2/1878.

125 AS 1891, 930, Erzeroum for 1889–90, Hampson, 6/16/1890; A&P 1905, 93, Shipley, Erzeroum district for 1904.

126 A&P 1908, 116, 7252, Wylie at Konya.

127 Buhi, 9, 8/20/1907.

128 k und k, VIII, 1, 1907, Aleppo.

129 E.g., k und k 1901, X, 3, Aleppo.

130 Unfortunately, the source reporting the strike does not state with total clarity if the strikes were in Aleppo only or in the other production centers as well.

131 k und k, 1904, X, 1, Aleppo.

132 A&P 1893–94, 97, 5581, Jago, Aleppo, 4/7/1893.

133 A&P 1893–94, 97, 5581, Aleppo for 1892, 4/7/93.

134 Buhi III, 10, 1/22/1902, Aleppo. In 1907, however, Aleppo was providing the southern part of Sivas province with locally dyed yarns. Buhi, x, Heft 9, 8/20/1907.

135 Buhi, Heft 13, 2/14/1902. The text says "Rohgarne" but the context makes clear that "Rothgarne" was intended.

136 k und k, VIII, 1, Aleppo for 1907.

137 Dyeing ten pounds of British yarn in Europe then cost *c.* 5 kronen while dyeing it "Turkish red" in Aintab cost only 2.5 kronen. k und k, 1904, I, p. 1. In 1902, Aintab had imported 600,000 kg. of better quality red yarn. Buhi Heft 13, 2/14/1902.

138 k und k, 1904, I.

139 k und k, 1907, VIII, 1, Aleppo.

140 E.g., k und k 1907, VIII, Aleppo; Buhi, 9, 8/20/1907, Aleppo.

4   Silk cloth and raw silk production

1 İnalcık (1969); Dalsar (1960); Owen (1984); Labaki (1984); Quataert (1984).

2 BBA HH 57568, 1212/1797–98.

3 BBA Cev İkt 1324, II 23 1222/May 1807. Tax farming data, however, reflects increasing silk cloth production only after 1808. See Genç (1975).

4 BBA Cev İkt 245, V 23 1217/1802.

5 Genç (1975), however, argues that the period generally was dominated by increasing government restrictions and involvement in the economy.

6 Dalsar (1960), p. 307.

7 BBA Cev İkt 1642, IV 900 1231/1 February 1816; 36 piasters/*top* while the İstanbul cloth cost 41 piasters.

8 Hammer (1818), p. 69, states that production was 100,000 pieces. This figure included all varieties of silk products, from velvet cushion covers to semi-transparent gauzes. Later enumerations, such as those by Sandison (q.v.), note production levels of particular kinds of cloth and thus cannot be directly compared with the Hammer figure. Genç (1975) p. 273 is the source for the 1811–33 comparison. The annual *muaccele* for tax farms of the Bursa silk cloth industry was 58,000 piasters during the 1740s–50s and 60,000 in 1808. In the 1811–33 era, it annually was 76,000 piasters. These data support the impression given by comparing Hammer's figures with those

of Sandison – that the 1810s and 1820s were record years for Bursa silk cloth output.

9 BBA Cev İkt 1776, V 26 1261/July 1845.

10 BBA Cev İkt 1642, III 9 1231/1816; I MV 99, VI 21 1256/1840.

11 BBA HH 16756, 1225/1810. Cev İkt 1112,III 11 1230/1815.

12 BBA Cev İkt 1174, IV 1231/1816; Cev İkt 1924, II 1246/1830; Cev İkt 22, III 7 1251/1835.

13 BBA HH 16756, 1225/1810; Cev İkt 1112, III 11 1230/1815. The amount was 76,000 kg./year (5,000 *kıyye*/month at 65 piasters/*kıyye*).

14 BBA Cev Har 5147, IX 21 1216/1802; Cev İkt 399, 1219/1804–5; Cev İkt 1419, VI 1231/1816; Cev İkt 1240, 7 VI 1242/1826; Cev İkt 996, X 20 1242/May 1826; Cev İkt 1298, 9 VI 1244/1828. FO 78/131 "Defense d'exporter de la soie" that quotes an English translation of the text of the 12/16/1802 and several other prohibitions just noted and the translated text of a firman dated VIII 1240/April 1825. FO 78/355, Posonby at Therapia, 4/3/1839; FO 78/346, Posonby at Therapia, 5/19/1839.

15 Respectively near the Koca Mustafa Pasha and Selimiyye mosques. BBA HH 16756, 1225/1810. The decision of the judge and its approval by the supervisor of the Tersane, who had jurisdiction in the case, apparently was overturned later by imperial decree.

16 Urquhart (1833), p. 183.

17 Personal correspondence from Carlo Poni, 45/1/1988; Hammer (1818), pp. 69–70; Pallis (1951), p. 75; Braudel (1986), II, pp. 312–13.

18 Urquhart (1833), p. 183. Silk spinning, that is, unravelling the single cocoon thread, is simpler than cotton spinning but supplies were comparatively limited.

19 FO 195/113, Sandison at Bursa, 2/15/1840; FO 78/490, Sandison at Bursa, 2/10/1842.

20 FO 195/113, 2/15/1840, Sandison at Bursa; FO 78/490, Sandison at Bursa, 2/10/1842; USNA 1847, Film T 194, r. 2, Schwaabe at Bursa, 10/1/1847. Whether the recorded increases in 1839 were due to the Convention or were part of an existing trend can be debated; I hold the latter position.

21 FO 195/113, Sandison at Bursa, 2/15/1840; MacGregor (1847), p. 107.

22 FO 78/750, reports on trade of Bursa for the year 1847. FO 195/208, 3/10/1844, Sandison at Bursa. In 1855, the *kazaz* guild of İstanbul complained, unauthorized persons were selling silk goods, *ipek* and *kazaz*, in their shops. As a result, it said, the guild daily was becoming more disorganized and confused. BBA I MV 13965, VI 25 1271/1855. As in the case of most guild complaints, it is difficult to assess the significance of the complaint.

23 BBA: Cev İkt 424, VI 20 1251/1835; I MV 99, VI 21 1256/1840; I Dah 1606, 1256/1840–1. FO 195/113, Sandison at Bursa, 2/15/1840.

24 With the departure of Consul Sandison, the detailed reports on the silk industry that traced cloth production ceased. His successors and other observers focused their attention on efforts to reverse the plummeting level of cocoon and raw silk production.

25 Turkey (1970), p. 161, states that there were 1,400 looms in the city in 1917; but this was wartime and the figures reflect exceptional times in which the Ottoman Empire was nearly totally self-reliant for its textiles.

26 Dalsar (1960) says 1910 while Turkey (1970) gives the year as 1908.

27 Dalsar (1960), pp. 432–34; Turkey (1970), pp. 161–63; Eldem (1970), p. 130, includes

the Hereke cloth production in the 1.1 million piaster figure. He states the value of hand-woven cloth from Syria and Lebanon at 16.0 millions.

28 See chapter 3; also BCF Trebizonde for 1889, pp. 219–20.

29 USCR, LXVI, 249, June 1901, p. 281; Buhi, 9, 8/20/1907; Mamuret ul Aziz VS 1325/1907, pp. 146–48.

30 UPA, Vol. 16, 1908, Mesopotamia, p. 104; Buhi, 9, 8/20/1907, p. 712.

31 BCF 1889, Diarbekir for 1888, 7/1/1889.

32 For Aleppo and Diyarbakır, see chapter 3; for the case of Damascus, see the work of Sherry Vatter.

33 Bursa VS 1325/1907, pp. 258–60; Stich (1929), p. 96.

34 FO 195/113, 2/15/1840 and FO 195/208, 2/24/1844, Sandison at Bursa.

35 FO 195/208, 2/24/1844, Sandison at Bursa.

36 FO 78/868, 3/31/1851 and 195/393, 3/16/1853. Sandison at Bursa.

37 FO 195/393, 3/20/1854, Sandison at Bursa; A&P 1862, 58, Sandison at Bursa for 1860.

38 FO 195/113, 2/15/1840, Sandison at Bursa.

39 FO 195/208, 2/24/1844, Sandison at Bursa.

40 FO 78/868, 3/31/1851 and 195/393, 3/16/1853. Sandison at Bursa.

41 FO 195/774, Sandison for 1864, 8/16/1865. In 1901, 103 hand reels still worked in the city of Bursa, 4 percent of all reels operating. AE CC Turquie, Brousse, 3/25/1898.

42 Dalsar (1960), p. 373. The famed silk rugs made at Kayseri after 1870 were produced from foot-reeled raw silk. Ibid. p. 374. RCL reports of the Bursa district after World War I similarly report the presence of many hand reels. My thanks to Çağlar Keyder for this information.

43 Delbeuf (1906); Cuinet (1890–94) IV, pp. 57–58; USNA Film T 194, r. 2, 10/1/1847, Schwaabe; FO 195/205, Sandison at Bursa, 6/25/1845. Stich (1929), p. 96. The sources state that short reels came in 1838, the same year the Glaizal family opened a silk reeling factory. It seems reasonable to assume that the mill contained the first short reels used in Bursa region. Dalsar (1960), pp. 410–12. The migration of the Glaizal family and general establishment of the French silk producers' colony at Bursa certainly is tied to the great strikes in the silk center of Lyon between 1831–34 and in subsequent years. Sewell (1980), pp. 207–8, 217.

44 FO 195/205, 3/17/1846, Sandison at Bursa. The Falkeisen mill apparently (was?) burnt down and was rebuilt. FO 78/701, 7/6/1847, Bursa. USNA Film T 194, r. 2, Schwaabe at Bursa, 10/1/1847.

45 Stich (1929), p. 96.

46 In the same year, silk production was the largest in several years. FO 78/701, Report on Trade of Bursa for 1846 as well as for 1847 and for 1847–48. The stagnation in the silk trade finally subsided, with steady sales and rising prices. FO 195/299, 10/7/1848.

47 FO 778/441, 3/18/1841.

48 FO 778/441, 5/29/1841. This was proportionately less than in England.

49 USNA Film T 194, r. 3, Brousse, Schwabe, 12/31/1850.

50 FO 295/393, 3/16/1853. In his report for 1851–2, Sandison states that "Gesairli" owned two mills at İstanbul, one each at Mudanya and Bilecik and rented another from the former governor of Bursa, Sarım Pasha. FO 78/905, 8/6/1852.

51 BBA I MV 12045, V 15 1270/1854. A decade before, the government had summoned experts from France and Switzerland to help develop the industry. Dalsar (1960), p. 411.

52 Delbeuf (1906), p. 131.
53 Urquhart (1833), pp. 180–81; GB FO 195/100, 12/31/1838 and FO 195/176, 2/2/1843 and FO 195/240, 3/27/1846, Blunt at Salonica; FO 78/441 and CR US 1851, T 194, Reel 3. Edirne possessed three steam powered mills in the early 1870s, that were functioning in the early twentieth century. Compare FO (1873) with RCC 1905, # 412 and RCC 1910, Adrianople province for 1903 and 1909.
54 Owen (1981); Labaki (1984).
55 FO 195/241, Werry at Smyrna, July 1845. Georgiades (1885), p. 65; Scherzer (1873), p. 150.
56 Buhi 1904; BBA Cev Har 2497, IV 1265/1849; GB FO 195/304, trade of Samsun, 12/31/1852; BCF 1877, p. 557.
57 UPA, Vol. 16, 104, pp. 212–13, 1908 report.
58 Cochran (1887), p. 178, quoting Lady Claud Hamilton.
59 Cochran (1887), p. 176. This contains very lengthy and extraordinary descriptions of silk raising in the İzmir area during the mid-1880s.
60 French national production averaged *c.* 4 million kg. of cocoons. In Italy, by contrast, cocoon production averaged *c.* 40–50 million kg. in the pre-World War I period. *The Manchester Guardian Commercial.* "European Textiles", 12/10/1925, pp. 36–38.
61 FO 78/868, 3/31/1851, Sandison at Bursa. FO 195/393, report on Bursa for 1855, Sandison at Bursa, 1/15/1856, shows the importance of Britain in the Bursa silk market. Farley (1862) states that Bursa formerly had sent 75 percent of its raw silk to England, but now France received this amount. Warsberg (1869) asserts that France then was buying 65 percent of the total. This process was a part of the ongoing international division of labor, in which Britain focused on cotton textiles and France on silk.
62 A&P 1854–55, LV, 2264, Sandison at Bursa for 1854. Dry cocoon output fell when producers needed money and contracted to sell all or nearly all their fresh cocoons. RCL 7/31/1901, pp. 154–55. On 20 July, a Bursa correspondent wrote, the fresh cocoon harvest was over with 1.4 mil. kg. RCL 6/30/1898, pp. 207–8. At İzmit, first arrivals were on 17 June. My thanks to Çağlar Keyder for his analysis of the post-World War I RCL reports.
63 AE CC Turquie, Brousse, 3/31/1897. Although this quote comes from late in the period, it seems to explain why families in the 1850s became and remained involved in providing materials for raw silk production.
64 Dutemple (1883), pp. 196–7.
65 Cochran (1887) for the İzmir region. DeKay (1833), Appendix, Salonica, 28 August 1832. For Bursa, see RCL 3/31/1902, pp. 506–8. Contributors to this journal of French Chamber of Commerce complained of the cheating peasant who, at harvest time, lied that the yield had been poor or altogether absent. This happened increasingly, the journal reported, as the number of egg raisers rose during the period of Debt Administration control over the industry. This early twentieth-century source provides unusual detail and reflects the general situation of the later nineteenth century as well.
66 FO 195/774, Sandison report for 1863, 5/28/1864.
67 FO (1873), J. Maling at Brussa, 10/5/1872.
68 Georgiades (1885), p. 66; Scherzer (1873), p. 150.
69 Buhi 1904; BCF 1877, p. 557.

70 FO (1873).

71 FO 195/648, 6/12/1860, Calvert at Salonica; BCF 1878, 7/1/1878, pp. 839–40.

72 FO 195/774, Sandison, 8/16/1865.

73 Dutemple (1883), pp. 209–10.

74 Cochran (1883), p. 108.

75 See Cochran (1883) for a full description of Pasteur's research and the control procedures.

76 Gueneau (1923), p. 217. Also, see table 4.5.

77 Quataert (1984) and sources therein.

78 The encouragement that the Ottoman Public Debt Administration offered to the silk industry has been studied in Quataert (1984).

79 FO (1873); RCC 1910, Adrianople for 1909, pp. 8–9. RCC 1910, #838, Adrianople for 1908.

80 Gueneau (1923), pp. 217–18.

81 Owen (1984), pp. 477–78.

82 RCC 1910, Adrianople for 1909, pp. 8–9.

83 FO 195/240, Blunt at Salonica, 3/27/1846.

84 FO 195/299, report on Bursa in 1850–51, 5/24/1851.

85 FO 78/905, report for 1851–52, 8/6/1852. FO 198/774, report for 1863, Sandison, 5/28/1864.

86 USNA Film T 194, r. 2, Bursa, 10/1/1847, Schwaabe.

87 Warsberg (1869), p. 149 and Delbeuf (1906).

88 FO 195/299, report on Bursa for 1850–51, enclosed in Sandison, 5/24/1851.

89 Mordtmann (1925), p. 296; Clark (1969), p. 47.

90 These dormitories are present on a detailed map of Bursa prepared in 1861–2 by the Ottoman General Staff. Erder (1975) is uncertain of the gender identity of the dormitory residents. Delbeuf (1906), pp. 139 and 139 n. 1, is explicit, asserting that they were young unmarried girls.

91 Delbeuf (1906), pp. 139 and 139 n. 1.

92 A&P 1862, 58, Sandison at Bursa for 1860 and 1/28/1861 for first half year, 1860. Delbeuf (1906), pp. 139–40 and 139 n. 1.

93 FO (1873), J. Maling at Brussa, 10/5/1872.

94 Ibid.

95 *İştirak*, 20 Şubat 1325 and 27 Mart 1326 give the higher figures for the workday and shorter break times. Turkey (1970), p. 157, states the average workday was 14 hours, including two hours of breaktime and meals.

96 Akbay (1983); Clark (1969), p. 34; Owen (1984), p. 476.

97 Warsberg (1869), pp. 144–45, contains a rosy analysis of the liberating effects of wage work on the status of Turkish working women; 1857 voyage by Perrot quoted in Galante (1985), IV, p. 333. Dumont (1982), p. 224, recounts an 1899 effort by the Bursa Jewish community to reel and weave silk that ran into the active opposition of the Greeks who sabotaged the effort. The 3 percent Jewish share of the workforce, however, does not seem disproportionately small. At this time, Jews formed under 1 and 2 percent respectively of the population of Bursa province and the central district of Bursa. Bursa VS 1321/1903, pp. 368–71.

98 A&P 1862, 58, Sandison for 1860, seems to place full blame for the crisis on the

part-time nature of work, ignoring the dependence of the mills on seasonally available supplies of cocoons.

99 FO 195/700, two reports by Sandison on the first and the last half of 1861, 12/21/1861. In the first, he reports that the Bursa region was "more or less exempt from the disease rampant in other countries." This is puzzling since 1860 cocoon production already had fallen to half of 1855 levels. See table 4.3.

100 FO 195/721, Sandison at Bursa, reports dated 7/24, 26 and 30/1862. The night after the factory sacking, Turks from an adjoining village attacked an Armenian village near İnegöl. Ibid., 6/28/1862. In December, he reports that the sultan had visited the city earlier in the year and made liberal purchases of bath cloths and silk hand-kerchiefs. This appears to have been a means of mitigating the economic crisis in the town. Dalsar (1960), p. 413 has a slightly different version of the attack. He says that dirty water used in the newly built factory ran into graves underneath the building.

101 E.g., BCF, Brousse, 2/26/1877, pp. 288–89.

102 This figure is indirectly derived by comparing raw silk production figures in the peak years of the 1850s and with those of the 1870s and 1870s and assuming a correspond-ing decline in the workforce.

103 RCL 5/31/1907, p. 846 notes that 19,000 persons were employed in the mills of Bursa province and İzmit district. Various sources, including Dalsar (1960), p. 410, state that 154–80 workers were required for every 100 reels in the factory. These ratios indicate that between 14,600 and 17,134 persons worked in the mills in 1909.

104 k und k 1901, X, 4, Brussa.

105 FO 195/649, Charles Calvert at Salonica, 6/12/1860.

106 The industrial survey of 1913 states that it is reporting the founding dates of silk mills at Bursa. Rather than date of foundings, these are the dates of the transfer of ownership from one party to another. As table 4.4 shows, the number of mills in the town of Bursa fell from 47 to 1901 to 38 in 1909, with 2,350 and 2,083 basins respectively.

107 FO 78/905, 8/8/1852 and other Sandison reports from Bursa; FO (1873); Turkey (1970), pp. 21–23.

108 Turkey (1970), 1917 table 8, p. 23 and table 8, p. 21. J. Maling at Bursa, 10/5/1872 in FO (1873).

109 RCL 6/30/1910, pp. 686–87.

110 RCL 6/30/1910, pp. 686–87.

111 The cocoon harvesting season is given in Akbay (1983). Arrivals of 120–150,000 kg. of fresh cocoons/day are noted in AE CC Turquie, Brousse, 7/10/1872. Also see RCL 6/30/1898, letter of 6/29/1898.

112 J. Maling, 10/5/1872 report in FO (1873) and RCL 8/31/1901, pp. 353–54; k und k 1901, X, 4, Brussa, says that the industry required 8.5 million kg. of cocoon but had only 4.5 million kg.

113 RCL 1/31/1901, pp. 488–90, 493. The French merchants at this time were pressing the Ottoman regime to ease restrictions on the import of silkworm eggs. To make their case, they argued that the mills were standing vacant for lack of eggs and they proposed import from Caucasus, Persia and Turkistan. Hence, although it is clear that lengthy shutdowns were common in the industry, our sources here are biased and must be treated accordingly. Ibid., 7/31/1901, pp. 154–55.

5 Carpet making

1 This chapter is a substantially revised and amplified version of Quataert (1986). This study is not art history but social and economic history and does not differentiate between rugs and carpets. Except when directly relevant, I will not refer to the truly vast literature on carpets/rugs as art objects.

2 Annette Ittig, personal correspondence, 1/24/1989 and 9/10/1990.

3 Turkey (1968), pp. 254–60; Banaz (n.d.), pp. 4–5; p. 6 gives the date as 1792. BBA HH 56146, 1204/1789–90.

4 Turkey (1968), p. 267.

5 USNA Film T238, reel 2, carpets were included on the list of exports to the U.S.

6 Hamilton (1842); quote from Arundell (1834), 104.

7 BBA Hüdavendigâr eyaletine dair mesaili mühimme #2281, 1262/1845–46 and Cev İkt 1520, IV 1261/1846; quote is from I, MV 8422, VII 13 1268/1852, report of VII 7 1268.

8 Farley (1862) p. 94.

9 This is an estimate, based on data in tables 5.4, 5, and 7 and the sources therein. It counts only the 2,000 looms in the city of Sivas as commercial looms and does not include the other 8,000 counted in the province.

10 For examples from the Uşak region, see FO 195/288, statement of the sums due to Messers. Werry, Keun and Company, 1846.

11 Buhi, 9, III, Januar 1902. Unlike raw silk spinning, carpet making was dependent on imports for some of its raw materials, for example, indigo and cochineal dyes.

12 Scherzer (1873), p. 171; Salaheddin (1867), p. 45.

13 Turkey (1968), p. 268.

14 *Bursa Sergisi*, Nr. 4, 10 Temmuz 1325, pp. 44–45 and #6, 14 Ağustos 1325, pp. 67–72. Jeancard (1919), p. 68, in 1914, reports this to be the invention of the Isparta director of the Oriental Carpet Manufacturers. More likely, it was developed elsewhere and adopted by the trust.

15 Buhi 1904; Buhi 1906.

16 Church (1892), pp. 4–5.

17 Beattie (1981), p. 132.

18 Van Lennep (1870), II: pp. 258–59.

19 Anon. (1904), p. 72.

20 Luckerts (1906), p. 32. Compare with Ittig (1985), illustrations on p. 113 showing a 1909 Kirmani carpet knotted after Watteau's "Les Fetes Venitiennes."

21 Atalay (c. 1952), pp. 44–45 and p. 45 n. 28; this probably is the source for a similar description in Turkey (1968), p. 261.

22 GB (1919), p. 122, based on Fitzner (1902).

23 Anon. (1904), pp. 60–72.

24 Stoeckel (1892), p. III.

25 Dutemple (1883), pp. 222, 224.

26 Turkey (1968), p. 261.

27 Buhi 1904, p. 293.

28 BBA, I MV 8422, VIII 7 1268/April 1852. A 1840s' visitor to Uşak, however, spoke of workers knotting solely from memory. Hamilton (1842).

29 Salaheddin (1867), p. 41.
30 Işıksaçan (1964), p. 12.
31 Scherzer (1873), p. 172.
32 Church (1892), p. 5.
33 Stoeckel (1892), p. III; HHStA, Januar 1896.
34 Van Lennep II (1870), p. 258. RCC 1911, Sivas, #953, pp. 4–5.
35 Luckerts (1906), p. 32.
36 RCC Reel #33, #130, Smyrna for 1900.
37 von Scheinitz (1906).
38 Atalay (*c.* 1952), pp. 51–52; at Kula, dyeing was done by the individual knotters. *İkdam*, 2 IV 1325/4/15/1907, pp. 2–3, notes these dyers were organized into guilds.
39 Buhi, III, 9, Januar 1902.
40 BBA I MV 8422, VIII 13 1268/1852.
41 USNA T238, Reel 7, Smyrna, 1/4/1868. The reference to machinery is obscure. An undated document from the palace archives of the Sultan may provide a clue. It lists the equipment for machines and tools to spin and dye wool yarn, at the rate of 1700 kg./day, for the manufacture of 545,000 kg. of Anatolian rugs per year. The equipment to be imported included machines for spinning warp and woof threads and for wool washing, dyeing, carding. The document also gives price of the dyes: madder, sumac, cochineal, indigo. BBA Yıldız 18, 525/636 128 30.
42 Scherzer (1873), pp. 171–72; Buhi 1904; Stich (1929), p. 110.
43 Brian Huffner, Oriental Carpet Manufacturers, London, interview of 7/25/1985.
44 AS 3931 for 1906, p. 10, quoting a British merchant in the rug business.
45 In 1904, Germany shipped 5.3 million piasters worth of German aniline and alizarin dyes to the Ottoman Empire. *The Board of Trade Journal*, 5/23/1907, p. 352.
46 Scherzer (1873), pp. 171–72.
47 Import of indigo reportedly down sharply in recent years, only 160,000 kg. in 1886, because of increased aniline dye usage. FO AS 1887, #197, Constantinople for 1886, Fawcett, states that, twenty years before, local dyers abandoned vegetable for mineral dyes.
48 Atalay (*c.* 1952), p. 50; natural dyes, he says, vanished with the building of the European style yarn factories in the town.
49 Stoeckel (1892), pp. I–II. Since Uşak was in the province of Bursa, he reported, the 1888 prohibition of the Aydın governor was without force.
50 Mumford (1900), pp. 151–52.
51 Fitzner (1902), translated in GB Naval Staff (1919), p. 122. Mumford (1900), p. 150. Until a few years ago, a 1906 source reported, rug makers used imported indigo from India but that was being replaced by German synthetic indigo. A&P 1908, 116, 7252, İzmir for 1906 quoting a local British manufacturer of carpets.
52 k und k, 1903, Konstantinopel; 1907 report of the German consul in Konya in *Board of Trade Journal*, 9/12/1907, p. 517. Buhi 1904, pp. 294–95. But RCL 8/31/1897, Lettre de Konia of 8/8/1897, p. 53, states that only rarely were dyes imported from Europe.
53 HHStA, AA, January 1896; Stich (1929), p. 110, is quoting the 1906 Buhi report on rugs.
54 AE CC, Turquie, 56, Report for 1895. GB, AS 4009, Constantinople for 1907, p. 12.
55 Church (1892), pp. 4–5.
56 Kurmuş (1974), p. 147.
57 Sivas vs 1321/1903, p. 181 and 1325/1907, p. 194; Buhi, 9, 1906, p. 725.

58 GB 3170, 1904, for years 1902–3.
59 *Board of Trade Journal*, 5/28/1914, p. 510.
60 A discussion of the problem is in USCR LXIX, 262, July 1902, "Decline in the Value of Turkish rugs," pp. 453–54. Also see, for example, Aydın vs 1306/1890 and k und k 1905, X, 2, Smyrna.
61 Buhi, 9, 1906, p. 727.
62 "Die anatolische Teppichindustrie," Buhi, 9, 1906, 713; this long and detailed report is the source for Stich (1929).
63 Buhi, 9, 1906, pp. 720–21.
64 *Bursa Sergisi*, #4, 10 Temmuz 1325, pp. 44–45 and #, 14 Ağustos 1325, pp. 67–72.
65 *Revue du monde Musulman*, III (May 1907), pp. 54–55. For more details on the company, see Ford (1988).
66 Jeancard (1919), pp. 66–67. The trip was completed in 1914. At Isparta, he said, the company provided workers with wool dyed in its İzmir factory, made with chemical dyes. Vegetable dyes formerly gave more solid colors and, he adds, chemical colors have replaced the more brilliant but more durable vegetable colors. His statement seems supported by the continued high volume of synthetic and artificial dyestuffs imports after the firm took over most of the industry in Anatolia. The GB *1919 Report on Trade and Economic Conditions*, p. 65, states that about 50,000 kg. of German-made aniline and alizarin annually were being used in Uşak during the immediate prewar period.
67 Ibid.; RCC 1910, #868 for 1908–9, İzmir, Pierre Valet, pp. 44–45.
68 Junge (1916), p. 305.
69 RCL Lettre de Sivas, 8/8/1900, pp. 106–107; Buhi 9, 1906, pp. 712, 723, 728.
70 CRUS XXXVI, #128, 1891, pp. 97–104; Stich (1929), pp. 112–13.
71 Buhi 1904, pp. 293–94.
72 Buhi 1904, p. 294.
73 Stoeckel (1892), p. I.
74 du temple (1883), p. 224.
75 Buhi 9, 1906, p. 720; k und k 1906, X, 2, Smyrna; Bursa VS 1324/1906.
76 Sami (1983), p. 205.
77 Buhi 1906 and *Board of Trade Journal* 12/27/1906, p. 617 on 1905 high wool prices in İzmir. Tillman (1916–17), pp. 8–9.
78 Serious mortality among sheep in 1907 substantially reduced the flocks; GB AS 4009, Constantinople for 1907; RCC 1907, p. 613, Smyrne for 1905.
79 BBA Hüdavendigâr eyaleti mesaili mühimme #2281 and 2282, 1262; I MV 8615, VII 16 1268/1852; Cev İkt 1520, IV 1262/1846. Stich (1929), p. 105, for weaving reference. Since mechanical carpet weaving had been invented in the United States just two years before, the reference probably was to equipment for mechanically spinning wool yarn.
80 See page 10 of the 1886 Baker catalog, reproduced in Ford (1988), p. 16.
81 Cochran (1887), p. 101.
82 US Special Consular Reports, I (1890), p. 308.
83 According to the 1913 survey, the founding dates are: Bıçakzade Biraderler ve Mehmet Zeki Kum. in 1905; Yılancızade Biraderler ve Şürekası in 1910 and another in that same year by Hamzazadeler ve Şürekası (which had a flour mill attached). Turkey (1979), p. 141. But Banaz (n.d.), p. 12, says Tarakçıoğlu established the first factory in 1895,

otherwise agreeing with the dates of the survey. Turkey (1968), p. 173, gives the founders' names as Hacıgedik, Yılancı and Bacakoğlu.

84 Atalay (*c.* 1952), p. 47.
85 *İkdam*, II 24 1324.
86 Stich (1929), p. 112.
87 Turkey (1968), p. 273.
88 k und k 1905, X, 2, Smyrna; Buhi, 9, 1906, pp. 731–32.
89 *Bursa Sergisi*, Nr. 4, 10 Temmuz 1325, pp. 44–45 and #6, 14 Ağustos 1325, pp. 67–72.
90 See Quataert (1986) for more details.
91 Atalay (*c.* 1952), pp. 46–47.
92 Salaheddin (1867). Kurmuş (1974) basing his account on Salaheddin Bey, mistakenly assumes that Hacı Ali was the controller of this particular network, an assumption that I followed in Quataert (1986). The 1867 source, however, simply says that Ali was an important dealer and later speaks of one large operation controlling 84,000 meters of production.
93 RCC 1907, #613, Smyrne for 1905 and Buhi 1906, 9, p. 719.
94 Stich (1929), pp. 23–24; and personal interview with Howard Reed, August 1983, about his ancestor, Blackler.
95 Mumford (1900), p. 151. Stoeckel (1892), however, says Demirci was almost wiped out by bad dyes.
96 The Bandırma factory that he and his Bosnian partners opened in 1902 became the exclusive source of the yarn used at Kütahya; *Bursa Sergisi* #9, Eylül 1325. *İkdam* II 24 1325 shows that the factory then supplied 86 percent of the yarn consumed there.
97 US D of C&L, B of Mfg., Turkey for 1907, AS #30, pp. 19–20. USCR LXIX, 262, July 1902; Harput, 4/7/1902, Norton. AS 4741, Aleppo for 1910, p. 5.
98 Dirik (1938), pp. 80–81, quoting the memoirs of Bucizade Süleyman Sami (1983).
99 RCL Lettre de Sivas 8/8/1900. The governor, Memduh Pasha, also worked to develop rug making while governor of Ankara province, but details are lacking. He later rose to become Minister of the Interior. US Spec C Report, I (1890), p. 309, states explicitly that all the looms in the town of Sivas were in homes.
100 A&P 1901, 85, 6450, Trebizond; also RCL Lettre de Sivas, 8/8/1900, p. 207; repeated in German translation in Buhi 1906, 9, p. 727.
101 RCC reel #34, Nr. 149, Sivas in 1901, p. 14. In the 1900 Konya rug exhibition, Sivas rugs won first prize; Sivas vs 1321/1903, p. 180.
102 Buhi 9, 1906, p. 727; Lewis (1911), pp. 55–56.
103 Sivas vs 1321/1903, p. 180; Luckerts (1906); Buhi 1906, 9, p. 727.
104 RCC 1911, #953, Sivas province.
105 RCL 1897, 8/31/1897, Lettre de Konia, 8/8/1897.
106 RCL 1900, Lettre de Koniah, 8/28/1900, pp. 238–39. RCC 1907, #613, Smyrne for 1905. Originally stated as 500,000 francs.
107 RCL Julliet 1899, #148, pp. 97, 130; Buhi 1904, p. 296; Buhi, 9, 1906, p. 730. *Revue du monde Musulman*, III (May 1907), pp. 54–55.
108 Buhi 1906, 9, p. 729. Luckerts (1906), p. 32.
109 ZStA, AA 8728, 1900, Bl. 264, s. 11–12. Scheinitz (1906).
110 AS 4009, Constantinople for 1907, Konia, p. 28.
111 *Levant Trade Review* June 1912, p. 92.

112 Beattie (1981), p. 130.

113 Işıksaçan (1964), p. 17; Beattie (1981), p. 130.

114 Buhi, 9, 1906, states only that a family migrated; RCL 1900, Lettre d'Ismidt, 8/29/1900, dates the migration and says one Uşak resident moved.

115 Bursa vs 1302/1884, p. 456; Sami IV (1311), p. 3155.

116 Atalay (*c.* 1952), pp. 44–45; Banaz (n.d.), p. 7, states that the spinning mills lowered workers' incomes.

117 Atalay (*c.* 1952), p. 44.

118 Scherzer (1873), pp. 171–72, 179; duTemple (1883), pp. 223–24.

119 Buhi 9, 1906, pp. 733–34.

120 Pittard (1931).

121 This is a revision of my own analysis in Quataert (1986), p. 479.

122 Stoeckel (1892), p. IV. It is likely that Pittard's figure reflects the workforce mainly of these traditional centers.

123 But the official yearbook for the province states that the veiled Muslim women in Sivas were particularly skilled in rug making. Sivas vs 1321/1903, p. 180.

124 RCL Lettre de Sivas, 8/8/1900, pp. 204–7.

125 Atalay (*c.* 1952), p. 46.

126 Cochran (1887), p. 102.

127 HHSt, PA, XII, Turkei, Karton 172, 1/4/1896, p. 139. A major fire had destroyed two-thirds of the town in either 1894 or 1895 and apparently halted carpet making. Perhaps it was this crisis that brought men into spinning. Banaz (n.d.), p. 7 and Işıksaçan (1964), p. 12, offer the different dates.

128 RCL Lettre de Sivas, 8/8/1900, p. 203.

129 Atalay (*c.* 1952), pp. 48–53. Among the eight large dyeing works in the town was that owned by the Giraud house of İzmir, noted for its fast and stable dyes. Dutemple (1883), p. 223.

130 Ford (1988), p. 16, reproducing the Baker catalog published between 1878 and 1895.

131 Buhi 1906, 9, p. 719.

132 The following is based on Quataert (1986).

133 Stoeckel (1892), pp. II–III.

134 Salaheddin (1867).

135 Turkey (1968), p. 270.

136 Buhi 9, 1906, pp. 719–20.

137 Stoeckel (1892), p. IV; Sivas vs 1321/1903, p. 180.

138 k und k 1906, X, 2, Smyrna.

139 Turkey (1970), pp. vii–viii; *Das Handelsmuseum* 8/24/1914; Kurmuş (1974), pp. 150–52.

140 Jeancard (1919); Ford (1988), p. 18. Eldem (1970), pp. 141–42, says that 60,000 persons worked in carpet making in 1913 and only 15,000 for OCM at that time.

141 Atalay (*c.* 1952), p. 54.

142 HHStA, Januar 1896; Turkey (1970), p. 136; Ford (1988), p. 23, quoting the Baker journal.

143 RCL Lettre de Sivas 8/8/1900; GB AS 4009, Constantinople for 1907, p. 28.

144 Jeancard (1919), pp. 66–67; Liebetrau (1963), p. 17.

145 Buhi 9, 1906, p. 727.

146 Compare data in table with Jeancard (1919), p. 238. The rate is stated as one para per

20 knots, usually o fr 92 or 4 piasters for a seven- to eight-hour day. Between the two dates, there had been a very severe inflation. And so, the Isparta wages were relatively even still lower than the Uşak wages. The costs of living in the two towns probably were comparable.

147 USNA, 8/17 and 26/1908, Smyrna.

Conclusion

1 Mitchell (1976), p. 782, and Turkey (1970).
2 FO 78/298, 6/22/1836, Treasury to Nouri Efendi.
3 Tomlinson (1985), Chandavarkar (1985).
4 Here, we would insist on comparing output in geographic units of the same size and not on an empire-wide basis; the empire, overall, shrank considerably during the long nineteenth century.
5 Quataert (1973).
6 Hanson (1980), p. 148.
7 Some Ottoman manufacturers worked for the very bottom of the market and price easily was the most important factor. But there were many reasons. For example, hand-spun yarn sometimes was preferred not for its cheap price but for the qualities that it imparted to the final woven textile.
8 FO 195/177, Brant at Izmir, 8/1/1843; Sami (1983).
9 Chandavarkar (1985).
10 In the 1860s, for example, a prominent Armenian moneylender (*sarraf*) at Arapkir obtained permission to build an additional dyehouse to handle the demand. But, because the dyes produced would stink and spoil the air, the government stipulated that the dyehouse be built away from the town center. BBA I, MV 21959, XI selh 1279/1863.
11 BBA I MM 2274, IV 12 1292/1875.
12 FO 195/687, 4/20/1861.
13 Quataert (1986) and Buhi 1904.
14 Buhi, X, Heft 9, 8/20/1907.
15 AS 4579, Salonica for 1909.
16 AS 4538 for 1909, Trebizond.
17 Goody (1982), pp. 4–5.
18 Mendels (1972).
19 See, for example, Quataert (1983).
20 Çağlar Keyder's analysis of the silk industry after 1914, based on RCL reports, however, shows measurable quantities of hand-reeled silk, probably made at home.
21 Goody (1982), p. 34.
22 It is important to stress that the sources were biased in favor the export industries, on which they provided infinitely greater detail than for manufacturing focused on the domestic markets.
23 Whenever possible, this book has stated the gender identity of the workers.
24 Anon. (forthcoming).
25 Herlt (1918), p. 58; Buhi 1902, 4/10/1902 and 1904; Junge (1916), p. 446, states that a Turkish shoemaking guild was functioning in the early twentieth century.
26 This interpretation differs from that presented in Quataert (1979).
27 Berg (1985), p. 20.

Bibliography

Archives

Turkey: Başbakanlık Arşivi, Prime Ministry Archives, İstanbul.
    Bab-ı Âli Evrak Odası.
    Cevdet Tasnifi, Belediye
    Cevdet Tasnifi, Dahiliye
    Cevdet Tasnifi, İktisat
    Cevdet Tasnifi, Maliye
    Cevdet Tasnifi, Nafıa
    Hatt-ı Hümayûn Tasnifi
    Kamil Kepeci Tasnifi
    İradeler Tasnifi
    Yıldız Tasnifi
    Ankara eyaletine dair mesail-i mühimme
    Hüdavendigâr eyaletine dair mesail-i mühimme
Austria: Haus-Hof und Staatsarchiv, Vienna.
    Politisches Archiv, Türkei XII, K 195, 196, 352.
France: Archives du Ministère des affaires étrangères,
    Quai d'Orsay, Paris.
    Correspondance consulaire et commerciale, 1873–1901.
    Constantinople, 106–7, 115–17.
    Trèbizonde, 9–13.
    Smyrne, 55–57.
    Brousse, no nr.
    Erzeroum, 4.
Germany, (formerly Democratic Republic) Zentrales Staatsarchiv, Potsdam. Auswärtiges
    Amt.
Great Britain: Foreign Office, The Public Records Office,
    London. *Foreign Office Papers*, The Public Records Office. FO 195.
United States: National Archives, Washington, D.C.
    Brusa, 1837–40.
    Constantinople, 1820–70.
    Salonica, 1832–40.
    Smyrna, 1802–75.

Bibliography

Published government documents

Austria: *Berichte der k. u. k. Österr.- Ung. Konsularämter über das Jahr.* Herausgegeben im Auftrage des K. K. Handelsministeriums vom K. K. Österr. Handelsmuseum. Vienna, 1900–12.

France: *Bulletin consulaire français. Recueil des rapports commerciaux adressés au Ministère des affaires étrangères par les agents diplomatiques et consulaires de France à l'étranger.* Paris, 1877–1914.

Germany: Deutsches Reich. *Handel und Industrie. Berichte über Handel und Industrie.* Berlin, 1900–15.

Great Britain: Parliamentary Papers, *Accounts and Papers.* London, 1876–1913; selected reports from Foreign Office 78 and 424.

Diplomatic and Consular Series. Annual Series, 1903–14.

Foreign Office (1871), *Further Reports from Her Majesty's Diplomatic and Consular Agents of the Industrial Classes and the Purchase Power of Money in Foreign Countries,* London.

Foreign Office (1873), *Reports ... respecting Factories for Spinning and Weaving of Textile Fabrics Abroad,* London.

(July–September, 1919), Naval Staff Intelligence Department, C. B. 847a–b, *A Handbook of Asia Minor,* 2 vols. In part, this is a translation of Rudolf Fitzner (1902), pp. 86–96.

(1919), Department of Overseas Trade, *General Report on the Trade and Economic Conditions of Turkey for the Year 1919,* London.

Italy: Bolletino Consolare. Publiccato per cura del Ministero per Gli Affari Estri di S. M. il Re d'Italia. Torino/Roma, 1863–86.

Turkey: *Düstur* (1289–1302), Birinci Tertib, 4 vols. and 4 appendix vols., İstanbul.

Düstur (1939–43), Birinci Tertib, 4 vols., Ankara.

(1968), *Uşak İl Yıllığı 1967,* İstanbul.

(n.d.), *Rapport du Ministre du Commerce et de l'Agriculture au Grand Vizer. Statistique Judiciaire du Ministère du Commerce pour l'Année 1285,* Constantinople.

(1970), *Osmanlı Sanayii. 1913, 1915 yılları sanayi istatistiki,* a modern Turkish rendering by A. Gündüz Ökçün, Ankara, of an Ottoman industrial survey.

Ziraat Vekaleti (1936), *Pamuk ve Pamukçuluk Hakkında Rapor,* Ankara.

Provincial Yearbooks (*vilayet salnameleri*) for the following provinces, various years and places of publication:

Adana, Ankara, Aydın, Bitlis, Edirne, Hüdavendigâr, Diyarbakır, Halep, Karesi, Kastamonu, Konya, Mamuret'ül-Aziz, Selanik, Sivas, Trabzon.

United States: Department of Commerce and Labor. Bureau of Foreign and Domestic Commerce. *Special Agent Series,* 1912.

Bureau of Foreign and Domestic Commerce. *Special Consular Reports.* Washington 1889–1911.

Department of State. *Commercial Relations of the United States.* Washington, 1856–79.

Daily Consular Reports. Washington, 1901–2.

Department of Commerce and Labor, Bureau of Manufactures, *Monthly Consular and Trade Reports.* Washington, 1907–14.

Contemporary newspapers and journals

Adana, 1307; 1311; 1318–20; 1325
Ankara, 1301; 1306; 1321; 1325
Ahenk (İzmir), 1896–1909
Aydın (İzmir), 1297–1301; 1306–7; 1312; 1313; 1325
Betail, 1910–11
Bitlis, 1310
Board of Trade Journal, 1906–14
British Chamber of Commerce of Turkey and the Balkan States. Balkan State Reports, 1913, 1921–27
Bursa, 1302; 1307; 1310–11; 1315; 1321; 1324–25
Bursa Sergisi, 1325
Capker (İzmir), 1909
Diyarbakır, 1302; 1312; 1317; 1321; 1327
L'Economiste d'Orient, 1920–23
Edep Haher, 1908
Edirne, 1300; 1309–10; 1313; 1314; 1319
Ertuğrul, 1910
Eskişehir, 1910
Fevarid, 1895–96
Das Handelsmuseum, 1914
Hüdavendigâr, 1302; 1307; 1315; 1310; 1321; 1324–25
Halep, 1302; 1317; 1321; 1324
Hitasa, 1910
İkdam, 1907
İmtiyaz, (İzmir), 1909
İştirak, 1325–26
İtidad (Adana), 1908
Le journal de la chambre de commerce de Constantinople (İstanbul), 1885–87 and 1908
Karesi, 1305
Kastamonu, 1310–12; 1317
Kokorok (İzmir), 1908
Konya, 1298; 1310; 1317; 1322
The Manchester Guardian Commercial, 1925
Le Mouvement Economique, Bucharest, Dec. 1904–15
Levant Trade Review, 1911–15
Mamuret'Ül-Aziz, 1310; 1325; 1909
Maşrik-i İrfan, 1910
Müsamver emel, 1898–99
Nilüfer, 1895–96
Peyman, 1909
La Revue Commerciale du Levant, Bulletin Mensuel de la chambre de commerce française de Constantinople, 1896–1912, İstanbul
Revue de Constantinople, 1875–76

Bibliography

Revue Technique d'Orient, 1910–14
Revue du Monde Musulman, 1907
Sivas, 1902–8; 1910; 1916
Silmik, 1307; 1315; 1322
Şule-i Edep, 1899
Teceddirt, 1910
Trabzon, 1309; 1318; 1320–22
Tütün İnhisar Dairesi, 1928–29
Ziraat ve sanaat tercüme fünun odaları, 1302

Secondary sources

Abidin, İhsan (1928) *Anadolu Ziraat ve Yetiştirme Vaziyeti*, İstanbul, 3 vols.
Abou el-Haj, Rifaat (1991) *Formation of the Modern State*, Albany.
Akbay, Rana (1983) "Silk Production Process in Bursa," Master's Thesis, Middle East Technical University, Ankara.
Anon. (1904) *Oriental Rugs and Carpets*.
Anon. (forthcoming) "Women's Work, Men's Work and Uneven Class Formation in the Irish Linen Industry 1780–1840," *Signs*.
Arundell, F. V. J. (1834) *Discoveries in Asia Minor*, Volume I, London.
Atalay, B. (c. 1952) *Türk Halıcılığı ve Uşak Halıları*.
Baer, Gabriel (1982) *Fellah and Townsmen in the Middle East: Studies in Social History*, London.
Banaz, Remzi, (n.d.) *Uşak'ta Dokuma Sanayii ve Dokumacılık*, Uşak.
Barkan, Ö. L. (1975) "The Price Revolution in the Sixteenth Century," *IJMES*, VI, 1975, pp. 3–28.
Barnett, R. D. (1974) "The European Merchants in Angora," *Anatolian Studies*, 24, pp. 135–41.
Baykara, Tuncer (1984) *Yatağan. Her Şeyi ile Tarih Yaşatma Denemesi*, Tokyo.
Beattie, May (1981) "Hereke," *Halı*, 4, 2, pp. 128–34.
Beinin, Joel (1983) "An Approach to the Study of the Working Class in the Arab World," unpublished paper.
Bensoussan, Pamela (1985) "The Masterweavers of Istanbul," *Halı*, 26, pp. 34–38.
Berg, Maxine (1975) *The Age of Manufactures: Industry, Innovation and Work in Britain, 1700–1820*, New York.
Bigham, Clive (1897) *A Ride Through Western Asia*, London.
Blunt, Mrs. John Elijah (A Consul's Daughter and Wife) (1878) *The People of Turkey: Twenty Years' Residence Among Bulgarians, Greeks, Albanians, Turks and Armenians*, 2 volumes, London.
Bowring, John (1840) *Report on the Commercial Statistics of Syria*, London.
Braudel, Fernand (1986) *Civilization and Capitalism*, II, *The Wheels of Commerce*, New York.
Brewster, Josiah (1830) *A Residence at Constantinople in the Year 1827*, New Haven.
Burnaby, Fred (1898) *On Horseback Through Asia Minor*, London.
Caillard, Vincent (1911) "Turkey" in *Encyclopaedia Britannica*, 11th edn., vol. 27, New York, pp. 429–34.

Cevdet, Ahmet (1309) *Tarih-i Cevdet*, 12 vols., İstanbul.

Chakrabarty, Dipesh (1989) *Rethinking Working Class History: Bengal, 1890–1940*, Princeton.

Chandavarkar, Rajnarayan (1985) "Industrialization in India before 1947: Conventional Approaches and Alternative Perspectives," *Modern Asian Studies*, 19, 3 pp. 623–68.

Chevallier, Dominique (1962) "Les Tissus Ikates d'Alep et de Damas: Un Exemple de Résistance Technique de L'artisanat Syrien aux XIX et XX Siècles," *Syria*, 39, pp. 300–34.

Childs, W. J. (1917) *Across Asia Minor on Foot*, London.

Church, A. H. (1892) "A Short Treatise of the Development of Oriental Carpet Weaving During the Last Hundred Years," reprint from *The Portfolio*.

Clark, Edward C. (1969) "The Emergence of Textile Manufacturing Entrepreneurs in Turkey, 1804–1968," unpublished Princeton Ph.D. dissertation.

Clifford, C. R. (1911) *Rugs of the Orient*, New York.

Cochran, William (1887) *Pen and Pencil in Asia Minor*, London.

Collignon, Maxime (1880) "Notes d'un voyage en Asie-Mineure," *Revue des deux mondes*, 37, pp. 150–77; 38, pp. 891–917.

Conder, Josiah (1827) *The Modern Traveller. Turkey*, London.

Cönker, Orhan et Emile Witmeur (1937) *Redressement économique et Industrialisation de la Nouvelle Turquie*, Paris.

Cook, M. A., ed. (1970) *Studies in the Economic History of the Middle East*, Oxford.

Corancez, L.-A-.A. (1816) *Itinéraire d'une partie peu Connue de l'Asie Mineure*, Paris.

Cox, Samuel S. (1893) *Diversions of a Diplomat in Turkey*, New York.

Coxon, Herbert (1884) *Oriental Carpets, How They are Made and Conveyed to Europe*, London.

Cuinet, Vital (1890–94) *La Turquie d'Asie; Géographie Administrative Statistique Descriptive et Raisonnée de Chaque Province de l'Asie Mineure*, 4 vols., Paris.

Cunningham, A. B. (1983) "The Journal of Christophe Aubin: A Report on the Levant Trade in 1812," *Archivum Ottomanicum*, 8, pp. 5–132.

Çizakça, Murat (1976) "Reflections of Sixteenth-century European Price Revolution on Ottoman Textile Markets," Paper delivered to Middle East Studies Association.

Dağlaroğlu, Rüştü (1941) *L'Industrie Textile Turque*, Thèse, Friburg.

Dalsar, Fahri (1960) *Bursa'da İpekçilik*, İstanbul.

Darüşşüfeka (1927) İstanbul.

DeDreux, Robert (1925) *Voyage en Turquie et en Grèce*, Paris.

DeKay, James E. (1833) *Sketches in Turkey in 1831 and 1832*, New York.

Delbeuf, Regis (1906) *Une Excursion à Brousse et à Nicée*, Constantinople.

Denny, W. B. (1973) "Anatolian Rugs. An Essay on Method," *Textile Museum Journal*, IV, 3, pp. 7–25.

Dernburg, Friedrich (1892) *Auf Deutscher Bahn in Kleinasien*, Berlin.

Dirik, Kazım (1938) *Eski ve Yeni Türk Halıcılığı ve Cihan Halı Tipleri Panoraması*, İstanbul.

Dumont, Paul (1982) "Jewish Communities in Turkey during the Last Decades of the XIXth Century in the Light of the Archives of the Alliance Israelite Universelle," in Benjamin Braude and Bernard Lewis, eds., *Christians and Jews in the Ottoman Empire*, I, New York.

Dunn, Eliza (1910) *Rugs in Their Native Land*, London.

Dutemple, Edmond (1883) *En Turquie d'Asie: Notes de Voyage en Anatolie*, Paris.

Eldem, Vedat (1970) *Osmanlı İmparatorluğunun İktisadi Şartları hakkında bir Tetkik*, İstanbul.

Erder, L. (1975) "Factory Districts in Bursa During the 1860s," Middle East Technical University, *Journal of the Faculty of Architecture*, 1,1; pp. 85–99.

Erdmann, Kurt (1960) *Oriental Carpets, An Essay on Their History*, translated by Charles Grant Ellis, New York.

(Ergin), Osman Nuri (1330–38) *Mecelle-i Umur-u Belediye*, 5 vols., İstanbul.

Ete, M. E. (1941) *Türkiye'de Pamuklu Ev dokuma Sanayii*, İstanbul.

Eton, William (1799) *A Survey of the Turkish Empire*, 2nd. edn., London.

Farley, James Lewis (1862) *The Resources of Turkey*, London.

Findley, C. V. (1986) "Economic Bases of Revolution and Repression in the Late Ottoman Empire," *Comparative Studies in Society and History*, pp. 81–106.

Fitzner, Rudolf (1902) *Anatolien Wirtschaftsgeographie*, Berlin.

Ford, P. R. J. (1988) "The Role of the O.C.M. in the Nineteenth- and Early Twentieth-century Revival of Oriental Rug Weaving," eight parts, April–December *Rug News*.

Franco, Moise (1897) *Essai sur l'histoire des Israélites de l'Empire Ottoman*, Paris.

Frankland, Charles Colville (1829) *Travels to and From Constantinople in the Years 1827 and 1828*, Volume I, London.

Fraser, David (1910) *Persia and Turkey in Revolt*, London.

Fukasawa, Katsumi (1987) *Toilerie et commerce du Levant d'Alep à Marseille*, Paris.

Galante, Abraham (1985) *Histoire des Juifs de Turquie*, 9 vols., İstanbul.

Garnett, Lucy M. J. (1909) *Home Life in Turkey*, New York.

(1904) *Turkish Life in Town and City*, New York.

(1914) *Turkey of the Ottomans*, New York.

Gavin, Carney E. S. (c. 1982) *The Image of the East, the Photographs of the Maison Bonfils*, Chicago.

Geister, Paul (1907) *Die Türkei im Rahmen der Weltwirtschaft*, Greifswald.

Genç, Mehmet (1975) "Osmanlı Maliyesinde Malikane Sistemi," in Ünal Nalbantoğlu and Osman Okyar, eds., *Türkiye İktisat Tarihi Semineri, Metinler, Tartışmalar*, Ankara, pp. 231–91.

(1987) "XVII–XIX Yüzyıllarda Sanayi ve Ticaret Merkezi Olarak Tokat," in *Türk Tarihinde ve Kültüründe Tokat Sempozyumu 2–6 Temmuz 1986*, Ankara, pp. 145–70.

Georgiades, D. (1885) *Smyrne et l'Asie Mineure*, Paris.

(1892) *La Turquie actuelle*, Paris.

Gerber, H. (1976) "Guilds in Seventeenth-century Anatolian Bursa," *Asian and African Studies*, 11,1, pp. 59–86.

(1980) "The Social and Economic Position of Women in Ottoman Bursa, 1600–1700," *IJMES*, 12,3, pp. 231–44.

Giraud, Edmund H. (1934) *Family Records: A Record of the Origin and History of the Giraud and Whittall Families in Turkey, and a Short History of the La Fontaine Family*, London.

Glavanis, Kathy R. G. and Pandeli M. Glavanis (1983) "The Sociology of Agrarian Relations in the Middle East: The Persistence of Household Production," *Current Sociology*, 31,2; pp. 1–107.

Goldberg, Ellis (n.d.) "Heroic Workers and Workaday Contracts," unpublished paper.

Gönül, M. (n.d.) "Caftans of the Sultans and Old Turkish Embroidery," Typescript, Textile Museum, Washington, D.C.

Goody, Esther N., ed. (1982), *From Craft to Industry. The Ethnography of Proto-Industrial Cloth Production*, Cambridge.

Göyünç, Nejat (1983) "The Procurement of Labor and Materials in the Ottoman Empire (16th and 18th Centuries)," in Jean-Louis Bacqué-Grammont and Paul Dumont, eds., *Économie et Sociétés dans L'Empire Ottoman*, Paris, pp. 327–33.

Greenberg, Dolores (1982) "Reassessing the Power Patterns of the Industrial Revolution: An Anglo-American Comparison," *American Historical Review*, pp. 1237–61.

Grothe, Hugo (1916) *Türkisch Asien und seine Wirtschaftswerte*, Frankfurt.

Gueneau, Louis (1923) *Lyon et le Commerce de la Soie*, Lyon.

Güran, Tevfik (1984–85) "The State Role in the Grain Supply of İstanbul: the Grain Administration, 1793–1839," *IJTS*, Winter, pp. 27–41.

Gurdji, V. (1913) *Threads from the Oriental Loom*, New York.

[H.K]. (1828) *Description géographique et historique de la Turquie d'Europe*, Paris.

Hall, W. H. (1918) *Reconstruction in Turkey*, New York.

Hamilton, William J. (1842) *Research in Asia Minor, Pontus, and Armenia, with some Account of their Antiquities and Geology*, 2 vols., London.

Hammer, Joseph V. (1818) *Umblick auf einer Reise von Constantinopel nach Brussa und dem Olympos, und von da zurück über Nicaa und Nicomedien*, Pesth.

Handelspolitische Flugschriften (1916) *Die Türkei und Bulgarien als Absatzgebiete der Deutschen Industrie*, Berlin.

Hanson III, John R. (1980), *Trade in Transition. Exports from the Third World, 1840–1900*, New York.

Harrison, Joseph (1978), *An Economic History of Modern Spain*, New York.

Hayri, Mehmet (1922/1338) *Niğde Sancağı*, Ankara.

Hellauer, Josef (1918) *Das Türkische Reich*, Berlin.

Herlt, G. (1918) "Die Industrialisierung der Türkei," *Das Wirtschaftsleben der Türkei*, II, pp. 41–80.

Hershlag, Z. Y. (1964) *Introduction to the Modern Economic History of the Middle East*, Leiden.

Herve, Francis (1837) *A Residence in Greece and Turkey; with Notes of the Journey through Bulgaria, Servia, Hungary, and the Balkans.* 2 vols., London.

Hoffmann, Friedrich (1919) "Die Industrie in der Türkei," *Weltwirtschaftliches Archiv*, 14, Heft 1, Januar, pp. 1–26.

Hogarth, David G. (1896) *A Wandering Scholar in the Levant*, London.

Honig, N. von (1916) "Über Industrie und Handwerk in Konstantinopel," in Reinhard Junge, ed., *Archiv für Wirtschaftsforschung im Orient*, I,3/4; pp. 421–48.

Hopkins, Eric (1982) "Working Hours and Conditions During the Industrial Revolution: A Re-Appraisal," *Economic History Review*, February, pp. 52–66.

Huart, Clement (1897) *Konia, la Ville des Derviches Tourneurs: Souvenirs d'un voyage en Asie Mineure*, Paris.

Hulme-Beaman, Ardern George (1898) *Twenty Years in the Near East*, London.

İnalcık, Halil (1969) "Capital Formation in the Ottoman Empire," *Journal of Economic History*, 19, pp. 97–140.

(1979–80) "Osmanlı Pamuklu Pazarı, Hindistan ve İngiltere: Pazar Rekabetinde Emek Maliyetinin Rolü," *Middle East Technical University Studies in Development*, Special Issue, pp. 1–65.

Işıksaçan, Güngör (1964) *Batı Anadolunun Başlıca Halı Merkezlerinde İmal Edilen Halıların Desen ve Kaliteleri üzerinde Araştırmalar*, İzmir.

Issawi, Charles (1966) *The Economic History of the Middle East, 1800–1914*, Chicago.

(1980) *The Economic History of Turkey, 1800–1914*, Chicago.

(1982) *An Economic History of the Middle East and North Africa*, New York.

(1988) *The Fertile Crescent 1800–1914. A Documentary Economic History*, New York.

İstanbul (1333) *Dersaadet Ticaret ve Sanayi Odasına Mukayyet Banker, Tüccar ve Komisyoncularının Esamisi*, Dersaadet.

Ittig, Annette (1981) "A Group of Inscribed Carpets from Persian Kurdistan," *Halı*, IV (2), pp. 121–27.

(1985) "The Kirman Boom – A Study in Carpet Entrepreneurship," *Oriental and Textile Studies*, I, pp.

Jeancard, Paul (1919) *L'Anatolie*, Paris.

Jeggle, Theodore (1926) *Der Internationale Teppichmarkt*, Duren.

Joyce, Patrick (1980) *Work, Society and Politics: The Culture of the Factory in later Victorian England*, New Brunswick, New Jersey.

Junge, Reinhard (1916) "Türkische Textilwaren" in *Balkan-Orient-Sonderausgabe der Zeitschrift, Die Textile Woche*, 1916–17, pp. 135–42.

Kalkas, Barbara (1979) "Diverted Institutions: A Reinterpretation of the Process of Industrialization in Nineteenth-Century Egypt," *Arab Studies Quarterly*, I, 1, pp. 28–48.

Kais, Firro (1987–88). "Alep, une ville traditionelle face à l'impact de l'Europe, 1830–1914," *Cahiers de la Méditerranée, Actes du Colloque*.

Karpat, Kemal (1985), *Ottoman Population 1830–1914, Demographic and Social Characteristics*, Madison.

Keyder, Çağlar (1989) "Creation and Destruction of Forms of Manufacturing. The Ottoman Example," Paper Presented to the Conference on "The Precocious Attempts at Industrialization of the Periphery (1800–90)," Geneva.

Knight, William (1839) *Oriental Outlines, or a Rambler's Recollections of a Tour in Turkey, Greece, and Tuscany in 1838*, London.

Konyalı, İbrahim Hakkı (1967) *Abideleri ve Kitabeleri ile Karaman Tarihi*, İstanbul.

Krauss, J. (1901) *Deutsch-türkische Handelsbeziehungen seit dem Berliner Vertag*, Jena.

Kurmuş, Orhan (1974) *Emperyalizmin Türkiye'ye Girişi*, İstanbul.

Kütahya İli 100. yıl kutlama Komitesi (1981–82) *Kütahya*, İstanbul.

Labaki, Boutrous (1984) *Introduction à l'histoire économique du Liban*, Beyrouth.

Lampe, John R. and Marvin R. Jackson (1982) *Balkan Economic History, 1550–1950. From Imperial Borderlands to Developing Nations*, Bloomington, Indiana.

Landau, Paul (1900) *An der Westküste Klein-Asiens*, Berlin.

Landes, David (1969) *The Unbound Prometheus: Technological Change and Industrial Development in Western Europe From 1750 to the Present*, London; revised and expanded version of his (1966) "Technological Change and Development in Western Europe, 1750–1914," in H. J. Habakkuk and M. Postan (eds.) *The Cambridge Economic History of Europe, Volume VI: The Industrial Revolutions and After: Incomes, Population and Technological Change*, London.

Leake, William Martin (1824) *A Tour in Asia Minor with Comparative Remarks on the Ancient and Modern Geography of That Country*, London.

Lewis, G. Griffen (1911) *The Practical Book of Oriental Rugs*, Philadelphia and London.

Liebetrau, Preben (1963) *Oriental Rugs in Colour*, New York.

Lockman, Zachary (1980) "Notes on Egyptian Workers' History," *International Labor and Working Class History*, Fall, pp. 1–12.

Luckerts, I. (1906) "Le développement industriel de la Turquie d'Asie," *Le Mouvement Économique*, 1er Juin, pp. 19–34.

Luke, Harry Charles (1924) *Anatolica*, London.

Lüfti, Ahmet (1292–1328) *Tarih-i Lüfti*, 8 vols., İstanbul.

MacGregor, John (1844) *Commercial Statistics*, 3 vols., London.

Mağmumi, Şerefeddin (1909/1327) *Seyahat Hatıraları*, İstanbul.

Masters, Bruce (1988) *The Origins of Western Economic Dominance in the Middle East*, New York.

Mavuna ve Mavunacılık (1339) İstanbul.

McCullagh, Francis (1910) *The Fall of Abdul Hamid*, London.

Mendels, Franklin (1972), "Proto-industrialization: The First Phase of the Industrialization Process," *The Journal of Economic History* 32, pp. 241–61.

Mitchell, Brian (1976) *European Historical Statistics, 1750–1970*, London.

Mordtmann, Andreas David (1878) *Stambul und das moderne Türkenthum*, Leipzig.

(1925) *Anatolien. Skizzen und Reisebriefe aus Kleinasien*, ed., Franz Babinger, Hannover.

Mumford, John Kimberly (1900) *Oriental Rugs*, New York.

Nuri, Hıfzı (1922/1338) *Kayseri sancağı*, Ankara.

Olivier, Guillaume Antoine (1801) *Travels in the Ottoman Empire, Egypt and Persia*, I (translated from the French), London.

Onay, Aliye (1972) "İlk Şeker Fabrikalarını Kurma Teşebbüsleri," *BTTD*, X, 55, Nisan.

Önsoy, Rıfat (1988) *Tanzimat Dönemi Osmanlı Sanayii ve Sanayileşme Politikası*, Ankara.

Osganyan, K. (1857) *The Sultan and His People*, New York.

Owen, Roger (1981) *The Middle East in the World Economy*, London.

(1984) "The Study of Middle Eastern Industrial History: Notes on the Interrelationship between Factories and Small-scale Manufacturing with Special References to Lebanese Silk and Egyptian Sugar, 1900–1930," *IJMES*, pp. 475–87.

Öz, Tahsin (1950) *Turkish Textiles and Velvets, XIV–XVI Centuries*, Ankara.

Pallis, Alexander (1951) *In the Days of the Janissaries*, London, New York.

Pamuk, Şevket (1984) "The Ottoman Empire in the 'Great Depression' of 1873–1896," *Journal of Economic History*, 44, pp. 107–18.

(1987) *The Ottoman Empire and European Capitalism, 1820–1913*, Cambridge.

Pech, Edgar (1911) *Manuel des sociétés anonymes fonctionnant en Turquie*, 5th edn., Constantinople.

Petmezas, Socrates (1989) "Patterns of Protoindustrialisation in the Ottoman Empire: The Case of Eastern Thessaly, c. 1750–1860," unpublished paper.

Pittard, Eugene (1931) *Le Visage Nouveau de la Turquie*, Paris.

Pollard, Sidney (1981) *Peaceful Conquest: The Industrialization of Europe, 1760–1970*, New York.

Porter, James (1854) *Turkey: Its History and Progress*, 2 vols., London.

Bibliography

Pouqueville, F. C. H. L. (1806) *Travels through the Morea, Albania and Several other Parts of the Ottoman Empire to Constantinople during the Years 1798, 1799, 1800 and 1801,* translated from the French, London.

Pretextat-Lecomte (1902) *Les Arts et Métiers de le Turquie et de l'Orient,* Paris.

Quataert, Donald (1973) "Ottoman Reform and Agriculture in Anatolia, 1876–1908," Ph.d. dissertation, University of California, Los Angeles.

(1979) "The Economic Climate of the 'Young Turk Revolution' in 1908," *The Journal of Modern History,* On Demand Supplement, September, pp. D1147–61.

(1983) *Social Disintegration and Popular Resistance in the Ottoman Empire,* New York.

(1984) review of Justin McCarthy, *The Arab World, Turkey and the Balkans (1878–1914): A Handbook of Historical Statistics,* Boston, in *Turcica,* 16, pp. 293–98.

(1986) Machine Breaking and the Changing Carpet Industry of Western Anatolia, 1860–1908, *Journal of Social History,* Spring, pp. 473–89.

(1988) "Ottoman Handicrafts and Industry in the Age of European Industrial Hegemony, 1800–1914," *Review,* Spring, pp. 169–78.

(1990) "Janissaries, Artisans, and the Question of Ottoman Decline, 1730–1826," Paper presented to the 17th International Congress of Historical Sciences, Madrid, August.

(forthcoming) associate editor and contributor, *The Ottoman Empire: Its Society and Economy, 1300–1914,* Cambridge.

Quataert, Jean (1985a) "Combining Agrarian and Industrial Livelihood: Rural Households in the Saxon Oberlausitz in the Nineteenth Century," *Journal of Family History,* Summer, pp. 145–62.

(1985b) "The Shaping of Women's Work in Manufacturing: Guilds, Households and the State in Central Europe, 1648–1870," *American Historical Review,* December, pp. 1122–48.

(1988) "A New View of Industrialization: 'Protoindustry' or the Role of Small-scale, Labor-intensive Manufacture in the Capitalist Environment," *International Labor and Working Class History,* Spring, pp. 3–22.

Rambert, Louis (c. 1926) *Notes et Impressions de Turquie. L'Empire Ottoman sous Abdul-Hamid II, 1895–1905,* Genève, Paris.

Ramsay, W. M. (1897) *Impressions of Turkey During Twelve Years' Wanderings,* New York & London.

Reimers, Heinrich Christian (1803) *Reise der Russich-Kaiserlichen ausserordentlichen Gesandtschaft an die Ottomanische Pforte im Jahr 1793,* St. Petersburg.

Ritter, C. (1841) *Briefe über Zustände und Begebenheiten in der Türkei aus den Jahren 1835 bis 1839,* Berlin.

Rougon, F. (1892) *Smyrne, Situation Commerciale et Économique,* Paris.

Russell, J. C. (1794) *The Natural History of Aleppo,* II (London).

Salaheddin Bey (1867) *La Turquie à l'Exposition Universelle de 1867,* Paris.

Sami, Bocuzade Süleyman (1983) *Kuruluşundan Bugüne kadar Isparta Tarihi* (transliterated by Dr. Suat Seren), İstanbul.

Sami, Şemsettin (1306–16) *Kamus'ül-Alam,* 6 vols., İstanbul.

Sarç, Ömer Celal (1940) "Tanzimat ve Sanayiimiz," in *Tanzimat. Yüzüncü Yıldönümü Münasebetile,* İstanbul, pp. 423–40.

Scala, A. v., ed. (1882) *Neue Volkwirtschaftliche Studien über Constantinopel und das Anliegende Gebiet,* Vienna.

Scherzer, K. von (1873) *Smyrna,* Vienna.

von Scheinitz, Hans Hermann Graf (1906), *In Kleinasien*, Berlin.

Schurtz, H. (1903) "Türkische Basare und Zünfte," *Zeitschrift für Socialwissenschaft*, VI, Berlin, pp. 683–706.

Scott-Stevenson, Mrs. (1881) *Our Ride Through Asia Minor*, London.

Sewell, William (1980) *Work and Revolution in France*, Cambridge.

Sherwood, John M. (1985) "Engels, Marx, Malthus, and the Machine," *American Historical Review*, October, pp. 837–65.

Shields, Sarah (1986) "An Economic History of Nineteenth-Century Mosul," Ph.D. Dissertation, University of Chicago.

Simmons, Colin (1985), "'Deindustrialization', Industrialization and the Indian Economy *c*. 1850–1947," *Modern Asian Studies*, 19,3, pp. 593–622.

Slade, Adolphus (1833) *Record of Travels in Turkey and Greece*, 2 vols., Philadelphia, Baltimore.

Smith, Grace Martin (1980) "The Özbek Tekkes of İstanbul," *Islam*, 57,1, pp. 130–39.

Stavrianos, L. S. (1958) *The Balkans Since 1453*, New York.

Stern, Bernhard (1909) *Die Moderne Türkei*, Berlin.

Stich, Heinrich (1929) *Die Weltwirtschaftlich Entwicklung der Anatolischen Produktion seit Anfangs des 19. Jahrhunderts*, Keil.

Stockel, J. M. (1892) "Modern Turkey Carpets. A Monograph," in C. Purdon Clarke, ed., *Oriental Carpets*, Vienna, pp. I–IV.

Svoronos, N. (1956) *Le commerce de Salonique au XVIIIe Siècle*, Paris.

Synvet, A. (1872) *Traité de Géographie Générale de l'Empire Ottoman*, Constantinople.

(Şanda), Hüseyin Avni (1937) *Türkiye'de Sanayiin İnkişafı*, İstanbul.

Şerif, Ahmet (1325) *Anadolu'da Tanin*, İstanbul.

Şirket-i Hayriye (1330/1914) *Boğaziçi*, İstanbul.

Tarbassian, Hratch A. (1975) *Erzurum (Garin): Its Armenian History and Traditions*, Boston & New York.

Texier, Charles (1862) *Asie Mineure. Description Géographique Historique et Archéologique*, Paris.

Thieck, Jean-Pierre (1985) "Décentralisation Ottomane et Affirmation Urbaine à Alep à la Fin du XVIIIème Siècle," in Mona Zakaria et al, eds., *Mouvements Communautaires et Espaces urbains au Machreq*, Beirut, pp. 117–68.

Thomas, Macolm J. (1974) *The Town Laborer and the Industrial Revolution*, New York.

Thornton, Thomas (1807) *The Present State of Turkey: or a Description of the Political, Civil, and Religious Constitution, Government, and Laws, of the Ottoman Empire; the Finances, Military and Naval Establishments; the State of Learning, and of the Liberal and Mechanical Arts; the Manners and Domestic Economy of the Turks and other Subjects of the Grand Signor, etc., etc ... From the Observations Made, during a Residence of Fifteen Years in Constantinople and the Turkish Provinces*, London.

Tillmann, Hugo (1916–17) "Türkische Textilrohstoffe," in Reinhard Junge, ed., *Balkan-Orient-Sonderausgabe der Zeitschrift, Die Textile Woche*, pp. 128–34.

Todorov, Nikolai (1983) *The Balkan City, 1400–1900*, Seattle, Washington.

Tomlinson, B. R. (1985) "Writing History Sideways: Lessons for Indian Economic Historians from Meiji Japan," *Modern Asian Studies*, 19,3, pp. 669–98.

Twomey, Michael J. (1983) "Employment in Nineteenth Century Indian Textiles," *Explorations in Economic History*, 20,1, pp. 37–57.

Ubicini, M. A. (1856) *Letters from Turkey*, 2 vols, London.

Urquhart, David (1833) *Turkey and its Resources: Its Municipal Organization and Free Trade; the State and Prospects of English Commerce in the East*, London.

Uşak Necm-i Ticaret Osmanlı Anonim Şirketi (1323) *Uşak Necm-i Ticaret Osmanlı Anonim Şirketi Nizamname-i Dahilisi*, İstanbul.

Üster, M. F. (1940) *Tiftik ve Tiftikçiliğimiz*, İstanbul.

Van Lennep, Henry (1870) *Travels in Little-known Parts of Asia Minor*, II, New York.

Veinstein, Gilles (1989) "Les Relations Commerciales Entre l'Inde et l'Empire Ottoman (Fin XVe-Fin XVIIIe s.)," Unpublished Paper, École des Hautes Etudes en Sciences Sociales, Paris.

Vienna, Österreiches Handelsmuseum (1882) *Neue Volkwirtschaftliche Studien über Constantinople und das Anliegende Gebiet*, Vienna.

(1892–96) *Oriental Carpets*, Vienna & London.

(1895) *Teppich-Erzeugung im Orient von Sir George Birdwood etc.*, Vienna.

Vives, Jaime Vicens (1969), *An Economic History of Spain*, Princeton.

Walsh, Robert (1836) *A Residence at Constantinople during a Period including the Commencement, Progress, and Termination of the Greek and Turkish Revolutions*, 2 vols., London.

Warsberg, Alexander Freiherrn von (1869) *Ein Sommer im Orient*, Vienna.

Warburg, O. (1918) "Die Landwirtschaft der Türkei," in Josef Hellauer, ed., *Das Türkische Reich*, Berlin, pp. 152–91.

Wiedenfeld, Kurt (1915) *Die Deutsch-Türkischen Wirtschaftsbeziehungen und ihre Entwicklungsmöglichkeiten*, Munich, Leipzig.

Yavuz, Erdal and Ümit Nevzat Uğurel (1984) *Tarih İçinde Ankara*, Ankara.

Yurt Ansiklopedisi (1981–84) 11 vols., İstanbul.

Index

Cambridge Middle East Library

Printed in the United States
57438LVS00004BA/146